Flooding the Courtrooms

LAW IN THE AMERICAN WEST

Series Editor

John R. Wunder,
University of Nebraska–Lincoln

Series Advisory Editors

Lawrence M. Friedman,
Stanford University
Kermit L. Hall,
University of Florida
Harry N. Scheiber,
University of California, Berkeley

Volume 4

M. CATHERINE MILLER

Flooding the Courtrooms

Law and Water in the Far West

University of Nebraska Press Lincoln and London

© 1993 by the University of Nebraska Press
Manufactured in the United States of
America
The paper in this book meets the minimum
requirements of American National
Standard for Information Sciences—
Permanence of Paper for Printed Library
Materials, ANSI Z39.48–1984.

Library of Congress
Cataloging-in-Publication Data
Miller, Mary Catherine.
Flooding the courtrooms: law and water
in the Far West
M. Catherine Miller.
p.   cm.—(Law in the American West; v. 4)
Includes bibliographical references
and index.
ISBN 0-8032-3153-9 (cloth)
  1. Water rights—California—History.
  2. California—History—1850–1950.
  3. Miller & Lux.
I. Title. II. Series.
KFC162.M54   1993
346.79404'32—dc20
[347.9406432]   92–33048
                 CIP

CONTENTS

M A P S

ACKNOWLEDGMENTS

A number of agencies and individuals provided funds for my work on this project. Initial research was supported by a John H. Wheeler and Elliot H. Wheeler Fellowship (Bancroft Library Study Award) and a Graduate Opportunity Fellowship from the University of California. During 1986, a Littleton–Griswold Research Grant for Research in American Law and Fields of Law and Society from the American Historical Society helped finance additional research at Stanford University and at the Bancroft Library. Work at the Huntington Library in 1987–88 was aided by a Huntington–Haynes Fellowship. Jennie Parnes Miller made it possible for me to take a leave of absence from my teaching duties to write the last third of the book.

Many individuals have offered valuable comments and insight into the issues considered here. The work was begun under Harry Scheiber, then at University of California, San Diego. Paul Gates, who years before had found the collection of Miller & Lux Papers housed in a damp library storage center, insisted on the importance of the collection. Mort Rothstein, John Wunder, Donald Pisani, Charles McCurdy, Christian Fritz, and especially James Sherrow provided valuable critiques of the research and the manuscript as it was being revised. A number of my colleagues and former colleagues at Texas Tech University also provided comments and suggestions, though my research often fell outside their areas of expertise. Chester Pach, Ben Newcomb, Joe King, Ed Steinhart, and David Troyansky all offered criticism or discussion of issues and problems (large and small) raised in the study.

The staff of the Bancroft Library also must be acknowledged. When I began this project, the Miller & Lux Papers were virtually unprocessed. The staff of the Bancroft Library provided invaluable help. Estelle Rebec, former head of the manuscripts division, provided access to the uncataloged, dusty, and difficult collection. During my summer trips to the Bancroft, librarians and clerks put up with requests for the huge numbers of boxes and cartons that filled their vans and storage vaults. And with wry good humor, Richard Ogar and his assistants photocopied the thousands of pages of often less-than-memorable documents that made possible long-distance research in a massive collection.

For the last decade, debate has raged over the role of law in society. Some scholars have presented law as an instrument, serving either the general will, the undefined majority, or the ruling elite, depending on one's ideological orientation. For others, law is more autonomous, operating according to internal rules or inherent contradictions, indeterminate and potentially available for use by the disadvantaged in a battle for power and protection. In the midst of the discussion of abstracts are unanswered questions about the role of lawyers, of the judiciary, and of ideology. Crucial to answering these questions are descriptions of law in practice, for it is in practice that legal assumptions and realities, and their role in society, can be observed. It is through the concrete that the abstract can be evaluated and more completely understood.[1]

This study looks at the particulars essential to understanding broad theoretical questions about law and the mechanisms of legal and economic power. It is the legal biography of a business, the prominent California land and cattle company Miller & Lux, during the period 1870–1930. It leaves the eastern and midwestern terrain of James Willard Hurst and Morton Horwitz[2] to look at the West, but like them examines law in an environment undergoing major economic development, where the rules governing resources are in contention. In this instance, water, made precious by scarcity, became a focus of conflict as California's mining camps, cattle ranches, and fields— where "there was nothing else to be seen but the limitless sea of wheat as far as the eye could reach"—were replaced by vineyards and citrus ranches, by growing cities and new industries.[3] While its environment was unique, California like the rest of the nation was struggling with the implications of corporate capitalism for government, law, and society, and Miller & Lux, like many others in the legalistic culture of the United States, looked to law to mediate its place in these changing times. Unlike most, Miller & Lux was a major actor in the legal arena, and the actions and reasoning of its lawyers and managers were recorded and preserved, revealing the impact of law on an individual player as well as on the broader society.

Miller & Lux was formed in 1858 by the immigrant butcher Henry Miller.

His was one of the bold, entrepreneurial enterprises that flourished in Gold Rush California. Resourceful and ambitious, Miller arrived in San Francisco in 1850. Eschewing prospecting, he went to work at his trade and within a few years had saved enough money to open his own butcher shop. Then, unhappy with the quality and quantity of cattle available in the city and eager to raise his own livestock, Miller embarked on an investigation of the ranches of upper California. In the San Joaquin Valley, he took an option to buy a quarter interest in a 48,000-acre Spanish land grant, and the cattle grazing it, from a man who hoped to leave for the gold fields. Jointly with a rival butcher, Charles Lux, Miller took this and a few other options he had collected to William Ralston at the Bank of California. Famous for his speculations, Ralston advanced Miller and Lux the money they needed to complete the purchases, helping to launch a partnership that lasted thirty years. Lux ran the business in the city, Miller that in the country, and they embarked on "a veritable orgy of land and cattle buying."[4]

In acquiring these first options, Miller proved himself adept at exploiting the distress faced by many owners of Mexican and Spanish land grants. Such grants had been under siege since 1851, when Congress required that the owners prove their titles. Heavily in debt as a result of the litigation that ensued, many of these ranchers were easy prey for anyone with ready cash. Miller often purchased a share of a *rancho,* becoming a tenant in common and filling the land with his cattle until he was able to buy out the remaining owners or force a partition. In this way he acquired portions of more than a dozen land grants in as many counties.[5] He was equally adept at exploiting loopholes in American land law, artfully benefiting from the largesse of the federal and state governments in this period, especially from legislation such as the Swamp Land Act of 1850, which provided easy, cheap access to land.[6]

On occasion Miller employed dummy entrymen to acquire tracts or to challenge homesteaders who were in his way. He used this tactic especially when he wanted to pick up small plots that controlled springs or the head-waters of small streams along the mountain valleys of his breeding ranches. However, Miller generally found the use of dummy entrymen messy and difficult. The method for making a dummy entry was well known—hire a man with no ambition and require that he sign a property transfer before actually filing his claim to land. But such men were unreliable. They did not always stay on the land as required, or they might spread rumors about Miller & Lux's interest in a piece of property or hold up the firm for more money before signing the necessary documents. Instead, Miller found it more convenient to rely on professional dealers in land scrip, like F. A. Hyde, for such services. Thus, though accusations of fraud often followed Miller, they were seldom proved. While Hyde was indicted and convicted of land fraud, Miller escaped the net by asserting that his purchases had been legitimate second- or third-party transactions.[7]

Ultimately Miller & Lux acquired almost a million acres of land and, according to Henry Miller's estimate, controlled at least ten times what it owned. The bulk of the land was in California's Central Valley, where the firm owned nearly a hundred miles of riparian footage along the San Joaquin River, as well as thousands of acres along the Kern and Fresno rivers. Miller & Lux's ranches and those of its subsidiary Pacific Live Stock Company dotted the mountain clefts and riverine valleys of eastern Oregon and western Nevada, and the foothills of California as well; the company also owned hundreds of parcels of land in San Francisco, Gilroy, Fresno, Bakersfield, and other small towns in California.[8]

In some ways, this accumulation of land merely followed a pattern common in frontier California. Large holdings had predominated in the Mexican era, when distance from markets and a small population had given land itself little monetary value. The pattern was repeated in the American period when gold rather than sod lured early migrants. William Chapman, for example, acquired over half a million acres of land in the 1860s and 1870s; James Ben Ali Haggin, Lloyd Tevis, Isaac Friedlander, James Irvine, and others each possessed hundreds of thousands of acres; and the Southern Pacific Railroad received more than 11 million acres in land grants. Many of these holdings survived intact well into the twentieth century, creating the distinctively skewed pattern of land use in California, where massive corporate farms, long dominant in agricultural production, stand side by side with a multiplicity of progressively smaller farms.[9]

As was common on the American frontier, California land was often acquired for speculation, not development, as a gamble at extracting the benefits of monopoly from those who followed. For Henry Miller, however, land played a different role. Miller did not want to sell his property but to exploit its use-value. He was an agricultural capitalist, for whom land was a means of producing commodities for sale on the market. His profits would come from transforming and extracting the natural assets of his soil and water in the form of beef and pork. Miller & Lux operated a fully integrated cattle company in which units of land were treated as elements of the larger whole, each specialized to best utilize its natural advantages. Cattle were bred on Miller & Lux's Nevada and Oregon highland ranches, which were relatively free of the cattle diseases that plagued the California ranches, and arrived on hoof and by the trainload in the San Joaquin Valley, to be fattened and readied for market; the company raised hundreds of thousands of cattle, sheep, and hogs on its valley pastures. Miller & Lux butchered and sold cattle as dressed meat from its own abattoirs in Los Banos and San Francisco; byproducts and wool were sold on both the national and international markets. The firm also raised fruit and grain, owned retail lumber and dry goods stores, banks and numerous canal companies—all as subordinate parts of the cattle operation.

The enterprise was both successful and powerful. Miller & Lux was large enough to get favorable shipping rates and rebates from its allies in the Southern Pacific Railroad. It also dictated the supply and price of cattle in northern California: during his lifetime, Henry Miller set the price of cattle for livestock dealers in San Francisco, furnishing the newspapers with a daily quotation of the price he credited his ranches.[10] Although the firm remained a regional one, never reaching the national prominence of the giant midwestern meat packers, in 1917 Miller & Lux was among the top two hundred industrial corporations in the United States, with assets of $35 million. Miller & Lux began selling its land after 1925 and ceased to be a major livestock producer in the 1930s; yet as late as the 1970s it still ranked among the twenty-five largest owners of land in California, holding some 90,000 acres.[11]

In the "land of little rain" that predominated in the West, the control of water provided the key to the profitability and success of such ventures as Miller & Lux. When buying land, Miller had carefully selected tracts along rivers and sloughs to ensure easy access to water. While some tracts included tule and alkali lands, most produced good forage, irrigated by regular seasonal overflows. At a time when the potential of irrigation was unappreciated by most settlers, Miller began building levees and ditches to reclaim land and to direct water to the most effective use. Eventually Miller & Lux improved thousands of acres of land along the banks and sloughs of the Kern, Fresno, and San Joaquin rivers. In Nevada and Oregon, where the firm's operations were smaller in scale and influence, it owned numerous isolated springs as well as land along rivers such as the Silvies in eastern Oregon and the Walker in western Nevada. As in California, control of water made irrigation possible; it also allowed Miller & Lux to dominate and graze wide areas of the public range. Miller & Lux's ditches, levees, and other capital improvements enhanced the benefits nature provided, letting the firm feed ever-larger herds and affording protection from the droughts that repeatedly plagued the arid West. Yet the growing size of Miller & Lux's fixed capital also required increasing sales to maintain profits, and it forced the firm into the courts to fight all challenges to its water rights.

Donald Worster has characterized the West, especially California, as a "hydraulic society." In his picture, water is the independent variable; the sheer effort of manipulating the environment generates a hierarchy in which power is based on the command of water.[12] This picture, however, is too simplistic. As Miller & Lux knew, the command of resources is not simply a matter of physical control, but one of law, particularly the laws defining property. As settlement increased and the practice of irrigation agriculture spread, water became an object of physical, ideological, and legal contention. These struggles were a complex interplay of forces tied not only to the local environmental problem of aridity, but also to the broader concerns of American law and political economy at the turn of the century.

California water issues are now dominated by state-sponsored and -subsidized projects, but during the period of California's industrial and agricultural takeoff, the development of water depended on private initiative and private capital. For most in the West, water, like land, minerals, and machinery, was an object to be exploited to generate income. But it was not clear how the benefits of this exploitation were to be distributed, nor was it clear who should bear the burden of cost, especially when promoters linked irrigation to social and economic democracy. Although zoning laws were beginning to modify the rights of landowners, the meaning of private property in land was a well-defined and understood part of American culture. Water rights, however, were different. As with land in earlier centuries, the laws governing water were in flux, and water was often portrayed as the common property of all. While in this period the image of water as commons omitted even the shadow of stewardship, it did confer important ideological incentives and power on those seeking access to a limited resource.

During the 1850s and 1860s, water rights had been acquired according to local custom, acquiesced in by the federal government as the main landowner and by the courts. As with mineral rights, the key factor in claims to water was the notion of first in time, first in right. These customs paved the way for the western doctrine of prior appropriation, which allowed claimants to acquire exclusive, transferable rights to finite quantities of water. Prior appropriation was accepted by the federal government in the mining code of 1866 and was adopted in arid states such as Colorado and Nevada, where legislators viewed appropriation as the legal doctrine most encouraging of rapid economic development. While many in California accepted prior appropriation as the doctrine governing western waters and while appropriation was provided for in California's water code of 1872, the state judiciary recognized the common-law doctrine of riparian rights as then practiced in the eastern states. Rather than recognizing ownership in a fixed quantity of water, riparianism traditionally restricted water rights to the use of flowing water and limited such rights to those owning riparian land. As these two doctrines competed for dominance and definition, the outcome of legal debate became a crucial parameter defining the costs and benefits of development, and each new use of water exposed new gaps in the laws governing it. Litigation became a strategy and courtrooms a theater for conflicts over economic power.[13]

As the owner of thousands of acres of riparian land, Miller & Lux was a major actor in this theater. During the period of its expansion, the firm used law consciously and aggressively to enhance and guarantee the value of its property. In this it followed a pattern noted in other areas dominated by extractive industries.[14] As a large commercial enterprise, Miller & Lux was involved in lawsuits to collect money owed, to foreclose on tenants and mortgagees, and to prosecute cattle thieves, but it perceived and treated such issues as petty, routine, and inconsequential. Its main concern was water law, for it was water that made its ranches so productive and so profitable. As a litigant the firm was overwhelmingly a plaintiff, picking fights and waging battles to protect and extend its control over the rivers it relied upon. Its fights were primarily intraclass contests against other, often large, landowners. On occasion Miller & Lux took on smaller farmers—all of them likewise hoping to capitalize on water as a source of profit.

Miller & Lux created a vast complex of litigation that illustrates the logic of self-preservation employed by a major firm and the complexities and contradictions inherent in the law as an arena of economic competition. The firm relied primarily on riparian rights and on a litigation strategy that stressed contracts and the protection of property rights. Its successes before the California Supreme Court formed the centerpiece of the judiciary's protection of riparian rights against the assertion that appropriation better served the "public." In Oregon and California, Miller & Lux actively opposed water law reform. Yet to strengthen its own position and improve its property, the firm later manipulated the very institutions and legal arguments developed by reformers. It used the doctrine of riparian rights both to prevent the development of reservoirs planned by competitors and to establish water storage systems that might benefit its land. While it denied any privileges for public utilities competing for water, winning judicial affirmation of its riparian claims against a public service company, Miller & Lux also sought to have the claims of its canal company raised above the rights of other, newer riparian water users. Throughout, Miller & Lux confronted the capriciousness of judges and manipulated the flexibilities of a federated, stratified court structure.

A general predilection among jurists toward protecting vested property rights aided the enterprise but could not always guarantee its success. The law was full of contradictions that gave judges power and autonomy. California and Oregon both elevated riparian rights and recognized prior appropriation. In addition to the uncertainties this duality imposed, each of these doctrines included concepts of reasonableness, allowing even more room for the play of ideology and judicial choice. The potential for independent decision making was enhanced by the reformism of the Progressive era, in which governmental and legal action were perceived as remedies for the problems of both concentrated capital and excessive competition. In the charged atmosphere that pervaded discussions of water rights in the West, those who lost in the courts did not easily accept defeat. Judicial endorsement of riparian rights did not legitimate the doctrine, which seemed tinged with the colors of monopoly. Laws could be changed, and the legislature became an important arena of struggle and the police power a tool for restricting riparian claims. Reformers and outsiders seeking access to resources raised notions of the public trust, of water as a natural resource held in reserve by the state for all the people, to counter the idea of water as capital, as simply part of the productive investment of enterprising property owners. As in the national arena, state judges could choose, on the one hand, a kind of sociological jurisprudence (in this case, an instrumentalist jurisprudence of aspiration) or, on the other, formalism, liberty of contract, and vested rights. Although most players shared the cultural attitude that water was to be exploited to advance economic development, law provided a forum for conflict, not consensus.

This book traces the struggle for power over resources and for influence over the laws governing them, a struggle that illuminates the dialectical interplay of legal and economic capacities. The first three chapters consider the period 1870–1919. For most of these years, Miller & Lux experienced physical and financial growth; dynamic and confident, it repeatedly brought its conflicts to court. Each of these chapters traces a major avenue of litigation pursued by the firm. The first focuses on Miller & Lux's bold assertions of its riparian claims against upstream appropriators, examining the impact of competing doctrines and exploring Miller & Lux's role in the judicial resolution of these contradictory conceptions of rights. The next chapter looks at Miller & Lux as the owner of the San Joaquin & Kings River Canal & Irrigation Company, a public utility that provided irrigation water to hundreds of farmers in the San Joaquin Valley. In this situation, Miller & Lux's power struggle with its customers hinged on the judiciary's willingness to recognize water rights as income-earning capital. The third chapter analyzes conflicts with rival riparians who had legal claims equal to those of Miller & Lux. In these cases, Miller & Lux's difficulty in translating its wealth into legal success serves as a corrective to simplistic evaluations of riparianism and of the relationship between law and wealth.

The last three chapters look at the period 1911–35, when Miller & Lux's economic power began to wane. In this period, Progressive reformers and entrepreneurial farmers looked to the legislature to grant the access to water that the judiciary had denied; their effort and Miller & Lux's response provide the focus for the fourth chapter. The last two chapters trace Miller & Lux's momentary retreat from litigation when it confronted financial disaster. Instead, it manipulated institutional reforms in an effort to raise capital for canal development and to co-opt opposition to its control of water. A reservoir was proposed to provide a technical solution to the conflict by increasing the available volume of water; but the proposal ultimately failed when competing interests proved unable to resolve the interwoven economic and legal issues that divided them. Again Miller & Lux and its rivals went into the courtrooms. This story fills in the background essential for understanding the modern state projects that dominate the delivery of water in California.

The battles described were never abstract. Power and wealth, present and future were at stake. Miller & Lux approached litigation with a consciousness of doctrine and its real impact. Doctrine was linked to daily life, interwoven into routine business decisions and social relationships as rivals competed for influence and strove to have their visions of economic growth and progress imposed on a larger region. The conflicts pitted Miller & Lux and its attorneys against opponents they knew—against neighbors, customers, and tenants; against lawyers who appeared again and again; before judges whose reactions they hoped to anticipate, predict, and influence. This is the real meat of legal history, of law as ideology, instrument, and a force in history at the most basic level.

1

Defining the Value of Riparian Rights

When Miller & Lux entered the murky legal arena of California water law, both the courts and the civil code had recognized two contradictory doctrines: riparian rights and prior appropriation. According to the doctrine of riparian rights, water was a part of property in land. Although the owner of the banks of a stream did not own the water per se, he had a right to a reasonable use of the water and, most important, was entitled to its continued flow over his land.[1] On the other hand, the doctrine of prior appropriation allowed water to be claimed (just as mineral rights could be claimed) by anyone who would put it to beneficial use, after filing the proper notices. For many in the West the latter doctrine was linked with prosperity and future growth. It had permitted the movement of water over vast distances to wash minerals from auriferous hills,[2] and it seemed most suited to the development of irrigation, which likewise required that water be transported to serve the state's arid regions.

However, neither the California constitutional convention of 1850 nor that of 1878–79 had adopted a single doctrine. The constitution and the civil code accepted English common law, of which riparianism was a part, as the rule of decision in the state; yet both riparian rights and prior appropriation were written into statutory law. Thus, as the demand for water rose, the courts were called upon to mediate not only between competing interests but also between competing legal doctrines.

Henry Miller owned extensive property along the banks of the state's rivers, property made valuable by the flow and overflow of these streams. Physical proximity, however, did not give him a monopoly on water, as farmers, ranchers, and hydroelectric interests dug upstream ditches and reservoirs that poured the benefits of water into new enterprises. To protect the natural advantages of his land, Miller took his complaints to court, asserting his legal rights as a riparian. Victory was not assured, however. Given the coexistence of competing doctrines, the battle for water gave the courts real choices, and judicial attitudes toward the law as an instrument of economic development and toward the meaning of private property played decisive roles in the fight for control. Persistence, the money to fund litigation, and the ability to link his cause to ideological concerns for stability and security eventually brought Miller success in court, and his repeated efforts to protect the value of his property indelibly marked California water law by fixing riparian rights at its foundation.

————

Miller & Lux's first effort to guard the borders of riparian rights came in Kern County, California. In the 1860s Miller and his partner had purchased 40,000 acres of overflowed lands along Buena Vista Slough and the lower reaches of the Kern River. Cheaply acquired under the Swamp Land Act of 1850, this land had long been favored by cattlemen; it provided secure water, naturally irrigated pastures, and shelter for cattle, sheep, and hogs, which also grazed adjoining public lands.[3] Miller & Lux soon intervened to improve on the advantages of its floodplain property. By 1873 Miller & Lux had organized a water company that dug a new channel to replace the shallow slough and operated canals to drain the swamps and to irrigate fields increasingly fenced and planted in alfalfa.[4] Farmers who began settling along the Kern in the 1870s also scratched out small canals to water their crops, setting the stage for conflict. When the region seared in the drought of 1877, the cattlemen, blaming the farmers for the severity of their losses, formed a riparian rights association to fight the new irrigators.[5] In 1879 the cattlemen filed seventy-eight lawsuits seeking to stop all interference with their rights. Their proposition was simple: as riparian owners, they were entitled to the full, uninterrupted flow of the Kern.[6]

Miller & Lux's main opponent in the various lawsuits was another large capitalist, James Ben Ali Haggin, a financier, speculator, and associate of George Hearst and Lloyd Tevis in a series of ventures that included the

profitable Anaconda copper mines in Montana. Haggin and his active partner in Kern County, William Carr, the Southern Pacific's political boss, had
arrived in Kern County with the opening of the railroad in 1874.[7] Haggin and
Carr took up vast tracts of railroad land, including one encompassing 59,000
of the valley's most fertile acres.[8] In 1877, with the collusion of the local land
registrar and dummy entrymen, they procured key parcels under the Desert
Land Act, despite swirling accusations of fraud that eventually forced a ten-
year suspension of such sales at the Visalia land office.[9] Quickly amassing
three-quarters of the irrigable lands,[10] Haggin also purchased controlling
interests in most of the existing farmer-initiated canals and by 1879 had
expanded one of them, the Calloway Canal, to supply his desert holdings.
Although most of the land Haggin acquired is still held as a single unit, part
of the oil-rich properties of Tenneco, Inc., in 1877 Haggin professed plans
to develop the land and sell it in small units that included water rights. While
the San Francisco newspapers attacked him, Haggin enlisted the support of
local boosters and businessmen in Kern County. His efforts had increased
the acreage under irrigation, and the local entrepreneurs welcomed both the
immediate cash he brought and the roseate vision of luxuriant family farms
and bustling towns that he conjured up, a vision dependent on the canals
challenged by Miller & Lux.[11]

The trial of *Lux* v. *Haggin* began in San Francisco in 1881, two years after
the initial filing of the suits. Stretching over forty-nine days, the trial involved a large portion of Kern County's citizenry and some of the leading
figures from the state bar. In general, cattlemen lined up with Miller & Lux,
while those testifying for Haggin were farmers, many of them defendants
in the other suits filed by Miller & Lux, or tenants of Haggin and Carr, or
customers of the canals they controlled. Both sides brought in surveyors,
engineers, and old-time residents of the state, and each side recruited an
advocate in the press. Much of the testimony focused on whether Miller
& Lux's property contained a watercourse or was a mere swamp caused by
the occasional overflow of the Kern River. The state had not surveyed its
swamplands before selling them, and each side vied to influence the state
engineer, who had begun a project to chart the state's rivers, hoping that the
official map would mirror the flow of its argument. The issue was crucial,
for if there were no watercourse on the Miller & Lux property, the company
could make no claim to water under riparian rights. Evidence was also taken
on the size and timing of appropriations of the Kern's waters, on the flow

of the canals and the amounts of land irrigated, and on past droughts and climatic conditions.[12]

Ultimately, however, the arguments focused not on these factual issues but on the questions of private property rights and public policy. Hall McAllister, a leading member of the state bar who represented Miller & Lux, argued that the company had paid $40,000 for its land, had built the Kern Valley Canal to control the water and reclaim the swamplands, and had used the area to graze cattle for many years. Miller & Lux had recognized the value of the land and developed it. Haggin, he maintained, was merely a speculator who had ruined the cattle company's property.[13] The defense, on the other hand, attached the label of monopolist to Miller & Lux and availed itself of the image of the enterprising pioneer "dedicated to freedom and liberty" and progress. Where Miller & Lux was merely exploiting the public domain for its cattle, Haggin and Carr, according to their attorney, were community builders who had taken "absolutely uninhabited and uninhabitable desert waste" and turned it into a "garden spot" on which thousands of families would one day live.[14]

In using this language, Haggin, himself a major landowner and speculator, linked his personal fight with Miller to the broad antimonopoly sentiments that characterized popular politics in California in this period. Since the 1850s many had railed against land monopoly, first pointing the finger at the large ranches of native Californians and then at the holdings of the railroads and land speculators. In 1871 Henry George fueled this sentiment with his pamphlet *Our Land and Our Policy*, which pointed out the abuses of American land policy that had aided many of the largest owners; in his 1879 book *Progress and Poverty*, George elaborated on his call for a massive single tax on land to restore it to the people. In 1877–78, sympathy for the national railroad strikes merged with anti-Chinese racism and distrust of the wealthy to spawn a wave of riots and a new political party, the Workingmen's Party, led by small-businessman and sandlot orator Dennis Kearney. The Workingmen's Party and farmers sympathetic to the national Grange movement were a major force in the California constitutional convention of 1878–79, which produced some efforts at railroad regulation amidst a great deal of anticorporate, antimonopoly, and anti-Chinese rhetoric. Although himself a target of populist criticism in 1878–79, Haggin later financed an antiriparian movement that linked monopoly and riparian rights in the popular mind.[15]

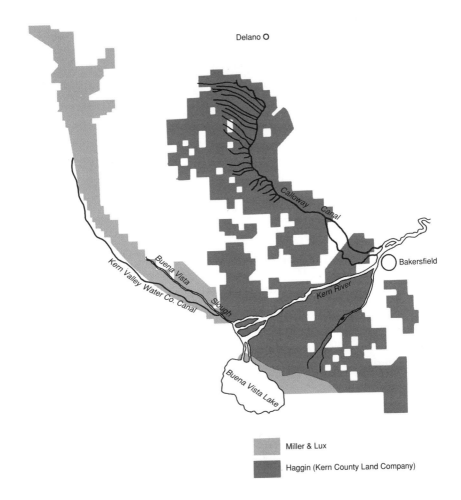

Map 1: Kern County lands of Miller & Lux and James B. Haggin ca. 1885. Based on the California Engineering Department, William Hammond Hall, Detail Irrigation Map, Bakersfield Sheet, Buena Vista Sheet, Delano and Poso Sheet (1885); Lux v. Haggin, Transcript on Appeal; Map of the Irrigating Canals in the Vicinity of Bakersfield, Kern County, California, "Agriculture by Irrigation," in Eleventh Census of the United States, 1890, vol. 5, part 2, p. 54.

The decision in the lower court went against Miller & Lux, refusing it an injunction against the Calloway Canal diversion. Judge Benjamin Brundage, a land agent and lawyer who had earlier written an effusive endorsement of Haggin's land and canal project,[16] accepted the facts as presented by the defendants. The Kern River, he found, did not flow through what he called the Buena Vista swamp, and thus no watercourse existed on Miller & Lux property. Although the lands had been purchased as swamplands, Brundage ruled that they had not actually been overflowed, having "never been wet or irrigated by any waters of the Kern River." He asserted, furthermore, that the diversion for the Calloway Canal had been properly made against the water rights of the state prior to Miller & Lux's acquisition of land.[17]

Endorsing the developmental argument Haggin had offered, Brundage reasoned that economic growth was the issue of the case, and future prosperity lay with irrigated farming, not with cattle ranching. The Calloway Canal served lands where irrigation was a "natural want," and no more water than was reasonable and necessary was taken. As a result of the canal, "the said lands had become profitable, productive, valuable, settled upon and occupied by a large number of persons and families, and covered with grain fields, vineyards, orchards, gardens, and homes; and . . . if deprived of such water, said lands will again become utterly barren, desert and worthless."[18] The desert bloomed; the injunction was denied.

As would become its pattern after defeats in its efforts to control water, Miller & Lux filed an appeal alleging numerous errors of fact and of law, including in this case Brundage's refusal to admit certain certificates of purchase. The certificates, the cattle company contended, proved that its land was in no way subject to Haggin's diversion. In the original presentation of its case, Miller & Lux had relied on a broad statement of rights—that, as a matter of law, appropriations were inferior to riparian rights and that, as the owner of riparian land, it was the "absolute owner of the water" flowing through its property.[19] Haggin, for his part, had submitted that since the Calloway appropriation had been made in 1875, three years before the cattle company acquired clear title to the swamplands, any rights that this land possessed assumed his prior use.[20] Miller & Lux had not addressed this argument and, surprised by the reasoning, tried to undercut it by belatedly demonstrating that its property had been in private hands since the 1850s, when the state had granted the Buena Vista swamplands to a group of speculators who promised to reclaim them. However, Brundage had ruled that the certificates of purchase offered by Miller & Lux were irrelevant and immaterial rebuttal evidence.

In 1884, the state supreme court ruled in favor of Miller & Lux. Writing for a narrow majority, Justice John R. Sharpstein declared that the common-law doctrine of riparian rights governed the case. Water was part of property in land, available and valuable to the owners, and transferable on sale just as were trees, rocks, and soil. While the appropriation of water was recognized in California, it could be exercised only against the rights of the state, not against those of private owners. The central issue here was a routine one of fact: Had Haggin first diverted water before or after the swamplands passed into private hands? Brundage, Sharpstein argued, had erred in refusing to admit the certificates of purchase and other evidence relevant to answering this question. Remanding the case for a new trial, Sharpstein concluded that "the only difficulty that need be experienced is in arriving at the facts. The law is plain enough." [21]

The question of law, however, could not be so easily dismissed. Led by Justice Erskine M. Ross, the only justice from southern California and himself an irrigator, three members of the court dissented.[22] Ross argued that custom, sanctioned by earlier decisions of the court and codified in the 1872 water statutes, established appropriation as the rule governing water rights in California. While the water code recognized riparian rights, this provision applied only to those holding Mexican or Spanish land grants whose property had been guaranteed by treaty. Beyond this narrow band of protection, common-law riparian rights were abrogated.[23] Such a reading, Ross argued, best served the dictates of the environment and best advanced the interests of the people. It reflected the spirit of the common law, which as "the perfection of human reasoning" should not impose a rule that left crops to "perish for thirst" while water went to waste.[24]

Given the depth of the division among the justices, at a time when Haggin and Carr were organizing and financing a statewide campaign against riparianism, the court agreed to rehear the issues. All interested groups were invited to present arguments, and the flood of briefs raised a debate on the role and source of law. Miller & Lux and its allies linked the attack on riparianism to the Kearnyite and Granger movements of the period: part of a broad assault on private property. They urged the court to protect property by recognizing traditional rights and following established precedent.[25] Their opponents called on the court to acknowledge physical and economic reality and yield to popular opinion: much of California was arid, needing irrigation to be fully and profitably developed for the people. The argument that law was an instrument of economic policy was dramatically illustrated in the brief submitted by William Stewart and Louis T. Herrin for a group of California irrigation companies.

William Stewart, who had earlier defended Haggin against charges of land fraud, was one of the most experienced mining lawyers in the West. In the 1850s he helped draft the widely copied quartz mining code of Nevada County and he had a hand in writing the federal mining law of 1866.[26] Both accepted local custom as determining legal rights to mining claims. The 1866 law also applied this reasoning to legitimate the appropriation of water on the public domain.[27] On the part of the irrigation companies, Stewart asserted that the usages of "reasonable men" should govern California water, whether or not these customs had been codified. California was a state of widely varied geography and climate, and neither precedent nor statutes could adequately reflect the natural differences. The courts and the legislature had recognized both riparian rights and appropriation, and while riparianism might well serve the conditions of the wettest regions, appropriation was best suited to most others. The determination of which doctrine was appropriate, he argued, should be left to the courts and juries of each county, which could then rule in "the best and paramount interests of their different localities."[28] The role of law was to set the stage for economic growth by endorsing the general will and the standards of each community.

In 1886 the state supreme court rejected these appeals to localism and popular sovereignty. In *Lux* v. *Haggin*, it emphasized the formal rule of law and the security it gave to property owners.[29] In principle, wrote Justice Elisha W. McKinstry for the same four-person majority as in the first hearing, neither geography nor public policy should influence the court to neglect the letter of the law. Examining the history of water in California from the first Spanish settlement of the region, he concluded that the determining event was the adoption of the common law by the state's first legislature. This gesture incorporated the rules of riparian doctrine. While riparianism had been modified by lawmakers to include irrigation and to concede certain limited rights of appropriation, it had never been abrogated. Moreover, the law had to be consistent. California was no longer a frontier state in which economic development occurred in isolated communities; rather, it had a statewide economy. Enterprises such as those of Miller & Lux stretched beyond the boundaries of any single county and even those of the state itself. If California was to continue to grow, the rights of citizens and the rights of property could not be left to the "whim or caprice"—or even to the honest judgment—of local courts and juries.[30]

Determined to protect property rights, McKinstry tried to settle each point of dispute, an effort that swelled the opinion to two hundred pages of rambling prose. In general, the court insisted that those challenging vested property rights bear the burden of proof. In one instance, Haggin had asserted that dams built by Miller & Lux to reclaim the swamps had cut off the flow of water through the firm's lands, thus eliminating its claim to the stream. McKinstry responded that the mere existence of a headgate that could be opened was adequate evidence of Miller & Lux's continuing right.[31] More important, he saw the statute allowing appropriation as a limited one. It had not expressly divorced property in water from land, nor could such a broad reading, with the incumbent injuries, be "based on any doubtful interpretation of language."[32] The statute had, in fact, recognized riparian rights; but even if it had not, McKinstry reasoned, the legislature could not strip the state or the federal government or private individuals of such claims. As common-law property rights, riparian rights were constitutionally protected and fully transferable to subsequent owners. In providing for appropriation, the legislature had merely agreed to grant water from state lands to those complying with the conditions laid out.[33] All such grants necessarily conceded existing private rights, an interpretation that precluded appropriation if downstream riparian land had already been sold.[34]

The question thus returned to one of timing. If Haggin's appropriation had occurred while the swamplands belonged to the state, he owned the water, but if the lands had been privately held at that time, Miller & Lux's riparian claims were controlling. The central issue in the dispute was the point at which title changed hands; in other words, what was the significance of the certificates of purchase issued when a buyer first filed and made partial payment on state lands? In many ways, these questions were as important as those of water law. Land titles in California had been in a state of chaos since the first attempts to settle claims to the Mexican land grants. Swampland grants, which required that the land be drained and reclaimed, were particularly troublesome because of the lax way in which California had disposed of the lands, often selling them before the federal government had identified which lands were in fact included in a grant.[35]

The case of the Buena Vista swamplands was typical. In 1857 the state had conditionally granted the lands to a speculator, W. F. Montgomery, who had promised both a grandiose reclamation and drainage project and a canal to link Kern County with San Francisco. The project was never completed. Ten years later the state issued patents for some 90,000 acres of this land to Thomas Baker and Harry Brown, who had succeeded to Montgomery's interest, only to challenge their title in 1868, when floods mocked their claim to have drained the land as the original grant required. Miller & Lux had purchased its land from Baker and Brown, but the litigation prevented Miller & Lux from receiving full title until 1877 and 1878. It was those dates that Haggin relied on to establish the priority of his water diversion.[36]

McKinstry rejected Haggin's argument that the swamplands had been state property until 1878. While acknowledging that the government held formal title to land until all conditions of sale had been met, McKinstry argued that the state only held title in trust for the purchaser. Equitable title to "all the incidents to land and ownership" was conveyed to a buyer at the time of the first payment and the filing of the certificates.[37] Such transfer of ownership was essential if landowners were to develop their property. Water rights were among the incidents transferred, since "to hold otherwise . . . would operate a manifest injustice."[38] Given this conclusion, Miller & Lux's lands and water rights had passed from state to private ownership long before Haggin began his diversion. Having accepted riparian rights as law, McKinstry in this case refused to restrict their application and recognized a broad definition of "private" property. Like Haggin's supporters, McKinstry was committed to the economic development of the state, but once again he insisted that the key to future development lay not in easing appropriation but in creating an atmosphere of stability and certainty that would encourage investment.[39]

Although *Lux* v. *Haggin* was a narrow decision, it was a tremendous victory for the cattle firm. The supreme court had called for a new trial, but the suit was not reheard, and the others filed by Miller & Lux were eventually dropped. Instead, a private settlement was reached that transformed legal success into capital improvements on Miller & Lux's ranches. Miller's goal was not merely to possess water, but to make it conform to his needs for irrigation, to exploit its economic potential. In its natural state, the Kern River delivered too much water to Miller & Lux's land in the winter and spring and too little in the dry months of summer and fall. So in 1888 Miller resolved both his natural and his legal problems by signing a contract with Haggin that divided the flow of the Kern River. Haggin was to receive two-thirds of the water, while the remaining third was allotted to Miller & Lux. In exchange, Haggin was to pay half of the construction and maintenance costs of a reservoir in which Miller & Lux would store, for its own use, water not consumed by the upper irrigators.[40] When completed, the shallow Buena Vista Reservoir covered some 23,000 acres. After this settlement, both Miller & Lux and Haggin continued to buy up land at the expense of small farmers. During the period of trials and appeals, Miller & Lux expanded its holdings in Kern County from 61,979 to 80,073 acres, much of it from its former allies among local cattlemen. By 1890 Miller & Lux had acquired an additional 40,000 acres, for a total of 120,587 acres in the county.[41] Haggin, Tevis, and Carr did not break up or subdivide their lands as they had promised in the 1870s. By 1890, when they set up the Kern County Land Company to administer their holdings, they owned 375,000 acres in the county.[42]

By recognizing riparian rights as property rights, *Lux* v. *Haggin* protected Miller & Lux's claims to all other streams flowing through its ranches. The firm did not need to file formal claims to water as required under the doctrine of appropriation but could use water at any time and in any manner, relying on the natural, physical advantages of its property. The victory, however, was far from final and marked only the beginning of Miller & Lux's litigation to protect its riparian claims against upstream appropriators.

In the decades following *Lux* v. *Haggin,* population growth and economic development repeatedly challenged Miller & Lux's command of rivers. By the 1880s many cattlemen had sold or lost land, and the cattle ranges that had dominated early California began to give way to irrigated vineyard, orchards, and dairy farms. In Fresno County, the area under irrigation rose from 100,000 acres in 1890 to 400,000 acres in 1910; the number of farms increased by 250 percent. A similar change took place in Merced, Stanislaus, and Madera counties, where the many new irrigated farms competed for water Miller & Lux relied upon.[43] Likewise, the rapid urbanization of southern and central California, especially the growth of Los Angeles, placed new demands on rivers, such as the Kern and the San Joaquin, that watered Miller & Lux's ranches.

The competition and the requirements of riparian doctrine became of furious concern as Miller & Lux confronted the new century. While irrigation promoters bewailed the victory of riparianism, insisting that it would throttle progress, the common law left riparians like Miller & Lux open to continual challenge. Riparian rights were subject to prescriptive, or adverse, use, by which an upstream user could gain a permanent right against all downstream proprietors. California law required only five years of uninterrupted use to perfect such a prescriptive title. The briefness of this interval greatly circumscribed the impact of riparianism in many areas because landowners failed to protest changes in water use.[44] Acutely aware of the dangers posed by upstream appropriators, Miller & Lux charged its employees to note all such activities along the rivers it relied on. Since riparian rights had been recognized as property rights, Miller & Lux could protest each new appropriation it detected, no matter how small. Where opponents were willing to concede its rights, it negotiated contracts to share the benefits of the rivers; where such concessions were rejected, it pursued new court battles that not only affected the pattern of water use, but also forced the state supreme court to further define the meaning and value of property in water.

Hydroelectric power interests began exploring the Kern and San Joaquin rivers in the late 1890s. Among the earliest to act were those working with Henry E. Huntington, who sought cheap, reliable electricity to fuel trolley and real estate enterprises in Los Angeles. By the turn of the century, the Los Angeles-based Edison Electric Company (later named Southern California Edison) and Pacific Light and Power Company (which merged with Southern California Edison in 1916), as well as the San Joaquin Light & Power Company (SJL&P) had filed claims for water and for reservoir sites along these rivers. In 1902, as Huntington's Pacific Light and Power Company (PL&P) prepared to open its Kern River generating plant, Miller & Lux and the Kern County Land Company filed a joint protest. They claimed that they used all the water of the river and threatened to take legal steps to stop any interference with their rights. As Huntington proposed negotiating a settlement, the two cattle companies obtained an injunction to shut down his plant without even raising the central question of water rights. PL&P carried water to its turbines through a twelve-mile-long canal that even its own attorney admitted "leaked like a sieve," and Miller & Lux convinced a local judge that if the canal were allowed to open, its seepage would undermine public roads.[45]

Financial pressures impelled Huntington to compromise rather than fight the cattlemen over this issue. Believing that Miller & Lux would pursue its protest, he reluctantly agreed to line the channel with cement. The lining, which more than doubled the cost of the canal, eliminated the loss of water that Miller & Lux had protested and in the process increased the generating capacity of the power plant, thus paying for itself. More important, however, were the long-term financial considerations. Huntington's attorney, H. W. O'Melveny, had projected that a court fight with Miller & Lux would last two to three years. During this time, PL&P would lose the interest and profits on its investment of more than a million dollars, as well as risking the deterioration of an idle plant. The alternative—settlement—not only eliminated "the hazards and delays of litigation" but also, by securing the company's title to water, made its bonds "absolutely safe and sound" and its stock "of immediate value." [46]

However, as quickly as the dispute with the PL&P was settled, the more substantial issue of water rights reemerged. Sometime in 1905, the Edison Electric Co. began working on a dam and generating system just upstream from the PL&P plant. On searching the records of Kern and Inyo counties, Miller & Lux found that the various power companies had made a series of filings on storage sites along the Kern and its tributaries. Miller & Lux and the Kern County Land Company then filed a complaint challenging all existing and planned water developments along the river and obtained an injunction against the Edison project. When the hydroelectric interests again proposed negotiations, the riparians raised the stakes, seeking a comprehensive contract covering the development and use of the entire stream.[47]

By the end of 1906, a contract had been devised that met all of Miller & Lux's terms. The agreement with Edison Electric specified both the timing of all the utility's diversions of water and the manner of constructing and operating all reservoirs and conduits; in addition, Edison was to pay Miller & Lux and the Kern County Land Company $350,000, ostensibly to allow them to buy up the remaining independent riparian properties. More important, the utility recognized and accepted the riparian proprietors as controlling the river, as no other upstream rival had done before. Agreeing to join Miller & Lux in all litigation necessary to defend riparian rights and to pay one-third of the costs of such litigation, Edison Electric conceded that its rights depended on the "assertion and protection of the rights of Miller & Lux and the Kern County Land Company as *riparian proprietors*." When combined with the Lux-Haggin contract, Miller & Lux attorney R. E. Houghton argued, the agreement with Edison gave "to the Kern River a status that does not exist as to any other river in the world. . . . [It] is in so far as the flow and use of its waters are concerned, practically held in private ownership,—the property of Miller & Lux, Inc. and of the Kern County Land Company."[48]

As it settled the Kern River deal, Miller & Lux opened talks about the San Joaquin River with Huntington's Pacific Light & Power and other power-generating interests. Initially skeptical, both Henry Miller and his son-in-law J. Leroy Nickel, who supervised the firm's legal affairs, had been persuaded that upstream storage on this river would benefit the cattle company by providing late-season water.[49] PL&P promised that its proposed reservoirs would increase the flow of the San Joaquin by as much as 300 second-feet during its lowest stages.[50] The reservoirs, argued attorney Frank Short, who mediated many of the negotiations, would make the San Joaquin "the most uniform and valuable in its flow in the state, barring only the Sacramento."[51] The arrangements, however, were more complex than those regarding the Kern. For one thing, the San Joaquin's many tributaries and the greater value of both its reservoir sites and its overflow complicated even the required engineering studies. For another, Miller & Lux was already committed to protect the rights of the Scottish-owned California Pastoral & Agricultural Company (CP&A), a riparian neighbor, whose resident manager, Isaac Bird, was skeptical and often hostile toward the negotiations. Agreement had to be reached on measurements of the flow of the various tributaries to the river, the timing of storage, and the subsequent release of water, all within the context of the anticipated expansion of both irrigation and power generation.[52]

Bird continually pressed Miller & Lux to file suit asserting their joint riparian claims against upstream storage, but Nickel was reluctant to take such action against the hydroelectric interests, preferring to settle such matters by negotiations. In 1906 Miller & Lux's obligations toward CP&A prevented it from consummating an agreement with the San Joaquin Light & Power Company (SJL&P), which even at that time operated a small generating plant on the north fork of the river. The delay presented the risk that this upstream user might perfect a part of its right; but rather than go to court, Nickel hoped to protect himself against such a loss through a negotiated stipulation in which the SJL&P disclaimed any rights that might accrue during the period of discussions. Nickel consistently refused to support the actions Bird eventually filed against the hydroelectric interests, insisting that the reservoirs benefited riparian proprietors.[53]

While litigation was the most direct method of protecting his title, Nickel based his decision in favor of negotiation on broad political and economic concerns. Water law, given the hostility to riparian rights that Haggin had tapped, had continued as an important element in California politics, and Miller & Lux wanted no more enemies. Although the Huntington's attorneys saw Nickel's attitude toward them as arrogant and disdainful, Nickel in fact hoped to build an alliance with the power companies. Litigation, Nickel argued, would be an unnecessary expense that "antagonizes people I desire to work with."[54] More important, it was politically dangerous. Even if the cattlemen succeeded in enjoining the reservoirs, the power companies had "ample resources" to contest the move. Such a well-financed suit would be dangerous in that "a powerful sentiment would be created throughout the state with a view to influence the Supreme Court as to the folly of letting all the flood waters from melting snows in the high mountains run to the ocean without any benefit being derived from them."[55] Legal rights could not be divorced from popular politics and pressures, and Nickel did not want another fight like that with Haggin.

Instead, in 1906 he struck the first in a series of deals covering the development of the San Joaquin: a secret, unrecorded contract that allowed PL&P (later Southern California Edison) to build a reservoir and generating plant at Big Creek on the river's south fork. The dam was to reach 100 feet by the fall of 1907 and 160 feet in 1909. Water would be restrained according to a schedule accepted by Miller & Lux; it would be released later to meet the needs of the firm's ranches. As in the case of the Kern River, the power company recognized the validity of riparian rights and Miller & Lux's ownership of the stored waters.[56]

However, not all reservoir builders were so tractable. Reservoir projects to irrigate arid lands presented a more serious threat to Miller & Lux's exploitation of the floodplains. While the power companies held water only temporarily, irrigators consumed it, taking it away from downstream landowners. The Madera Canal and Irrigation Company, for example, diverted and sold the water of the Fresno River upstream from Miller & Lux's Madera County ranches. This river, like many others in California, dried up in the hottest months of the year; to supply water during such periods, the irrigation company by 1904 had excavated a series of shallow reservoirs to store the Fresno's floodwaters. Each foot of water that was stored imperiled Miller & Lux's pattern of land use. The cattle company relied on the river's annual overflow to produce a swath of grass up to one and a half miles wide through its riparian holdings; by 1899 it had begun improving on the natural benefits of the river by building levees, weirs, and canals to channel these waters to wider areas of its best lands and had begun seeding its fields in alfalfa. At the same time Miller & Lux had joined with the CP&A, its riparian neighbor, to build a canal that diverted the waters of the San Joaquin onto land in the western section of Madera County.[57] This system provided cheap and ample feed for the firm's herds, but since it relied on minimal technology, it depended on the flow of all the river's floodwaters over the company's lands. Confronted with the loss of water to Madera Canal and Irrigation, Miller & Lux filed suits in 1900 and in 1905 charging that the diversion and subsequent reservoiring of the Fresno had damaged its property.[58] In 1894 and 1899, the cattle company had initiated similar proceedings against the Fresno Flume and Irrigation Company to protest reservoirs on the San Joaquin.

These suits proved lengthy and difficult. While Huntington had conceded Miller & Lux's view of the law, both the Madera Canal and Irrigation Company and Fresno Flume challenged the broad application of riparian doctrine and denied that they had interfered with the legitimate rights of the cattle company. In fact, the law governing floodwaters was more uncertain than the easy concessions from Huntington would indicate. Riparian owners were entitled to the "usual flow" of water, but that did not necessarily encompass overflow waters. In humid regions, floodwaters were seldom sought after, and efforts at flood control had produced little clarification of their status as property. In California, the appropriation of floodwaters had been allowed in some cases where riparian lands had sustained no consequent damages, and *Lux* v. *Haggin* had suggested that such overflows were not a part of the riparian right and were thus available for storage [59]—a point quickly seized upon by the proponents of storage in these cases.

Like Haggin before them, the promoters of the Madera Canal Company relied on ideological arguments to defend their exploitation of water. The Madera Canal Company's profits depended on the subdivision and irrigation of former wheat ranches. It sold water to small commercial dairy farmers and raisin growers as well as to the Standard Oil Company and the vintner Italian Swiss Colony, which owned 8,600 acres and a large processing plant in Madera County. The evidence before the trial court clearly demonstrated that the reservoirs interfered with the watering of Miller & Lux's grasslands, and the cattle company easily won an injunction shutting them down.[60] How-

ever, when the Madera Canal Company appealed this injunction, it shifted
the focus from fact and evidence to public policy and legal doctrine. By
the turn of century, irrigation (and with it water storage) had emerged as
a great panacea for the nation's ills, a new frontier for the expansion of
family farming, which promised economic growth, social equality, and political democracy.[61] This potential, the Madera Canal Company argued, was the
issue in the case. As Haggin had, the irrigation company contrasted Miller &
Lux's vast fields of wild grasses, cropped by scattered herds of cattle, with the
towns, dairy farms, vineyards, and independent citizens it could serve. The
lawyers and promoters of the Madera Canal Company went on to link their
reservoir plan to the programs of Theodore Roosevelt and the Progressive
conservation movement. What was on trial, they argued, was "conservation,
storage and the economical use of the streams."[62] The reservoirs made possible a more intense use of water that extracted greater profits from the soil,
thus providing the very prerequisites of further economic development in
California, in the arid West, and in the entire nation, for that matter.[63]

As the self-appointed champions of the state's future prosperity, the
Madera Canal promoters attempted to eviscerate riparianism through a selec-
tive interpretation of *Lux* v. *Haggin* and the common law itself. Traditionally,
riparian rights were usufructory, meaning that the corpus of the water could
not be possessed but only utilized. Moreover, the exploitation of rivers was
limited by the caveat that the flow to others not be materially diminished, a
condition that precluded irrigation development. In *Lux* v. *Haggin*, however,
the California supreme court had recognized a riparian right to irrigate.[64]
Praising the "elasticity" of the common law, Madera Canal argued that in so
expanding traditional doctrine, the court had redefined it.[65] "Limited to the
rights the commonwealth gives," a riparian's entitlement, like an appropriator's, was tied to the water actually consumed.[66] The riparian could no longer
demand "to see the stream flow past his land" for his own pleasure but could
claim only the portion that he reasonably and beneficially employed.[67] Miller
& Lux's reliance on the overflow of the Fresno River merely to wash over its
pastures was wasteful and extravagant, even as a riparian use.

Ultimately the Madera Canal promoters asked the court to underwrite
reservoir development. Although it was privately owned, the Madera Canal
& Irrigation Company was a public service company and could thus employ the right of eminent domain to seize the water it needed. However, in
that case it would have to compensate Miller & Lux for such a taking, and

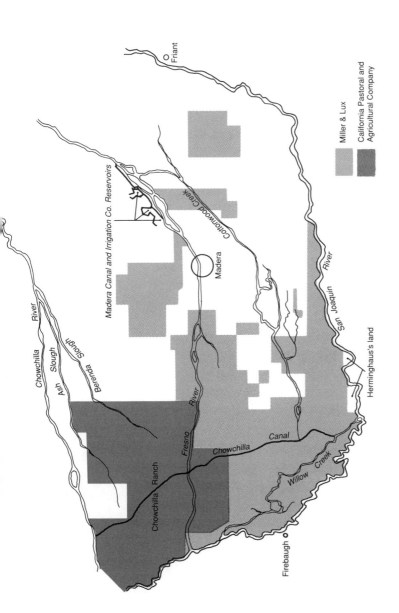

Map 2: The reservoirs of the Madera Canal and Irrigation Company and the land of Miller & Lux and its allies in Madera County, 1898. Drawn from the official map of Madera County, Frank E. Smith, county surveyor (San Francisco: 1898), Bancroft Library, University of California, Berkeley.

Madera Canal argued that this was too expensive. Capitalists would not invest in large irrigation projects if they had to pay for water rights because "the cost of acquiring such so-called rights w[ould] in most cases effectually obliterate the hope of profit."[68] Instead, because access to water was essential, the court should subsidize reservoir development with a "liberal" interpretation of doctrine, one that would divorce floodwaters from those belonging to riparians. Storm waters, Madera Canal argued, were not part of the "ordinary" flow of the stream, to which riparian rights attached; rather they were "unusual," belonging to no one and available to all. In this case, the Fresno River's annual overflow was not the property of Miller & Lux (in fact, Madera Canal claimed, it damaged the cattle company's land) but was rightfully open to appropriation and storage. Under this interpretation of the law, the river could provide the affordable water necessary for continuing growth.[69]

In a position to benefit from the judicial conservatism of the era, Miller & Lux rested behind the traditional citadel of private property. Reiterating principles it had successfully espoused in *Lux* v. *Haggin*, it asserted that riparian rights were property rights, part and parcel of the land.[70] Overflow and floodwaters constituted an essential element of this entitlement. Neither extraordinary nor unusual, they were annual, documented occurrences that enhanced the productivity and value of the fields they wetted. Even if the Madera Canal promoters were correct in maintaining that investments in new technology might lessen the need to divert water, Miller & Lux argued, a riparian was by law entitled to use the entire flow of the stream, whether the trickle of a California autumn or the torrent of its early spring. The issue properly before the court was not the public's concern for conservation or efficiency, but simply the right of a lawful owner to protect his property from injury and confiscation.[71]

Eminent domain, not judicial confiscation, Miller & Lux argued, was the proper remedy for any imbalance between public and private benefits. Rejecting the Madera Canal Company's plea that the cost of "just compensation" would preclude the commercial expansion of irrigation, Miller & Lux called for a policy of laissez-faire in which revenues would determine the pattern of development. "The state," attorney W. B. Treadwell argued, "is not interested in making any particular 'scheme' commercially profitable" but is instead interested in having water used "to do the greatest amount of good." If a new water project would really be of greater benefit, it would be more remunerative, and the user could "well afford" to pay for any damage caused.[72]

In reasoning that highlighted the importance of judicial ideology and public attitudes, Miller & Lux attorney Frank Short compared the issues in this case with the question of railroad development:

> It would be just as sensible and just as lawful to say that railroads could not be built and that the public interests were being injured thereby if it was not provided that the rights of way could be taken without just, or any, compensation for the construction of such roads as it is to say that public policy and public rights are offended against because it is insisted not that water shall not be taken for beneficial uses by non-riparian owners, but it is merely insisted that in the event of such a taking if the riparian owner is deprived of this valuable property right just compensation must be paid.[73]

At the time of this hearing, railroads, perceived often as monopolies that exploited rather than served the public, routinely paid compensation. However, both nineteenth-century railroads and transportation canals, then the hope of the future, were given both direct subsidies and the indirect aid the Madera irrigation promoters demanded for their reservoirs. Land was often taken with little or no compensation as courts and legislatures ruled that the economic growth promised by faster transportation offset part, if not all, of any losses incurred. The granting of eminent domain powers to irrigation companies throughout the western states was itself a product of this type of instrumental reasoning, under which the state should use law to meet the special needs of an arid environment and to foster rapid economic development.[74]

In 1909, however, the California Supreme Court refused the irrigation company's plea that it follow this tradition and employ the law as an instrument to ease reservoir development. In *Miller & Lux* v. *Madera Canal and Irrigation Company*, the supreme court strongly affirmed the property rights of riparian owners, including their claim to floodwaters. There was "no sufficient ground in principle," it reasoned, for restricting riparian rights to the lowest stages of the river. Riparians were entitled to the ordinary flow of the stream, including the regular periods of high water, which were no "less usual or ordinary" than the low waters that followed them.[75] Moreover, the supreme court rejected the irrigation company's attempt to limit Miller &

Lux to a reasonable use of water. Only in a conflict between two riparians, the court stated, could questions of reasonableness and waste be raised and considered; these issues were irrelevant in a conflict between a riparian and a nonriparian. As a matter of law, a riparian owner could restrain any non-riparian diversion that deprived him of the "customary flow of water," even if he then let water run to waste.[76]

As in *Lux* v. *Haggin,* concern about protecting private property from confiscation permeated the court's reasoning. The court accepted Miller & Lux's argument that market forces, not what the court called the "vague and uncertain guide" of public policy, should determine how water was used and what was a beneficial use. While storage might permit the cultivation of more land and might serve more people, this potential benefit did not empower the court or the legislature to take water from one group and freely give it to another. Eminent domain law provided a means for transferring water rights, once just compensation was paid. If the water provided little benefit to riparian claimants, the cost would be low; if the benefits of storage were great, as Madera Canal and its supporters argued, the beneficiaries could well afford to pay.[77] However, as the story unfolded in the following decades, the residents of Madera County were at no point willing or able to pay for the storage they continued to demand.

While the Madera Canal Company and the state's conservation interests protested this ruling, Miller & Lux attorneys pronounced it "the most comprehensive and valuable decision we have ever obtained."[78] By clarifying the nature of riparian property rights as first endorsed in *Lux* v. *Haggin, Madera* expanded the protections accorded the cattle company's pattern of land use. If riparian owners had been limited to a reasonable use, Miller & Lux could have been forced to invest considerable sums to replace systems of natural irrigation with more efficient, capital-intensive technology. The decision in fact strengthened Miller & Lux's control of upstream river development by forcing the Madera Canal Company to shut down its reservoir system entirely. Just as important, the decision protected Miller & Lux's relationship with Huntington and his hydroelectric companies, reinforcing the concessions the utilities had made to Miller & Lux's domination of both the Kern and the San Joaquin.

Miller & Lux had filed the suits against appropriation not out of greed but out of a recognition of the power and the limits of legal doctrine. Since under California law an adverse use of water became a right in only five years, the protection of riparian property required both a keen regard for injury and a relentless willingness to fight. Failure to challenge even the smallest user meant a loss of real property. Yet even a willingness to sue could not guarantee victory. As Nickel acknowledged when he declined to sue Huntington for control of the San Joaquin, the judiciary's commitment to riparian rights could not be taken for granted. The law provided judges with choices, not simply between riparian rights and appropriation, but also between what was "reasonable" and what was not. While the California Supreme Court's ideological commitment to property generally protected Miller & Lux's claims to water, alternative calls for the promotion of economic growth could not be dismissed, especially when injuries to the company were hard to prove. That was the case in the firm's suit against the Fresno Flume and Irrigation Company and in the continuation of its conflict with the Madera irrigators.

The Fresno Flume and Irrigation Company, a small manufacturer, employed eight hundred men in lumbering and the production of boxes, trays, and fence posts for the raisin industry. In 1892 Fresno Flume installed a dam in Stevenson Creek, a small mountain tributary of the San Joaquin River. The dam formed a shallow reservoir on the firm's timberlands and fed water into a flume system that carried logs down to its Clovis mill. In 1894 Miller & Lux initiated litigation charging that the dam interfered with the property rights of both downstream riparians and appropriators and asked the court to enjoin the diversion and to determine what rights, if any, Fresno Flume possessed.[79]

In defending itself, Fresno Flume made a broad assault on water law, rejecting riparianism as "an error committed by the legislature in 1850." The lumber company insisted that the water it stored was its "absolute property"; it had originated not as part of Stevenson Creek, which was dry most of the year, but as rainwater, runoff from the company's timberlands that had been collected and stored before it reached the stream. Such precipitation, Fresno Flume argued, should not be considered part of the ordinary flow of a watercourse. Moreover, the lumber company's reservoir benefited Miller & Lux by trapping water during the flood season, when the San Joaquin spilled over its banks, and releasing it later when water was scarce and in greatest demand. Enjoining the reservoir would decrease the available flow of the river as well as destroy a profitable lumber business.[80]

Miller & Lux was, of course, aware of the potential benefits of water storage. But as in its negotiations with Huntington, it insisted on the preeminence of riparian rights as the controlling force on the river. Because only such control would protect the continuing access to water that its enterprise required, Miller & Lux argued that it was entitled to an injunction against even the smallest upstream diversion. Fresno Flume's dam was a nuisance and by definition injured Miller & Lux's entitlement to the full flow of the stream. The lumber company's activities had to be stopped or "it would not be long before numerous small diversions would entirely fritter away the rights of riparian owners"[81]—a prophecy that even at that time had come true in many parts of the state.

In this case, the courts found the prospect of economic development more alluring than the stiff formality of doctrine. In 1905 Judge H. Z. Austin of the Fresno court ruled in favor of Fresno Flume; in 1910 the state supreme court, only a year after halting the use of the Madera Canal Company reservoirs, endorsed the lower court's decision.[82] Looking over earlier cases involving floodwaters, the supreme court declared that it had always "encourage[d] the impounding and distribution of those waters whenever it m[ight] be done without substantial damage to the rights of others."[83] It acknowledged Miller & Lux's argument that riparians were entitled to protection from injuries that might arise with the future development of a prescriptive claim; but it found that no harm had resulted from Fresno Flume's operations. The absence of measurable injury served to distinguish this suit from that against the Madera Canal reservoirs.

Both Austin and the supreme court accepted that Fresno Flume's reservoir had increased the flow in the river and took notice of the nature of the lumber company's enterprise. Riparian owners were not in every case entitled to the undisturbed flow of the river, as Miller & Lux had submitted. Although the common law allowed a riparian owner to let water run past his land simply for his own enjoyment, in *Fresno Flume* the state supreme court maintained that in California a claimant had to show that an upstream diversion caused real damage before the court would restrain a beneficial use. Injury had to be balanced against benefit, and if necessary, riparian doctrine would be modified. At issue was the profitable exploitation of the state's rivers, and the "fair apportionment and economic use" of water were of such importance to the development of the state that "if a rule of decision at common law shall be found unfitting to the radically changed conditions existing in this state, so that its application will work wrong and hardship rather than betterment and good, this court will refuse to approve and follow the doctrine." [84]

This decision was precisely the modification of doctrine, the kind of balancing, that the Madera Canal Company had demanded in the reservoir suit [85] and that Miller & Lux distrusted. Given the constant argument that the cattle company's use of water held back the state's economic development, the judicial adoption of a balancing test could transfer water to competing claimants. It was fear of this attitude that had made Miller & Lux's Nickel shrink from a court fight against the hydroelectric interests.

Undaunted by the adverse decision, Miller & Lux continued its efforts to limit all upstream diversions. In 1912 it filed another suit asserting that Fresno Flume interfered with its water rights. The lumber company charged Miller & Lux with harassment and protested that its rights had already been settled, but Miller & Lux convinced the courts that this was a new action dealing with new injuries. In 1918 the cattle company won an injunction that prevented Fresno Flume from taking any water that might ordinarily flow to the San Joaquin and required it to install measuring devices to ensure its compliance.[86] Around that time, Southern California Edison purchased Fresno Flume's reservoir, and it became the subject of negotiation and contract between Miller & Lux and the power company.

More important was the continuing litigation against the Madera Canal and Irrigation Company. Although its reservoirs had been shut down, the Madera Canal Company continued to divert water upstream from Miller & Lux's rangelands for direct irrigation of its customers' fields. This diversion had been the original cause of action between the two firms, and with the reservoir suit finally settled, it moved to trial. A conflict over the prescriptive rights of an upstream user, this case presented a different problem, that of defining such open-ended terms as "reasonable" and "beneficial," which qualified all water law. In doing so, the courts confronted the technical complexities of defining the specific amount of water needed for irrigation, as well as the demand that the law promote the public interest in irrigation development.

Challenges to prescriptive claims commonly focused on time: had the adverse use continued long enough to mature into a right? In this case, however, time was not at issue, since the Madera Canal Company had in fact diverted some water since 1872, eight years before Miller & Lux acquired riparian land along the Fresno River.[87] Miller & Lux's challenge instead stressed the legal requirement that all appropriations be "for some useful or beneficial purpose." While the canal company claimed to be entitled to 400 cubic feet per second (cfs) of water and to serve 40,000 acres of land, Miller & Lux argued that only a quarter of that volume of water was in fact needed for irrigation, thus limiting the amount that could be acquired.[88] Over the years western judges had restricted the often-extravagant claims of appropriators to such tangible limits as the capacity of their ditches and the specific uses of the water.[89] Miller & Lux hoped to build on this precedent. In the suit against the Madera Canal Company's reservoirs, Miller & Lux had protected its exploitation of the river by preventing the application of reasonable use to its own riparian rights; ironically, it later hoped to minimize its losses to Madera's diversion by insisting that the strictest standards of reasonable and beneficial use be applied to appropriators and prescriptive claimants.

Although a judge was brought in from San Francisco to prevent accusations of local bias from marring the resolution of the case,[90] a commonplace sympathy toward appropriation and smaller farmers undercut Miller & Lux's formalistic arguments. In a conflict between appropriators, Judge J. M. Seawell concluded, a strict application of "reasonable" use was appropriate, but in a conflict with a riparian, an appropriator need meet only the looser standard of "beneficial" use. In this case, the irrigation company was entitled to 250 cubic feet per second, the amount of water it had actually diverted for the last twenty-five years. While not the entire 250 cfs was needed to irrigate the limited acreage actually served by the Madera Canal, no water had been wasted. If of no other use, the water had at least filled underground reservoirs, aiding the increasing number of farmers who pumped groundwater to irrigate.[91] Although Miller & Lux insisted that the suit turned on the question of how much water was "reasonably necessary" to serve the irrigation company's customers, Seawell refused even to define this smaller volume.[92]

While even Miller & Lux's allies in this litigation saw Seawell's findings as a victory (after all, he had disallowed the Madera Canal Company's original claim of 400 cfs), Miller & Lux attorneys rejected the decision for two reasons. First, it granted the Madera Canal Company more water than the evidence supported. Second, it was based on an incorrect interpretation of the law of prescription. Highly conscious of the impact of doctrine, Miller & Lux attorneys Frank H. Short and Edward F. Treadwell pointed out that if Seawell's generous definition of appropriative rights were adopted by other courts, it would severely handicap the future defense of riparian property. Prescriptive users, Short insisted, were limited by law to the volume of water that in fact was reasonably used. Miller & Lux thus appealed Seawell's decision and attempted to make this alleged error of law as prominent as possible.[93]

Concerned as much with the physical control of water as with doctrine, Miller & Lux also initiated new litigation to restrict the Madera Canal Company's water right "no matter how the law is actually decided."[94] With this end in mind, Miller & Lux bought a piece of dry land in Madera County and arranged for one of its subsidiaries, the San Joaquin & Kings River Canal & Irrigation Company (SJ&KRC&ICo), to appropriate 150 cfs from the Fresno River to irrigate the land. In a contract with the SJ&KRC&ICo, Miller & Lux reserved its riparian rights and specified that the appropriation was filed against the water that the Madera Canal Company had not put to reasonable use. The SJ&KRC&ICo then sued in federal court to enforce its claims. By doing this, the attorneys manufactured a conflict between appropriators that Miller & Lux hoped would limit the Madera Canal Company's right to water. Even Seawell had conceded that in such a situation strict standards of reasonable use applied.[95]

The federal suit became superfluous in 1914, when the California Supreme Court endorsed Miller & Lux's interpretation of the law by ruling that the doctrines of reasonable and beneficial use applied to all appropriators, including those in conflict with riparians. Once again the court rejected arguments that would have restricted riparians in favor of alternative users of water. Additionally, the court narrowed the definition of beneficial use, constraining it to the amount reasonably necessary for the purpose at issue, rather than extending it to cover all water actually consumed. The court explicitly rejected the Madera Canal Company's contention that as a public service company it was entitled to liberal consideration of its claims. Whether an appropriator was an individual who diverted water for private uses or a canal company that diverted it for sale to the public was irrelevant; an appropriator could take no more water than was reasonably necessary to irrigate the land involved, regardless of the length of time the diversion had existed.[96] With each ruling, the court rejected an avenue for easing access to water.

Because Seawell had refused to determine the specific volume of water necessary to irrigate the land served by the irrigation company, the case was sent back to the Madera County court for a new trial. At this point the

Madera Canal Company tried to get the state water commission to inter-
vene (a goal thwarted by Miller & Lux's hostility to the new administrative
agency and by the water commission's limited mandate),[97] raised a claim to
be a riparian owner, and petitioned that the irrigators themselves be joined
in the suit as defendants who had both riparian and prescriptive rights to the
Fresno River.[98] Eventually a group of water users, including such well-known
companies as Standard Oil and Italian Swiss Colony, filed as intervenors.
The dispute then reverted to its beginnings, as the irrigation company and
its customers alleged that the company's diversion of 445 cfs was "barely
adequate" to water their lands.[99]

Establishing the Madera Canal Company's right under the standard of
reasonable use proved to be a difficult task. The specific duty of water, that
is, the amount of land that 1 cubic foot of water could irrigate, varied with the
quality of the soil and with the crop sown. Frank Adams of the Department
of Agriculture's Office of Irrigation Investigations was exploring this question for farms in the Sacramento Valley, but no such study existed for the
Madera County region. Adams insisted that the courts should not determine
such a technical question, and not wanting to lose the good will of either
side, he declined to testify in the lawsuit unless requested to do so by the
trial judge himself.[100] Unable to enlist the authority of government experts,
each side produced a variety of engineers—most of them current or former
employees of one of the parties—to attest to the legitimate water needs of
typical Madera County crops. Though Miller & Lux repeatedly asserted the
commonly accepted rule of thumb that 1 cfs was adequate to irrigate 160
acres, no clear consensus emerged.[101]

Even the comparatively simple question of how much land had been irrigated by the customers of Madera Canal Company brought in a spate of
contradictory evidence. The only indisputable answer seemed to be that
40,000 acres, the area the canal company formally claimed to serve,[102] had
never in fact been irrigated from the canal company's system. In 1900, the
year the suit was first filed, only 23,152 acres in the entire county had been
irrigated.[103] Both Miller & Lux's surveyors and employees of the Madera
Canal and Irrigation Company set the maximum area irrigated from its
canals at less than 9,000 acres.[104] Establishing the acreage irrigated was further complicated by the recordkeeping and billing structure of the Madera
Canal Company, which billed customers who had signed water rights contracts whether they received water or not. The Railroad Commission found

that in the irrigation season of 1912–13, only 2,813 acres out of 7,650 acres under contract had in fact received water; in all, the canal company irrigated only 4,327 acres that season.[105] Irrigators, in fact, had protested to the Railroad Commission that the company discriminated between customers, favoring new subscribers over old, and that it had neglected and mismanaged the canal system.[106] Such mismanagement, not an actual shortage of water, Miller & Lux argued, was the real problem confronted by local farmers.[107]

At the trial, Judge W. M. Conley of the Madera Superior Court set the canal company's water right at 200 cfs, 50 cfs less than granted by Seawell. Miller & Lux, however, still claiming that the disputed volume was only 100 cfs of water, again appealed to the state supreme court. This time the firm was unsuccessful; in 1919, the supreme court upheld the lower court's findings.[108] Beneficial use had traditionally been treated as a question of fact to be determined by the judge or jury.[109] Judge Conley's findings, the supreme court ruled, controlled the appeal, and his conclusions were supported by the evidence. The supreme court then cited what must have been the most galling section of its 1914 decision supporting Miller & Lux: a vague guideline for awarding water rights. Reasoning that "ordinarily one would not take the pains to use upon land any more [water] than was necessary under the circumstances," the court in 1914 had called for a presumption in favor of the appropriator.[110] Thus, although on the broadest legal points the court upheld the riparian arguments of Miller & Lux, it also granted the appropriator protection by placing the burden of proof on the riparian. Proving excessive use, unless such use was grossly negligent, was clearly difficult given the poor state of technical knowledge. Proof was also extremely expensive; both Miller & Lux and the Madera Canal Company had spent tens of thousands of dollars on this litigation.[111] Only the wealthiest and most committed could pursue such a strategy.

The disappointments in the Madera and Fresno Flume litigation, however, were small matters compared with Miller & Lux's repeated success in asserting its riparian claims against upstream appropriators. Riparian rights had been declared to be property rights and to extend even to the floodwaters of a stream. Overall, the advocates of prior appropriation had lost their case before the state supreme court. Their arguments that the courts should serve as an instrument of economic development, easing the establishment of new enterprises, had fallen victim to concerns about property rights and stability. In substantive terms, irrigation interests in Madera and

Kern counties were forced to rely on the more expensive process of groundwater pumping to develop their fields. Miller & Lux, on the other hand, had
not only retained control of the waters wetting its ranches but had built on
its victories by winning access to water storage that would serve its future
needs. In 1910 Nickel's only regret was that the lengthy negotiations to permit Pacific Light and Power (Southern California Edison) to develop the
hydroelectric potential of the San Joaquin had not yet produced the material
gain he had expected. Despite his disappointment, he continued to renew
the contracts that allied Miller & Lux with the power companies.[112] Though
not without problems, riparian doctrine had proved to be of immeasurable
value to the firm. Miller & Lux's wealth had allowed it to invest in litigation,
and successes before the courts had protected and enhanced its massive
investment in land.

2

Private Rights and Public Needs: The San Joaquin & Kings River Canal & Irrigation Company, Miller & Lux, and the Regulation of Utilities

Miller & Lux was not only a riparian proprietor but also the owner of one of the largest private canal companies in California, the San Joaquin & Kings River Canal & Irrigation Company. Unlike most of the small canal companies that Miller & Lux would eventually form,[1] the SJ&KRC&ICo was a public utility, supplying water to Miller & Lux and to hundreds of other customers in three counties. Like Miller & Lux, the SJ&KRC&ICo's "outside" customers viewed water as an economic asset. Irrigated agriculture promised greater profits and greater prosperity than dry farming, and access to water was crucial to maximizing the return on land. So were low water rates. Lacking physical control of water, yet ambitious for its benefits, the customers of the SJ&KRC&ICo looked to the government for help, demanding and winning the regulation of the canal company's prices. Miller & Lux again went to court, this time initiating a twenty-year fight to limit state interference in its business affairs that exposed the contradictions in the assumption that water would increase wealth.

With Miller & Lux asserting constitutional protections of private property, the struggle embodied the ideological and legal tensions between the belief that water should be available to all who needed it and the view that it was private property that could be bought and sold. The dispute raised the questions of what a fair rate of return was for a public utility, of how property should be valued, and most important, of whether water could be capitalized. Central to both rate-charging utilities and Progressive reformers, these questions were at that time new, and standards of judgment were "in an experimental stage."[2] In the end, regulatory efforts were bound by the judiciary's acceptance of the need to protect contracts and to guarantee a fair profit to private investors—the same property-centered ideology that had supported the riparian doctrine itself.

The SJ&KRC&ICo was incorporated in 1871, the creation of William Ralston, the ambitious director of the Bank of California; Isaac Friedlander, the "wheat king" of California; and William Chapman, another of the state's early land barons. Cast in the mold of many nineteenth-century canal projects, it was a grand speculative scheme to enhance the value of the proprietors' landholdings. Mixing giddy optimism with chicanery, its prospectus promised canals through Kern, Tulare, Fresno, Merced, Stanislaus, Contra Costa, and Alameda counties that would link the entire Central Valley with San Francisco and the markets of the Pacific basin. By connecting the great rivers of the valley, the canal system would also supply water for cities, for crops, and for the generation of electricity.[3] Notices were posted to appropriate water, the irrigation engineer and promoter Robert Brereton was hired to supervise construction, and land was leased from Miller & Lux for a model farm that would show "Californians the benefits to be derived from a proper system of irrigation."[4]

At its inception, Henry Miller was a minority stockholder in the canal company, as was Haggin, his Kern County rival. Miller, although certain that the overall project was unfeasible, nevertheless quickly established a special relationship with the SJ&KRC&ICo. Miller & Lux owned a fifty-mile stretch of land along the San Joaquin River through which some of the proposed canals would run; Miller himself had planned to install a weir at the site Brereton chose for the canal company's dam, in the hope of developing canals to serve his ranches as he had done in Kern County. Although his lawyers were uncertain about the standing of riparian rights in the state

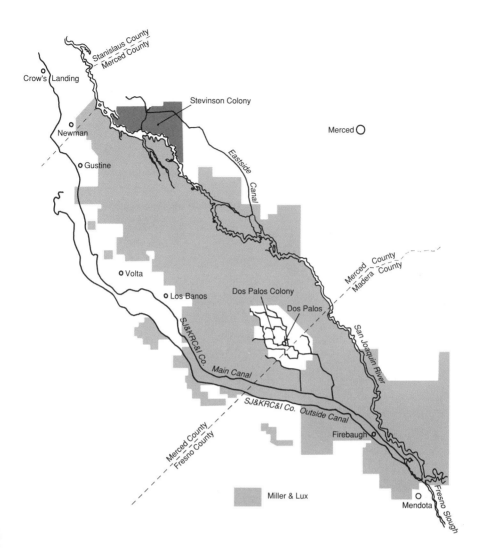

Map 3: San Joaquin Valley area serviced by the San Joaquin & Kings River Canal & Irrigation Company, ca. 1916. Drawn from Miller & Lux Inc., Map of portion of the San Joaquin Valley showing lands of Miller & Lux and others, compiled by Charles B. Gleaves (1916), Bancroft Library, University of California, Berkeley.

(*Lux* v. *Haggin* would not be decided for fifteen years), Miller asserted a riparian claim to the river and demanded compensation both for any loss of water and for the right of way through his property.[5] Miller also suggested that the canal company's system be built in stages, beginning with a branch canal, that would reflect the development of the San Joaquin Valley. In 1871 and 1872, he signed contracts giving the SJ&KRC&ICo a right of way, the use of all brush on his land, and a subsidy of $20,000; in exchange, the cattle company was to receive enough water to irrigate 50,000 acres of land at a maximum annual charge of $1.25 an acre, in addition to water at no charge to support livestock and to replace any overflow lost to its riparian lands by the diversion into the canals.[6] The first canal was built through Miller & Lux's west side ranches, where the water supplied made Miller & Lux the largest customer of the canal company. In 1873 SJ&KRC&ICo received less than $10,000 from the sale of water; of this, $2,500 came from Miller & Lux, which paid at the reduced rate. In the same year the canal company spent $109,000, almost half of it to rent land from Miller & Lux.[7]

The canal company was financially unstable throughout the 1870s. It possessed no land, only its water right—a limitation that Brereton later wrote had doomed the company from the beginning. Brereton, who believed that the canal company could not make a profit by levying charges for water, proposed that a mutual company be formed instead. He called on local landowners to join the canal company's venture by putting 100,000 acres of land into the enterprise. In exchange they would receive 100,000 shares of stock in the new company at a par value of $25 per share. Estimating that the cost of developing the land into marketable irrigated farms would be $25 per acre, Brereton traveled to London to borrow money, putting up the hoped-for land as collateral. His plan, however, never got off the drawing board. When Miller & Lux refused to join, other landowners who had initially favored the idea backed out.[8] In addition, the London financial interests rejected the scheme as too speculative: Brereton had arrived too late; London bankers, having learned of the shoddiness of many of the American enterprises in which they had been investing, had become cautious.[9] He was similarly unable to win congressional support for the project.[10]

During the 1870s the canal company's relationship with Miller & Lux, its major customer, was tempestuous. In 1874, the SJ&KRC&ICo announced that the agreement to provide Miller & Lux with water at $1.25 an acre had expired. It began billing the company at $2.50 and $3.00 per acre of cropland irrigated.[11] The canal company's directors decided, furthermore, that Miller & Lux had not fulfilled its financial commitments to them and thus rejected its application for water at no charge. The 1872 contract required that the canal company reserve enough water for Miller & Lux to irrigate 33,334 acres in 1873 and 50,000 acres by 1874. Payment for those volumes of water at Miller & Lux's special rate would have yielded over $70,000 for 1872 and 1873 and $72,000 in 1874, much more than the $2,500 Miller & Lux in fact paid for water in 1873. The discrepancy was explained by Miller & Lux's failure to take all the water guaranteed it. When the SJ&KRC&ICo sued to collect the $70,000 difference, the cattle company denied that it was obligated to pay for it. Miller & Lux won its argument when the court ruled that it was entitled to water free of charge to replace its normal riparian overflow, whether or not it purchased the reserved water.[12] Three years later, however, during the drought that provoked the filing of *Lux* v. *Haggin*, the SJ&KRC&ICo again refused to furnish water at no charge and demanded $1.25 per acre to irrigate Miller & Lux's uncultivated lands.[13] When Henry Miller returned from a European trip and saw his withered pastures, he took an ax to the offending stopgates and released water onto the fields. The canal company filed criminal charges, and a warrant was issued for Miller's arrest.[14]

The adversarial relationship between the two companies ended after the Bank of California failed in 1875. The bank held mortgages on the property of many of the canal company's promoters, who then faced foreclosure; Chapman, for example, lost his property to the Scottish investors who had backed him. Henry Miller seized the opportunity to take over the SJ&KRC&ICo. Brereton wrote that the financial disaster had forced him to sell Miller his 4,250 shares in the canal for $1,000, a mere fraction of the $34,000 he had paid for them.[15] In late 1877, Henry Miller became the majority owner of the canal system when he acquired a block of more than 28,000 shares for less than a third of their actual value. Within days the criminal charges filed against Miller earlier that year were dropped, and in 1879 the SJ&KRC&ICo executed a new contract making Miller's $1.25 rate perpetual for irrigation of as much as 33,333 acres.[16]

Miller continued to acquire stock until in 1908 he owned or controlled more than 80 percent of the company.[17] By that time the two companies had virtually become one. In 1905, when the SJ&KRC&ICo was reincorporated in Nevada, five of its seven directors were also directors of Miller & Lux.[18]

The two firms shared office space in San Francisco and in the San Joaquin Valley, and while the canal company employed its own clerks and book-keepers in Los Banos, by 1890 its managing officers, superintendent, and engineer served both companies.[19] Miller & Lux's employees, not the canal company's, controlled the stopgates that let irrigation water onto the cattle company's land. Its water bills had to be approved by ranch superintendents before they were formally written up and entered into the SJ&KRC&ICo's books, and they were then paid by the simple transfer of numbers from one account book to another in the San Francisco office. Under the scrutiny of the courts and the "outside irrigators," Miller & Lux eventually delegated more of this work to those on the payroll of the canal company and changed its bookkeeping practices to eliminate the appearance of underpayment and collusion.[20] However, the separation was merely technical; for all real purposes, the two companies were one.

Under Miller's ownership, the canal company increased both the area and the customers it served. By 1881 the Main Canal stretched seventy-one miles from its headgate in Fresno County through Merced County into southern Stanislaus County. In the 1890s engineering defects in the Main Canal were corrected, laterals were constructed to serve the small farms of Dos Palos Colony, and the Outside Canal, the second major conduit, was put into operation to the west of the original channel. As it expanded its physical plant, the SJ&KRC&ICo solicited new customers and promoted various uses of water at special rates. For example, the company offered low rates for irrigation of grain, which most farmers had abandoned as useless. Miller & Lux, however, saw the problem as one of timing: water should be applied in the winter, prior to plowing, not after the seed sprouted, as had been customary. Given the plentiful water supply during the winter, Miller & Lux hoped both to prove its point and to induce new patronage for the canals.[21] In any case, use of the canal system grew as rapidly as water was made available, and landowners repeatedly appealed for further expansion. In 1896 the company provided water to 37,000 acres; by 1908 it supplied 83,000 acres, of which 47,000 belonged to Miller & Lux and 36,000 to outside customers.[22]

In this period the west side of the San Joaquin Valley experienced some of the economic growth that the original promoters of the canal company had expected to profit from. Land on the west side had originally produced beef cattle or grain, but when water became available for alfalfa, commercial dairying developed in western Stanislaus County, where some 14,000 acres were irrigated by water from the SJ&KRC&ICo. After new creameries were built in the 1890s, farmers increased the size of their herds and began supplying butter, cheese, and cream to the San Francisco market. As settlers in eastern Stanislaus County struggled to establish irrigation districts, the value of west-side land served by the SJ&KRC&ICo soared; landowners there, in the "cream pitcher of the valley," clamored for the extension of the canals.

Miller & Lux encouraged similar developments to the south on its own land. Facing demands from Charles Lux's heirs for liquidation of the firm, Miller supported Bernard Marks's efforts to "colonize" southern Merced and northern Fresno counties by offering to sell a block of land in small units. The SJ&KRC&ICo constructed canals to irrigate the resulting Dos Palos Colony and, when the original location proved too alkaline for small-scale farming, Miller moved the settlers to a more fertile location. From 1890 to 1900, Miller & Lux sold more than 4,000 acres in the colony in the form of 20- and 40-acre irrigated parcels; from 1900 to 1930, it offered an additional 10,000 acres. In 1907 the firm took advantage of the interest in dairying by offering 40-acre farms in northern Merced County to both buyers and sharecroppers. It set up the town of Gustine, providing a bank, store, and creameries on the Southern Pacific line four miles south of the Stanislaus County dairying town of Newman. In three years the value of land in this area tripled.[23]

Despite (or perhaps because of) this growth, relations between the SJ&KRC&ICo and its customers were strained after Miller took control. Though the canal company facilitated the development of the west side, the rate of individual farm failure for smallholders was high,[24] and local farmers found the canal company a convenient scapegoat for economic woes, especially when Henry Miller began applying new businesslike rules and procedures to the company's operations. In the 1880s he cut wages while demanding more work and greater loyalty from SJ&KRC&ICo employees, who did not comply right away. Even as he insisted on his own entitlement to free water from the canal company, he attempted to hold its outside customers to the strict accountability of a market relationship. No longer would they receive water for livestock or wastewater free of charge, nor would they be allowed to graze or plow the canal company's right of way, as had become commonplace. The canal company also began refusing payment in kind.

Miller insisted on coin, "not jacknives and whetstones," and levied interest on overdue accounts. In the 1890s, when the canal company began suing to collect unpaid bills and threatened to cut off water deliveries to customers in arrears, disaffection turned into protest and a struggle for the control of water.[25]

Protest originated in Stanislaus County, where the canal company's customers were most independent of Miller & Lux. Many irrigators in Merced County were tenants or clients of Miller & Lux's banks and stores, and settlers in Dos Palos Colony had only recently moved to the region and were paying Miller & Lux for their land (and indirectly their water). Those in Stanislaus County were instead likely to be tied to rival firms such as the Simon Newman Company. Simon Newman, an early settler with no affection for Henry Miller, was one of the largest landholders in western Stanislaus County. Like Miller & Lux, he operated a store and bank, owned grain elevators, rented land, and gave credit, competing with Miller & Lux for the trade and the allegiance of farmers there and in northern Merced County. The Simon Newman Company and its managing partner, E. S. Wangenheim, who himself owned more than 3,000 acres of land, exerted a great deal of influence over their numerous debtors and tenants.[26]

The Newman Company and Wangenheim were also among the SJ& KRC&ICo's largest customers in Stanislaus County. Hoping to capture more of the wealth that water promised, they led the challenge to Miller & Lux's control of water. Conflict began in 1893, when Thomas Crow, a member of one of the founding families on the west side of the San Joaquin, frustrated the canal company's efforts to collect payment for what he said was wastewater. He easily convinced a jury of Stanislaus County farmers that the charges were unfair because Miller & Lux paid little or nothing for similar water.[27] Between 1893 and 1896, Crow and Wangenheim organized a Water Users' Association, which galvanized the vague dissatisfaction of other customers into a movement to force down the cost of water. An 1885 statute empowered county supervisors to set irrigation rates upon the petition of twenty-five taxpayers. When Crow had first raised the issue of lowering water rates in 1893, he had had no success. In 1896, however, the Stanislaus County Board of Supervisors held a public hearing on the question and listened to testimony criticizing the relationship between the canal company and Miller & Lux. After sending out their own engineers to evaluate the canal company's property, the supervisors accepted the water users' arguments and lowered the SJ&KRC&ICo's rates from $2.50 to $1.50 per acre of alfalfa. Celebrating their victory, Wangenheim and others in the Water Users' Association insisted that while they had lost money on their operations at the old water rate, they could now make a profit.[28]

Miller & Lux called in its lawyers and moved to protect its customary privileges with new contracts. In 1897 it signed an agreement with the SJ&KRC&ICo explaining that under the 1879 contract Miller & Lux was to pay only half the rate charged others, not to exceed $1.25 per acre per crop. The earlier contract had specified only the $1.25 figure, not the half-rate formula. That formula was inferred from the fact that $1.25 was half the fee charged others in 1871, 1872, and 1879.[29] Two years later a contract was drawn up concerning wastewaters, that is, those unconsumed waters released from the canals to return to the river. Throughout the 1890s, Henry Miller had insisted that wastewaters belonged to the cattle company, and the canal company's waste outlets had been installed to discharge through his ranches. Since most farmers did not irrigate at night and many did not irrigate on Sundays, Miller & Lux opened the gates to its ditches at those times and claimed that those waters were waste and surplus—a generous and profitable definition of waste. Yet there was no written agreement on the matter.[30] In 1899, as conflict with its customers mounted, the canal company formally granted Miller & Lux the free use of this "surplus" in exchange for the 350 cubic feet per second of water diverted for the newly constructed Outside Canal. The SJ&KRC&ICo's directors did so despite advice that Miller & Lux had tacitly assented to the new diversion and could not successfully challenge it. C. Z. Merritt, secretary of the canal company, later explained that the minority directors had approved the contract, which Henry Miller signed twice—first as president of Miller & Lux and then as president of the SJ&KRC&ICo.[31] As the water rate issue developed, this set of contracts proved to be a crucial piece of legal foresight.

As it consummated these new contracts, the canal company filed suit in federal court challenging the regulation of its Stanislaus County rates. The issue was not the level at which rates were set but the locus of control. The 1885 statute set forth a method for reviewing rates, but Miller & Lux ignored this process. Rate review delayed any change for a year and, more important, left power in the hands of the elected officials who had already rejected the canal company's views. The company saw itself in a battle against "popular prejudice."[32] In the 1870s, the SJ&KRC&ICo had been a target of Grangers, whose antimonopoly crusade included calls for state control of water as well as promotion of a variety of state-sponsored canal projects on the west side. Private water companies had repeatedly come under attack, especially when drought or depression hurt farmers; voters and politicians in Stanislaus County, which was home to two of California's important irrigation districts, had endorsed various legislative efforts to promote public control and regulation of water.[33] To protect its water, the SJ&KRC&ICo sought to eliminate the law that authorized the supervisors to set the canal's water rates, or at least to restrict the flexibility and power given them.

In filing its suit, the SJ&KRC&ICo draped itself in the mantle of the abused utility, raising the contract clause and citing the Fourteenth Amendment to the U.S. Constitution in its assertion that the 1885 statute violated constitutional protections of property. The firm's attorneys focused their arguments on an 1862 statute that declared that irrigation rates should return 1.5 percent per month. That statute, they contended, governed the SJ&KRC&ICo. It had been in force when the company was first organized and thus constituted a contract between the state and the canal company that Stanislaus County had violated. At issue was not so much the actual rate of return—the SJ&KRC&ICo at no point seriously expected an 18 percent profit—but the method for calculating the value of the canal company's property. The 1862 statute defined the base on which rates hinged as "the capital actually invested." The SJ&KRC&ICo had assumed this standard when approaching the county supervisors, naively believing that once it opened its books the supervisors would find it "impossible" to lower rates.[34]

The 1885 statute, however, based rates on "the value of all property actually used in and useful to the appropriation" and authorized the supervisors to determine just what the value was. This authority gave the supervisors, and through them the voting public, tremendous power over the corporation. The power to measure property included the power to devalue it, as Miller & Lux claimed had happened in its case. The supervisors and the water users had sent out surveyors who had decided that the property "useful to" Stanislaus County was worth only $337,000, one-third of the value the canal company placed on the same assets. While the supervisors' rate of $1.50 per acre generated a 6 percent return on $337,000, it yielded less than a 2 percent profit on the million-dollar value carried on the company's books.[35] The SJ&KRC&ICo thus argued that the supervisors and the law that empowered them had violated the promises of the 1862 statute and the guarantees of the Fourteenth Amendment.

While the canal company's argument stressed the constitutional protections accorded property, that of the customers reflected the antimonopoly reasoning of the Populists and Grangers. The customers' stance evoked notions of a just market, where the rights of small farmers were protected from the illegitimate and illegal activities that promoted bigness. In this case, Stanislaus County contended, the SJ&KRC&ICo had discriminated in favor of Miller & Lux and had thus limited the economic opportunity of other customers. More specifically, Stanislaus County asserted that the SJ&KRC&ICo had received net returns of 9–14 percent per year over a nine-year period and that with "prudent management" the canal company could have doubled these already substantial profits.[36] It cited the free water and the lower rates given to Miller & Lux as factors in reducing the returns on the canal company's investment; it justified the county's reliance on engineers, not company records, to assess the canal company's property by arguing that much of the money spent in the early years of the company had been squandered and lost through bad management. The real issue of the suit, Stanislaus County charged, was "that Miller & Lux by obtaining control of complainant's canal, are relieved of the cost of building their own canal, and are irrigating about 90,000 acres of their land at comparatively little cost and to a great extent free of charge at the expense of other customers."[37] The fight to reduce the water rates for outside customers was seen as one means to challenge Miller & Lux's control of the canal company and to fight "inequitable discrimination."[38] Equal access to water and equal opportunity to exploit it were the goals of the Stanislaus County ranchers, most of whom had begun irrigating from the SJ&KRC&ICo later than Miller & Lux and many others in Fresno and Merced counties.

In 1902 the canal company met with partial success in the circuit court. While his tortured opinion did not overturn the 1885 statute, Judge William Morrow ruled that the county must consider the monies actually invested when it appraised the canal company's property. Since the supervisors had not done so and since the $1.50 rate did not return 6 percent on the book value of the investment, Morrow enjoined the county rate. It "deprived the company of property without due process of law and denied it the equal protection of the law."[39]

In January 1904, however, the U.S. Supreme Court overturned Morrow's decision, declaring that the right to regulate and establish water rates was the equivalent of the state's right of taxation and thus could not be denied or restricted.[40] Justice Rufus W. Peckham's opinion echoed the legal majoritarianism of Justice Oliver Wendell Holmes. The language of the 1862 statute, he wrote, did not constitute a contract but was simply the judgment of the legislature at that time; it reflected the economic problems of an earlier period when investors in irrigation projects needed extra guarantees and protections. There was no such need in 1885, as the statute of that year demonstrated. In any case, any promises made in 1862 were subordinate to provisions in the state constitution regarding the alteration of specific and general acts of incorporation.

Stanislaus County had struck an ideological chord in the Supreme Court. During this period, the Court was divided over the role of corporations in the economy. One wing, identified with Peckham and John Marshall Harlan, distrusted corporations and favored an economy of small, independent producers. This ideology dominated antitrust rulings for over a decade and resonated through Peckham's opinion as he reiterated the suspicions of the canal company's customers. Getting to the heart of the disagreement between the SJ&KRC&ICo and Stanislaus County, Peckham endorsed the reassessment of the company's capital, ruling that there was adequate evidence to justify disregard of its book value. While not discussing the real relationship between Miller & Lux and the SJ&KRC&ICo, Peckham considered it likely that the canal's original costs were excessive because of errors of construction or improper acquisition of property; in one instance he related, a stockholder had accused the SJ&KRC&ICo's chief engineer of wasting $350,000 through mismanagement. More broadly, Peckham criticized the overcapitalization of utilities and held that the amount of money invested did not control the setting of rates. Although the state's right to regulate was not unlimited, the Court ruled that a "mere reduction of rates" was not prohibited as long as it allowed for just compensation. A 6 percent return on the total original investment was "more than most people are able to accomplish in any ordinary investment." A 6 percent return was not part of the definition of just compensation, nor was it a confiscatory action if rates were fixed to yield 6 percent on the property used.[41]

While this decision went against the canal company, it left room for continuing the fight against Stanislaus County. The real value of the

SJ&KRC&ICo's property had not yet been considered, and in sustaining the $1.50 rate, the Court had stated that its findings would not be binding if in the future the water rates set in all three counties failed to yield a combined return of 6 percent. In 1904 Miller & Lux moved to create such a situation for a continued assault on the SJ&KRC&ICo's ambitious northern customers. Miller & Lux, the largest taxpayer in Merced and Fresno counties, influenced the boards of supervisors to adjust rates in both counties. In Fresno County the supervisors reduced rates from $2.50 to $0.625 per acre, over the objections of District Attorney Frank Kauke. The new rate, the lowest in the San Joaquin Valley, was labeled "ridiculously low" by the *Fresno Morning Republican*. In Merced County, water charges were set at $1.08.[42] Within a month SJ&KRC&ICo filed suit in state court against the supervisors of all three counties—Stanislaus, Merced, and Fresno. Once again hoping to test the constitutionality of the statute, the canal company alleged that its income would be inadequate under the new rate structure, placing the blame on Stanislaus County's $1.50 rate.[43]

To a great degree the structure of the three-county complaint reflected Miller & Lux's evolving effort to impose more businesslike operations on the canal company, at least with regard to the outside customers. J. Leroy Nickel, vice-president of Miller & Lux and the SJ&KRC&ICo, felt that rates should reflect the cost of supplying water to each county; they should be lowest in areas close to the headgate and higher for those further down the canals. In addition, he reasoned that prices should reflect not merely the amount of water delivered, but the amount of water diverted at the headgates for each area, a method that would force customers to pay the cost of the seepage inherent in the company's earthen canals. This logic dictated proportionally higher rates in Stanislaus County. Not only was it a great distance from the headgates, but the extension to the north had required unexpected expenditures for a new channel when the Main Canal ran into a band of extremely porous soil. In 1907 the SJ&KRC&ICo calculated that, to sustain a 6 percent profit, the minimum acreage rates would be $0.95 for Fresno, $1.79 for Merced, and $2.21 for Stanislaus County.[44]

Initially, the move to base prices on the cost of delivery helped minimize opposition to the canal company from Fresno and Merced counties. The water users in Stanislaus, however, insisted that equity demanded lower rates, since only a small portion of the canal system lay in that county; they attributed seepage and the high costs of transporting water to poor maintenance, asserting that the SJ&KRC&ICo should bear these expenses.[45] While such arguments often unite customers, Miller & Lux attorney Frank Short persuaded officials in Fresno and Merced counties to separate their responses to the new three-county suit from that of Stanislaus County. Although irrigators in Fresno and Merced might differ with the canal company on the question of property valuation and general expenses, Short argued, they were "equally, if not more interested in opposition to Stanislaus County than is the canal company itself," the reason being that if Stanislaus County won, farmers in Merced and Fresno would have "to pay their part of the additional expense of irrigation in Stanislaus County."[46] In fact, until 1909, when the canal company raised its rates to a level that even Henry Miller labeled "exorbitant," large numbers of irrigators from Fresno and Merced counties refused to join the Water Users' Association, which had initiated the rate controversy.[47] As was common in disputes over railroad regulation, local rivalries limited organized protest against the utility.[48]

The SJ&KRC&ICo's new theory of rate setting went untested in the state courts. In 1904 Judge H. Z. Austin of the Fresno Superior Court dismissed the initial three-county rate suit because the SJ&KRC&ICo had not followed the statutory review procedures, and the company was finally forced to do so.[49] Although still reluctant to acknowledge any of the provisions of the 1885 statute or the authority of local politicians, in 1907 the SJ&KRC&ICo initiated the rate review process by requesting that the supervisors reconsider the 1904 rates. At that point Nickel became concerned that the supervisors in Fresno and Merced counties might grant too generous an increase; further judicial scrutiny of either the 1885 statute or the Stanislaus County rates would be impossible if the company's total income provided a 6 percent return. The company moved cautiously. Its formal applications for review in the two southern counties declared that the existing water rates were basically fair and requested neither an increase nor a decrease in fees. In 1907 Fresno and Merced counties quietly raised acreage rates to $0.85 and $1.65, respectively, levels just below the minimum rates necessary to generate a 6 percent return. In Stanislaus County, the canal company asked for a 50 percent increase, to $2.25 per acre. After a heated hearing, the supervisors there refused the request, retaining the old rate of $1.50.[50]

Miller & Lux's attorneys now began drafting their third suit to overturn the $1.50 rate and disempower the protesting Stanislaus customers. Disgusted with local magistrates, whom he judged to be either hostile to Miller

& Lux or too "weak" to defend the law when it was unpopular, Nickel insisted on returning to the federal courts. Miller & Lux and the SJ&KRC&ICo had been reincorporated in Nevada to guarantee this option,[51] but given the U.S. Supreme Court's recent criticism of the canal company's original costs, the tactic carried serious risks of its own. Although Frank Short, the Miller & Lux attorney, still believed that the 1885 statute was unconstitutional, at least when applied over more than one county, the Supreme Court's earlier decision ruled out further arguments on this question.[52] Instead the canal company's 1907 lawsuit focused on securing a high value for the capital on which its rates were to be based.

While there was ample disagreement over the appraisal of the firm's physical property, the key legal issue in the new federal suit was the value of the company's control of water—its water right. This question lay at the core of much of the philosophical and economic controversy between Miller & Lux and other private irrigation companies, on the one side, and the many proponents of water reform on the other. The Water Users' Association and its allies had from the beginning proclaimed that water was a gift of nature. It belonged to all the citizens of the state and could not be capitalized by a private company. While such a view might justify conservation or even the socialization of the resource, it was in this case a self-serving argument that promoted the entrepreneurial goals of local boosters and landowners: water should promote the economic development of the many—in this case the profitable exploitation of land by the many potential customers of the canal company. The SJ&KRC&ICo, on the other hand, considered its diversion to be private property that it had purchased, at least in part. Assigning its water right a monetary value of $1 million, the canal company claimed that it was entitled to earn 6 percent on this asset, just as it did on the land, canals, buildings, and machinery it owned. In Henry Miller's words, the case would determine whether the canal company could "lawfully collect enough money as to pay us a fair percentage on our investment."[53]

Despite Miller's long-standing belief that the SJ&KRC&ICo owned property in water, the legal status of this claim was uncertain. Under California law, water was generally viewed as property attached to land. This was true of both riparian and appropriative claims. Riparian rights, such as those Miller & Lux had secured in its earlier litigation, were the consequence of owning a piece of land that bordered a watercourse; the water was part and parcel of the land and could not be detached from it. On the other hand, appropriators claimed water under statutory provisions for transferring the rights of the state to private parties. In the case of irrigation, the water appropriated had to be put to beneficial use on the land specified in the state permit. Because water rights were so intimately linked to land, irrigation companies were often treated as mere agents of the landowners and water users they served, in whom the water right vested. In fact, Erskine Ross, the dissenter in *Lux* v. *Haggin* who in 1907 sat on the federal circuit court with Judge William Morrow, had ruled a decade earlier that there was no authority in law to grant a canal company a capitalized, property right in water such as the SJ&KRC&ICo's third suit was seeking.[54]

In other instances, Miller & Lux and the SJ&KRC&ICo had themselves linked water to land. In 1893, when first confronting the issue of rate regulation, the canal company had argued that its rates should not be reduced because the main benefits of the canal had gone not to its stockholders but to the customers, in the form of increased land values.[55] Three years later, when a group in Stanislaus County asked that the canal be extended, the company insisted that the landowners grant it a free right-of-way and pay the total cost of construction. While both the canal company and the irrigators would profit from the sale of water, the canal company's C. Z. Merritt argued, the benefits of construction would accrue "solely [to] the owner of the land."[56] In later attempts to limit the claims of the Madera Canal and Irrigation Company[57] and the East Side Canal,[58] Miller & Lux insisted that water held under prescriptive and appropriative claims must be beneficially used, inexorably joining the water claims of these public utilities to their customers. Similarly, when a downstream riparian landowner, James Stevinson, sought to shut down the SJ&KRC&ICo's diversion, the canal company was forced to establish the actual and necessary use of water on its customers' land in order to defend its water right.

Given this background, Frank Short argued that SJ&KRC&ICo should make no claim for a water right. In his view, neither the 1885 statute nor the decisions of the California courts contemplated such an allowance. The canal company had earlier dropped its assertion of a water right to focus on the 1862 law. Now Short proposed relying on the value of the firm's franchise— its right to do business—as the basis for establishing the value of its intangible capital. As the attorney for many other water and power companies, he saw the franchise as an issue of "tremendous future importance." Because utility companies were taxed on their franchises, he envisioned the possibility of a tax that could wipe out all earnings unless rates were also based on the franchises. Henry Miller, in fact, was in that period complaining about the increasing "burden" such taxes were placing on both Miller & Lux and the SJ&KRC&ICo.[59] To Short, a victory on the issue of the franchise was both desirable and possible. The recognition of the franchise, he felt, would "put the company definitely and permanently beyond the reach of harmful regulation."[60]

However, the formal complaint focused on establishing the value of the water right; it subordinated any claim to a franchise.[61] While the reasons for this are not explicit, one possible explanation is that Miller & Lux in the same period initiated a protest against the taxing of its franchise by the state, insisting that since it was incorporated in Nevada it had no taxable franchise in California.[62] More important, the defense of Miller & Lux's supply of free water and its low water rates seemed to impel this approach. As a public utility, the SJ&KRC&ICo could not lawfully discriminate in favor of any customer but had to sell water on an equal basis to all within its service area. The franchise argument provided no defense of its discriminatory contracts, which could only be justified as compensation for allowing the canal company to pass through Miller & Lux's property and to divert adversely to Miller & Lux's riparian right. Miller & Lux's various contracts with power companies relied on similar reasoning that allowed the contractual transfer of riparian right to a commercial user. In this case, Miller & Lux again asserted that the riparian right should be recognized not merely as a guarantee of necessary waters, but as an income-producing and marketable commodity.

In 1908, Judge Morrow granted the canal company a temporary injunction that suspended the county rates, in the belief that the Stanislaus fee might not even cover the cost of water, let alone provide an adequate return.[63] Morrow then submitted the case to E. H. Heacock, the master at chancery who frequently worked with him.[64] Assigned to examine the detailed financial issues, Heacock completed his report in May 1910.

Heacock's report was a major setback for Miller & Lux and the SJ&KRC&ICo. Heacock appraised the canals at the cost of reproducing them minus depreciation, a method that eliminated any possible return on monies invested but lost through mismanagement; because the canal company had no accurate records of its maintenance costs, he allowed no credit for depreciation in its annual costs. Most important, Heacock granted the company no amount of money for its water right, seeming to sustain

Short's fears about relying on this concept. Valuing the firm's capital at only $900,000, less than half that claimed by the company, he reported that the canal company was earning 8 percent on its property and had no cause for action.[65]

The canal company had presented three schemes for assigning a value to the water right, each of which confirmed its claim of $1 million. The first looked at the difference between the value of the land served by the canal company had it been without water and the greater value of the land as supplied with water. Half of the difference in value was assigned to the land, to reflect improvements, the other half to the canal company as the value of the water right. The second technique of valuation relied on expert testimony, in this case that of Samuel Fortier, professor of hydraulic and irrigation engineering at the University of California. The third method calculated the money expended in acquiring the water right, first from John Benchley, who had posted some of the original notices of appropriation, and later from Miller & Lux.[66]

Heacock rejected all three methods of valuation. In his view, the canal company had acquired water by appropriation; like all other water distribution companies, it had benefited from provisions of state law that transferred the state's interest in water to those who put it to use. Beyond this, the canal company had received the privilege of a franchise to sell water and the power of eminent domain. While agreeing that the water right was valuable and could not be taken without compensation, Heacock did not accept it as the property of the canal company; the canal company had devoted its water right to a public use and was not entitled to a return on it.[67]

Ignoring the power of riparian owners to stop such appropriations, Heacock denied that the SJ&KRC&ICo had purchased either water or a right-of-way from Miller & Lux, and his evaluation of the contracts linking the SJ&KRC&ICo with the cattle company further undermined Miller & Lux's efforts to protect its cheap water. The canal company had argued that it had paid $174,929 for its right-of-way through the granting of lower water rates to Miller & Lux. It also claimed that the $10,000 worth of wastewater that it delivered to the cattle company free of charge each year, as required under the contracts of 1871, 1872, and 1879, should be considered an essential part of its investment; it was a necessary payment for the company's riparian claims. However, having denied that the SJ&KRC&ICo had purchased anything from Miller & Lux, Heacock declared that the canal company should have treated the $10,000 a year as income due from Miller & Lux, rather than charging it to the value of the water right. The free water was a gift to the cattle company that should have been charged against income, not a necessary part of the canal company's capital outlay.[68] Heacock viewed the situation as Stanislaus County did: the irrigators were being overcharged to subsidize Miller & Lux.[69]

In protesting Heacock's report, Miller & Lux relied on the property-centered ideology that had previously served it well. Again the SJ&KRC&ICo pleaded the public's interest in protecting entrepreneurship, contrasting the cases defining water companies as the agents of their customers with the legislative and judicial actions encouraging private irrigation development. There was, the canal company argued, no overwhelming obstacle to its claim to the water right. None of the decisions denying a water right dealt with a situation exactly like that facing the SJ&KRC&ICo, and none had been extensively argued. In other instances when appropriators had purchased water rights, they had been granted a return on the investment. Those were the precedents that applied, for although no cash had changed hands, the SJ&KRC&ICo had paid for its water rights. To Miller & Lux's attorneys, economic and legal logic dictated that the water belonged to the utility: "It is difficult to see how the rule can be different when it [the canal company] was enterprising enough to acquire the [water] right before others realized the value thereof. If after it had expended its money it had been enjoined from diverting the water, it would have been the loser; and having been fortunate to escape that risk it should have the benefit of its success."[70] Both law and justice, the irrigation company argued, rewarded successful venture capitalists for the chances they took.

To emphasize its position, the SJ&KRC&ICo pointed to its concurrent litigation against the riparian landowner James J. Stevinson, an effort that the irrigators themselves supported. In 1906, Stevinson had won an injunction limiting the canal company's diversion of water from the San Joaquin River to 760 cfs. The company had responded with an eminent domain suit aimed at seizing 500 cfs against Stevinson's riparian rights to restore the original flow in its canal system. Where eminent domain was concerned, there was no doubt that the water right had a monetary value and that Stevinson must be compensated for his loss. Conflict centered on how much the canal company would have to pay. The SJ&KRC&ICo argued that the rules of valuation applied in eminent domain cases should also be the rules applied in rate cases: namely, the value of all property, both tangible and intangible, should be considered.[71] Privately, the attorneys advised the SJ&KRC&ICo that if the court refused to recognize the water right as property, the canal company should not continue the eminent domain suit; it could not afford to pay for Stevinson's water if it must then "donate" it to the public, as a loss in the rate case would require.[72] The SJ&KRC&ICo ultimately paid Stevinson $90,000 for the rights to 500 cfs of water, money on which it could not claim a return under Heacock's interpretation of the law.[73]

As arguments were prepared for Judge Morrow, political and economic conflict along the canal escalated. Hostility to the canal company had increased after the 1908 injunction that permitted the company to collect new rates based on the specific amount of water each customer used. In addition, the Stevinson injunction made it difficult for the canal company to deliver water to all its customers. Not only was the volume of the company's diversion limited, but the consequent reduction in the flow of water in the canals aggravated the losses to seepage. This problem intensified Nickel's emerging concern about efficiency and waste, and he proposed that the company switch from billing by the acreage irrigated to a system of billing based on measurement of the volume of water delivered. In April 1907, the canal company notified all irrigators that payments received at the county rates would not be considered payment in full. It announced that it would begin charging rates of $1.25, $1.90, and $2.35 for each unit of water delivered at the water user's lateral canals[74] and intended to collect any money owed under this system when the lawsuits were concluded. The impact of this change was dramatic. Whereas many had freely let water flow onto their land under the per-acre system, such practices caused soaring water costs under the new method of billing. In some cases, charges equivalent to $9.00 per acre were reported.[75]

J. F. Clyne, superintendent of the SJ&KRC&ICo, worked to educate customers in the advantages of the new system, pointing out that landowners and tenants would benefit from using less water, more carefully. In many cases, he blamed high bills under the new system on the irrigator's lack of skills and on poor maintenance of laterals, and he repeatedly urged irrigators to hire *zanjeros* to manage and maintain shared ditches. Eventually he even adjusted water rates for some of those facing high charges, reducing per-unit fees for many cooperative customers who were unfortunately saddled with porous soil. Despite Miller & Lux's efforts to promote the new scheme, the attempt to impose efficiency through pricing intensified customer discontent, and more irrigators joined the Water Users' Association. After meeting with customers, Clyne reported that many of the "kickers" would never be brought around to see the rationality of the new system "because they are simply opposed to the Canal Company as they are to railroads."[76] By 1910 discontent and antimonopoly sentiments had spread, and numerous schemes to form Wright Act irrigation districts emerged, each proposing to seize control of the canals in the name of the public. The most ambitious scheme called for the formation of the Westside District to embrace more than a million acres of land in Merced, Madera, and Fresno counties, areas that initially had been friendly to the canal company.[77] The battle for access to the benefits of cheap water had escalated from a call for regulation to a demand that the customers take ownership of the system.

As Nickel and Clyne pondered the best response to these developments, E. S. Wangenheim approached them with a proposal. Wangenheim was the most prominent figure in the opposition, and Miller & Lux believed he had forced his debtors to join the rate protest. But Wangenheim also hoped to convince the SJ&KRC&ICo to extend its canals to serve land he was interested in. To this end he offered to raise a subsidy to aid in canal construction and to help settle the rate controversy. The conflict could be ended, he argued, if the firm returned to per-acre rates, abandoning the measurement system that was now the focus of anticompany hostility. Conceding that efficient use was desirable (in fact necessary if water was to be made available to additional lands, as he desired), he suggested that efficiency could be accomplished by placing a cap on volume of water to be furnished under acreage rates. Negotiations bumped along, almost breaking down when Miller balked at tying up his money in the proposed expansion, but by the end of April, Wangenheim and the SJ&KRC&ICo had arrived at a compromise to be offered to the Water Users' Association. In return for eliminating the measurement system, the proposal required irrigators to recognize that the SJ&KRC&ICo had a water right worth $500,000 and to limit their annual use of water to 1 ⅛ acre–feet.[78]

The deal fell through. Despite Miller & Lux's views, Wangenheim did not control the water users, and when faced with public opposition to the compromise, he denounced his own proposal. Instead, the Water Users' Association petitioned the counties to reimpose acreage rates. Once again they went into the political arena for a solution to economic problems. By

July 1911 Fresno, Merced, and Stanislaus counties had instituted per-acre charges of $1.25, $1.75, and $2.00, respectively. In doing so, Stanislaus County moved closer to the $2.25 rate the canal company had originally demanded, and all three counties recognized the company's franchise, though placing its value at $60,000, not the $190,000 value at which it was taxed. However, they continued to deny the company a return on the water right, the issue that Nickel then became determined to win.[79]

The failed compromise fanned the flames of hostility. Acreage rates had gone into effect, yet no concession had been made on the issue of efficient use. Clyne began to cut off water to those who wasted it by allowing water to run down ditches,[80] and though Judge Morrow had not yet ruled on the 1907 rates, the SJ&KRC&ICo filed to enjoin the higher 1911 rates. In Stanislaus County, irrigators threatened to hire James Peck, an attorney who had represented many anti–Miller & Lux interests, including Stevinson in his effort to enjoin the canal company's diversion. Charging that the new suit was the product of Nickel's "egotism and stubbornness" in insisting on the measurement system against the true interests of the canal company, Wangenheim even called on the SJ&KRC&ICo's minority stockholders to oust Nickel from the management. The water users, he threatened in a letter to Nickel, would move to condemn the canal system, a situation that "your personality has forced . . . upon our people." Calm returned only when Miller & Lux publicly promised to take no further legal action until Morrow had reached his decision—and only after it threatened to expose Wangenheim's self-interest in the earlier negotiations.[81]

On 18 September 1911, Morrow announced his decision, a decision that underscored the vulnerability of even powerful interests to judicial independence. Edward F. Treadwell, Miller & Lux's corporate attorney, was shocked by the ruling: Judge Morrow, a man who "ha[d] always shown very sound views on questions of this kind,"[82] rejected the company's arguments for a return on the water right. Citing decisions made throughout the West and relying heavily on the ideas of his colleague Erskine Ross, Morrow ruled that the water right could not be held by the canal company. As an appropriator, its claim to water was limited by the use of water on land, and thus, Morrow reasoned, the water right belonged to the customers, not to the canal company. The SJ&KRC&ICo was merely an agent of the irrigators and could charge only for delivering water, not for controlling it.[83] Claiming that Morrow did not grasp "the precise point upon which the valuation of the water right turned," Treadwell and Short sought a rehearing in which they could raise additional arguments to show that the water right was a franchise.[84] However, their efforts came to naught. Morrow remained convinced that the canal company had received an adequate rate of return. The temporary injunction he had granted in 1908 was lifted, and the county rates were again in force.

The negotiations that followed this ruling made it clear that both Miller & Lux and the water users saw water as an economic asset and were fighting to divide the spoils. For Miller & Lux, the argument that the water right was a property right was not simply a fight over the canal company's rates and income. Beyond that, it was an appeal to law to recognize the vested rights of those first on the scene, to respect contracts, and to allow owners to develop their property as they wished. On the other hand, the water users, who also wanted access to the water resources, denied the property right in water not because of concern about conservation or waste or the general public interest, although their rhetoric sometimes raised these issues; rather, their denial of the property right was a demand that the state, the law, provide new entrepreneurs with the tools for private gain, in this case a share in the exploitation of the river that Miller & Lux seemed to monopolize.

Even though the water users had won their point—that the canal company had no property right in water and had been overcharging them— Wangenheim proposed another deal. Wangenheim hoped to persuade the SJ&KRC&ICo both to accept Morrow's decision, since an appeal would be costly for all the water users, and to extend its service area to include additional land in which he was interested. Once again he proposed that if the rate case were dropped, the irrigators might agree to an increase in the valuation accorded the canal company's property and to limits on their water use. Nickel listened with some skepticism, given the last such proposals, but he refused to accept Morrow's reading of the law. Curiously, Nickel's attorney, Treadwell, advocated compromise. Wangenheim's proposal, he argued, would mandate efficient use and make more water available for sale. More important, Treadwell, who had earlier proposed an appeal of Morrow's decision, was by then having second thoughts about the possibility of winning. The Supreme Court's decisions on such questions, he wrote, "have been almost universally opposed to corporations." Nickel, however, would accept Wangenheim's new proposal only under two conditions: if the company might reopen the question of its valuation in five years and if it would reserve its right of appeal. When the irrigators rejected these demands, Nickel retorted that the SJ&KRC&ICo would not only appeal Morrow's ruling but would also file additional suits to determine standards of economical use and to establish the proper distribution of rates and income among the three counties.[85] Litigation was still the firm's weapon of choice for asserting its power and independence of action.

In mid-March 1914, Treadwell rushed to Washington, D.C., to argue the rate case before the Supreme Court. By then Treadwell claimed to "have no fear of it being decided against us."[86] The tenor of the Supreme Court was different than it had been when the first rate case was decided. John Marshall Harlan, leader of those favoring small producers, was dead, and the Court had adopted a "rule of reason" interpretation of antitrust doctrine that accepted corporations and bigness as part of the natural business order. In April, Treadwell's new confidence was rewarded. In a short opinion written by Justice Holmes, the Supreme Court reversed Morrow and recognized the SJ&KRC&ICo's property in water. Declining to consider the specific values involved, the Court declared that the canal company was entitled in principle to compensation for its water right. The issues were framed by the chain of railroad, gas, and other utility cases that the Court confronted in this period, not by the issues peculiar to western water law. To Holmes, the fact that the water was dedicated to a public use meant only that anyone who paid for it was entitled to water, not that the canal company had made a gift of the water right to the users. Ignoring environmental issues, such as waste and scarcity, that distinguished water regulation, Holmes drew an analogy with the nation's railroads. The canal company, he wrote, was entitled to a return for its control of water just as a railway corporation was entitled to a return for ownership of the track. With this, he sent the case back to the circuit court.[87] There Morrow placed a value of $900,000 on the canal company's water right and enjoined the 1907 rates.

Although the canal company had finally won judicial support for its claim to property in water, new rates were yet to be established by the Railroad Commission, which had assumed jurisdiction over all public utilities as part of a 1913 package of Progressive reforms. The SJ&KRC&ICo retreated from its call for efficiency and proposed new acreage rates of $1.25, $1.75, and $2.25, respectively, for Fresno, Merced, and Stanislaus counties. It issued a statement promising that if these rates were accepted, it would drop its demands for a measurement system and for back payments. The canal company, like many of the irrigators, was weary of litigation and its rising costs.[88]

However, approval of the proposal hinged on the support of the water users, which was not immediately forthcoming. Wangenheim announced acceptance of the $2.25 rate, but smaller landowners clung to the goal of cheap and abundant water. Thirty-two water users from Stanislaus County, who irrigated a combined total of fewer than 2,000 acres, appeared before the Railroad Commission to object to the canal company proposal. As a result, the Railroad Commission set the Stanislaus County rate at $2.00 per acre, the level established by the board of supervisors in 1911.[89] The SJ&KRC&ICo, however, attributed the protest to the unreasonableness of a single irrigator and continued to press for the $2.25-per-acre rate, contemplating new litigation to challenge the $2.00 rate in federal court.[90] In 1915 it won the consent of the Railroad Commission to the higher rate after demonstrating that all irrigators in Stanislaus County had signed contracts at $2.25 per acre.[91] After fifteen years of litigation, the Stanislaus County farmers and ranchers were finally paying the water rate the company had originally demanded.

The SJ&KRC&ICo had realized little improvement in the rates offered in 1911, and in 1915 was charging less overall than it had been in 1900, but Miller & Lux had won a major victory. Judicial acceptance of the claim to a water right gave Miller & Lux crucial protection for the canal company contracts that granted it water rates lower than other water users paid. A rejection of the argument that the water right was property to be bought and sold would have invalidated these contracts, making the relationship between Miller & Lux and the canal company even more vulnerable to intervention by the regulatory bodies of the state. In 1909, the California Supreme Court had struck down discriminatory rates and contracts entered into by public utilities. Later, in *Leavitt* v. *Lassen Irrigation Company*,[92] the state supreme court rejected a contract granting lower water rates to the original owner of a small canal company on grounds that the contract violated the state constitution. The contract, it declared, turned a public trust into a private right and would "result in the destruction of the public use itself." If such contracts were allowed, appropriations made under the guise of a public use could be transferred into private ownership. That decision had played a role in Morrow's 1911 ruling. Still later, in the decision of *Limoneira* v. *Railroad*

Commission,[93] the California court stated that the Railroad Commission, as an incident of its power to regulate, could prevent discrimination between users and ensure that water was furnished at fair and reasonable rates.

For Miller & Lux and the SJ&KRC&ICo, however, once the Supreme Court had recognized the water right, the low rates and free water granted to the cattle company were protected as valid payments for property. Contract and property rights arguments thus undercut the police power when applied to Miller & Lux's use of water. The acceptance of the water right as property gave added legality to the contracts of 1871, 1872, 1879, and 1899. Although these contracts were attacked at later rate hearings, and although the ties between Miller & Lux and the canal company were under constant scrutiny as Stanislaus irrigators tried to win control of the canal company's water through irrigation district laws, Miller & Lux was able to preserve its favored status.

Through these suits, Miller & Lux was able to negate some of the effects of regulatory efforts and to maintain a system clearly favorable to it and, at least by modern theories of efficient distribution, hostile to economic development on the west side of the San Joaquin Valley. Miller & Lux, in essence, received water on the west side at no cost. Miller & Lux was relieved of the expense of maintaining the canals that delivered water to its San Joaquin ranches, and while it paid some water fees to the SJ&KRC&ICo, the profits of the SJ&KRC&ICo (which it owned) generally exceeded these payments. In 1915, for example, the canal company billed Miller & Lux $70,000 for the irrigation of 65,000 acres of land, yet the canal company's average net annual income for the five-year period 1912–16 was only $80,000.[94] If Miller & Lux had paid the full water rate for the almost 90,000 acres it irrigated from wastewaters, the canal company's income would have risen significantly. Payment for the wastewaters, even at the low rate of $1.25 per acre, would have increased the annual revenues of the canal company by more than $100,000. Such payment would have benefited the SJ&KRC&ICo's outside customers, since a doubling of the canal company's profits would have allowed a significant reduction in rates. Instead, the receipt of the water at no charge was an essential element in Miller & Lux's profits. In 1915, Miller & Lux's balance sheet recorded a net gain of only $151,000 on a capital investment with a book value of $12 million and an actual value of almost triple that amount.[95] The $100,000 saved by receiving water free of charge was two-thirds of the firm's acknowledged earnings.

The effect of this favoritism on the west side's development has never been quantified. Although the canal system supported the early growth of irrigated dairy farming in Stanislaus County, local newspapers credited the "turmoil" created by the lawsuit with scaring away "timid investors."[96] In 1929, charges were made that the canal company's rate system in general, being based on the acreage irrigated rather than the volume of water received, led to "extravagant and wasteful" use.[97] Advocates of efficiency models for rate setting insist that economic development is maximized if the cost of water represents the true cost of delivering it and is equal for all customers of a given class (based on delivery costs).[98] Clearly such standards did not operate on the west side, where Miller & Lux received water free of charge. However, neither would this model of rate setting have appealed to the water users who protested Miller & Lux's use of water. The measurement rates that the SJ&KRC&ICo imposed during the struggle against the Stanislaus County rate met the requirements of the efficiency model but were vociferously opposed by all other irrigators on the west side.

While the rate suit raised the rhetoric of reform and conservation, the goal in fact was self-serving, the litigation no more than a struggle between rival interest groups. The smaller ranchers and farmers of the west side of the San Joaquin Valley demanded rate regulation in the name of equity and justice and, more specifically, as a remedy to Miller & Lux's monopolization of water. Yet in doing so they shared important goals with Miller & Lux. For Miller & Lux, water was a source of profit, a resource to be mined and sent forth in the form of beef and pork. The SJ&KRC&ICo's customers accepted this view of water but wanted to turn it to their own economic benefit. They raised the right of the public to regulate utilities, denied that water could be capitalized, and insisted that the state's streams belonged to the people in general—all as a tactic to get a bigger share of the profits that irrigation promised. They lost this effort to democratize exploitation, however, in the face of the persistent demand that property rights be protected.

The efforts to release water to the broader public were undermined when the Supreme Court declared that the SJ&KRC&ICo's water right was a property right. Given the judiciary's commitment to traditional concepts of property and contract, the ruling ensured Miller & Lux's control of water and water rates. When coupled with the recognition of riparian rights as property rights, the decision that the water right could be capitalized hampered the efforts of Miller & Lux's rivals to lower the rates they paid or to increase the costs to the cattle company. Ironically, the commitment of the courts, of the state, to private property also rendered inoperative efficiency models of pricing and economic growth in a capitalist system. Instead, riparian property rights made ownership of a public utility an effective technique for ensuring a cheap supply of private water, and Miller & Lux's repeated litigation helped maintain a system that restricted access to water by skewing the pricing mechanism. As in the contests with appropriators, Miller & Lux did not win every battle in this area; frequently it found itself confounded by hostile readings of the law. Ultimately, however, it was able to maneuver the law to protect its uses of water against the demands of rivals that the state promote their enterprises as a part of public policy.

3

The Power of Doctrine:
Conflict Among Riparians
and the Exploitation of Public Necessity

Critics often argued that riparianism was undemocratic: by tying water to certain pieces of land, it allowed a few to monopolize a resource needed by the many. Miller & Lux, with its huge ranches and legal battalions, lent notorious support to this argument. The critique, however, was too facile. A riparian right by its nature was no secure haven for those wanting to hold water. Not only could a riparian claim be lost to a prescriptive user but, as Miller & Lux learned at the turn of the century, it could be seriously damaged by other riparians. In this period, neighboring cattlemen, who like Miller had purchased long stretches of cheap swamp and overflowed land, were breaking up their ranches. Ambitious to maximize their returns, they speculated in canals that promised to turn their unimproved pastures into irrigated family homesteads. Such riparian canals posed threats to Miller & Lux as real as those of upstream appropriators, yet the legal remedy was neither obvious nor simple. Riparian doctrine did not allow landowners a fixed amount of water but only the opportunity to use it. The right to water was correlative, shared by all riparians, who could begin exploiting a stream at any time, unrestricted by the history of their neighbors. While Miller &

Lux boldly challenged rival appropriators, its own dependence on riparian rights precluded such a direct assault on its new competitors.

Instead Miller & Lux fell back upon its ownership of the SJ&KRC&ICo, whose outspoken customers both demanded the protection of the water that irrigated their land and embodied an answer to the threat posed by the increasing diversion, or taking, of water from the San Joaquin. Trying to badger its opponents into compromise, Miller & Lux used any weapon it could, eventually latching onto the concept of public rights as a doctrinal club. Challenged by a downstream riparian owner, Miller & Lux attempted to seize his water rights by invoking the power of eminent domain as devolved upon irrigation companies; fighting to restrict upstream riparian irrigation, it argued that the rights of a public use were greater than those of a mere private owner; allied with Southern California Edison and other power companies, it tenuously supported efforts to restrict riparian owners to a reasonable amount of water. These efforts produced a tangled thicket of lawsuits, countersuits, and appeals as Miller & Lux plaited its need for immediate victory against riparian rivals with the requirements of the legal doctrines that protected its own property rights. Unlike the appropriative challenges Miller & Lux faced, riparian claims proved difficult to defeat. Despite Miller & Lux's efforts and other critics' complaints, riparianism gave access to water to new interests. In no case did litigation provide clear-cut, doctrinal victories, as had the assertions of riparian rights. On the contrary, litigation underscored the limits of Miller & Lux's power, the potential dangers of independent judicial action, and the relative autonomy of legal doctrine.

———————

Miller & Lux's struggle against other riparians began after the dry winter of 1898–99, when parts of southern California received less than half the normal rainfall. While less destructive than the drought years of the 1860s and 1870s, 1898 and 1899 were some of the driest on the west side of the San Joaquin Valley. Despite its irrigation systems, the shortage of feed forced Miller & Lux to move half its cattle. In March 1899, the cattle company filed suit against an upstream landowner, Jefferson G. James, who was constructing a canal above both Miller & Lux's San Joaquin ranches and the headgates of the SJ&KRC&ICo. This litigation, which will be considered later, became a battle between riparians when James asserted a riparian entitlement as a defense.

A few months later James J. Stevinson, a cattleman and riparian owner, challenged the SJ&KRC&ICo's diversion of water from the San Joaquin River. Stevinson owned more than 25,000 acres of grasslands on the east side of the river, just downstream from Miller & Lux and the SJ&KRC&ICo. Hoping to sell his property in small irrigated units, he proposed to increase the diversion of the underutilized East Side Canal, which had opened twenty years earlier amidst great, as-yet-unfulfilled promises for the future of Merced County.[1] Meanwhile, the SJ&KRC&ICo had been expanding its service area, opening the Outside Canal in 1897, and was in the process of installing a new, stronger dam. These actions, Stevinson charged, interfered with his riparian rights and deprived him of his legitimate and beneficial property in water.[2] For the first time, Miller & Lux confronted a riparian claim like its own.

Stevinson's challenge to the SJ&KRC&ICo placed Miller & Lux on the defensive, a position it occupied awkwardly, and brought it one of its first defeats. Any assertion of the SJ&KRC&ICo's rights restricted Miller & Lux's own riparian claim to the entire flow of the river and enhanced the position of the outside customers. Miller & Lux, which had recently signed contracts recognizing the SJ&KRC&ICo's right to take more than 1,000 cubic feet per second (cfs), thus answered Stevinson's charges hesitantly, first asserting that the canal company had a prescriptive right to 900 cfs of water and later that it was entitled to 1,260 cfs. This response proved inadequate. In 1905 Stevinson won an injunction limiting the canal company's diversion for nonriparian use to 760 cfs, well under the 1,400 cfs it frequently carried at the time.[3]

This injunction had an immediate impact on the canal company and its customers. As Stevinson's men began prowling the canals to detect violations of the new limit, the company was forced to measure the water it carried and to determine the rights of each piece of land it served. Miller & Lux's water was also carefully measured. Routinely diverting more than the injunction allowed,[4] the canal company hoped in this way to get the data necessary to establish its permanent title and to show that all water carried in excess of the 760 cfs belonged to Miller & Lux. The company encountered obstacles. Henry Miller railed that these measurements were useless, the canal company could find few men qualified and willing to do the work at the wages it paid, and complaints about unfair treatment and high rates intensified. But the firm's attorneys insisted that water measurement was necessary to protect the company from future challenges.[5]

In fact, Stevinson's initial success inspired even more litigation. The injunction obtained by Stevinson applied only to water used on nonriparian land and set no limit on the water carried through the canals for riparian irrigation. Bent on securing rights for his East Side Canal and thus enhancing the value of his property, Stevinson filed two additional suits asking the court to determine his and Miller & Lux's relative riparian rights. Miller & Lux met these lawsuits with more of its own: it quickly reincorporated in Nevada and filed suit in federal court asking that the riparian entitlements to the San Joaquin be fixed; it petitioned in state court to limit the diversion through the East Side Canal to the water "beneficially used"; and it appealed the injunction. Miller & Lux had no real intention of pursuing all of this litigation; in fact, J. Leroy Nickel, vice-president of Miller & Lux, hoped to avoid a determination of Miller & Lux's riparian rights because a determination might restrict its use of water. But Nickel had also resolved to take control of any effort to define entitlements, and he wanted the fight to take place in a federal court, not before the elected, local judge who had already favored Stevinson with an injunction.[6] More important, the firm's attorney, Frank H. Short, felt that the Stevinsons were bringing "unnecessary" litigation in an effort to get "more than they are entitled to" and argued that it was "entirely reasonable . . . to give them all [the trouble] they are hunting for and more."[7] Nickel agreed. Uncertain about the strength of his defenses, he hoped to "overwhelm" Stevinson with so much litigation "that he would be compelled to compromise."[8]

This strategy, however, quickly threatened to overwhelm the legal capability of Miller & Lux. In 1905–06, when it began the actions, the firm did not have in-house counsel. Like most of the interests it dealt with, Miller & Lux relied on a changing array of private attorneys; Miller, in fact, frequently hired lawyers who had impressed him with their skill in opposing his suits. In the litigation against Stevinson, the firm employed Frank H. Short of Fresno, Houghton & Houghton—who also represented the Kern County Land Company and played an important role in the negotiations with Southern California Edison—and W. B. Treadwell. Unfortunately these attorneys bickered among themselves to the detriment of the litigation, and in 1906, W. B. Treadwell, who had coordinated the firm's litigation in the valley despite his habit of being irritating to judges, suffered a debilitating stroke.[9] In the suit to limit the diversion via the East Side Canal, Miller & Lux had to demonstrate either that Stevinson had not actually taken water or that he had not put it to a beneficial use. With no single attorney clearly responsible for coordinating the case, the firm had difficulty in providing the necessary records, data, and testimony. Further complicating matters, F. W. McCray, the firm's engineer for twenty years, quit when Henry Miller insulted his work; he refused to testify in the case, depriving the firm of its most knowledgeable expert.[10] While Stevinson's attorney, James Peck, produced numerous "well-coached" witnesses, many of them disgruntled former employees of Miller & Lux and the SJ&KRC&ICo, Nickel found that current employees made unconvincing witnesses for him. As Nickel worked to appease McCray and keep him from joining forces with Peck and Stevinson, he worried that Peck might win this litigation through the sheer "preponderance of testimony" even though much of it was unfounded.[11]

In 1907, Miller & Lux moved to end this confusion and to limit its legal expenses. Following a pattern set by the nation's railroads and large insurance companies, it hired Edward F. Treadwell, W. B. Treadwell's son, as its full-time attorney. He was put on salary and given an office and staff in return for working exclusively for the corporation. Miller & Lux continued to hire some outside attorneys: local lawyers in Oregon and Nevada, where distances made such help imperative; Frank Short to assist with the water disputes in the San Joaquin Valley; the San Francisco law firm Pillsbury, Madison, and Sutro, and an East Coast firm to handle some of its protest against federal claims on Henry Miller's estate. But it was Edward Treadwell, who had studied with Judge McKinstry, author of *Lux* v. *Haggin,* at San Francisco's Hastings College of Law, who framed and carried to trial Miller & Lux's major water law disputes. Until his resignation in 1922, Treadwell was on intimate terms with Nickel and was a key figure in legal and business decisions.[12] Other California corporations followed this pattern as well. The Southern Pacific Railroad first employed corporate counsel in the 1880s; Huntington's Southern California Edison, which relied on the O'Melveny firm in its negotiations with Miller & Lux over the Kern and San Joaquin rivers, hired its own in-house counsel in 1919.[13]

The early results of this combat by litigation reflected the initial confusion and underscored the vulnerability of Miller & Lux's control of water.

In 1908, Judge Olin Wellborn of the federal district court dismissed Miller & Lux's suit to apportion the San Joaquin River for want of jurisdiction. Under the Constitution, the jurisdiction of the federal courts extends to trials of lawsuits between citizens of different states; Stevinson's company was incorporated in California, and Miller & Lux had reincorporated itself in Nevada to gain the forum of federal courts. Wellborn, however, ruled that there had been no legitimate change of citizenship because Miller & Lux's California corporation still existed in 1905, when the federal suit was filed. Miller & Lux appealed the decision, only to lose before the U.S. Supreme Court.[14] That same year, Judge E. N. Rector of the Merced County Court recognized Stevinson's East Side Canal as having a right to 281 cfs of water, part of which attached to Miller & Lux's land.[15] That volume was four times the amount Miller & Lux was willing to concede to the East Side Canal but only half what Stevinson had claimed. The decision satisfied no one, and both sides appealed. In 1915 the state supreme court rejected Stevinson's claim, finding that the East Side Canal was entitled to no more than 281 cfs, and granted Miller & Lux's request for a new trial to determine whether it was entitled to even that amount.[16] However, other complicated litigation over the San Joaquin delayed further action in this particular dispute for over a decade.[17] In the intervening years, the two cattle companies physically battled over the use of water on the east side of the river, each employing armed men and dynamite to threaten the dams and weirs of the other.[18]

Equally problematic was the SJ&KRC&ICo's appeal of the injunction limiting its diversion. In this case, the firm began to tread new and delicate ground to assert the primacy of the SJ&KRC&ICo's public use over Stevinson's riparian right. Although most of Miller & Lux's litigation sought to protect its private rights against the public, in this action Miller & Lux donned the mantle of guardian of the public interest and clothed Stevinson in images of greed and wastefulness. Again rhetoric linked the public interest with the greatest exploitation of water. The canal company, Frank Short argued, had spurred the growth of a prosperous community of farms and small towns; to cut off its water would do harm "almost beyond computation." Stevinson, on the other hand, invoked the law to protect unimproved lands, on which any damages the canals might create would be "infinitesimal."[19] Through rhetoric traditionally associated with appropriators fighting Miller & Lux, Short set the stage for a claim that as a public utility the SJ&KRC&ICo had a preeminent right to expand its diversion.

The Stevinson injunction limited the SJ&KRC&ICo to the amount of water it had diverted from the San Joaquin in the 1870s, denying it the additional flow taken during its period of rapid expansion in the 1880s and 1890s. The SJ&KRC&ICo insisted that the later diversion must be recognized as a public right. It took time to prepare land for irrigation, and after a canal had been constructed and water offered for sale, it was too late to object, the canal company argued; in this case, Stevinson had ignored the diversion for twenty-five years, and the time for protest had passed. When Stevinson pointed out that Henry Miller had assured him that the canal company's new construction would not increase its diversion,[20] Short responded that the expansion was notorious and open, "almost as great an event to the county of Merced as [was] the construction of the Panama Canal to the people of the world."[21] To accept Stevinson's argument that he had no knowledge of such an event would mean that "no public use or prescriptive title could ever be secure" against a riparian owner who pleaded ignorance.[22] While acknowledging Miller & Lux's reliance on riparianism, Short denied that riparian rights were at issue. Such rights were recognized by the courts and had contributed to the development of the state. But a riparian who had "permitted the public to begin a use . . . and upon the fact of its continued use to make investments, improvements, and developments" could not later be allowed to destroy the benefits.[23]

This call for the primacy of the public use and the insistence that the riparian owner prove that he had not acquiesced to the use would be repeated throughout Miller & Lux's battles against riparians. It was a powerful argument, appealing to antiriparian fears and to hopes for progress, and it had the potential to expand dramatically the rights of all utilities. However, it also exposed the contradictions inherent in Miller & Lux's ownership of the SJ&KRC&ICo. As a riparian proprietor, Miller & Lux had an independent entitlement to the river and had itself fought against similar assertions of public claims when defending its rights to the Kern and Fresno rivers against appropriators like Haggin and the Madera Canal Company. While Haggin's claims to a "public use" were purely speculative, the Madera Canal Company, like the SJ&KRC&ICo, in fact provided water essential to a growing community of irrigated farms.

The intervention of E. S. Wangenheim's Water Users' Association dramatized the contradiction. Even as they threatened to hire Stevinson's attorney to represent them in the fight to lower the SJ&KRC&ICo's rates, self-interest forced the irrigators into an uneasy alliance with the canal company's effort to lift the Stevinson injunction. They were totally dependent on water from the SJ&KRC&ICo canals, in many cases on the newer Outside Canal that had precipitated Stevinson's suit, and some in Stanislaus County wanted the SJ&KRC&ICo to expand its service and its diversion. The association argued that the injunction hurt the smaller users because it limited the water that the canal company could deliver to nonriparian lands and thus to the irrigating public. The water users suggested that Stevinson's complaint would properly be directed at Miller & Lux; yet as a riparian owner, Miller & Lux would benefit from the public's loss, as "any water which the canal company is enjoined from diverting and selling to the non-riparian land, Miller & Lux can and probably will take and place on its riparian land." [24] The water users were correct in much of this. While the SJ&KRC&ICo's canals were important elements in Miller & Lux's delivery system, its water rights were not. Miller & Lux's riparian rights had not been damaged by Stevinson's actions. However much their interests merged with those of the SJ&KRC&ICo, the Water Users' Association could never forget its own conflict with all riparians, especially with Miller & Lux.

Even as the SJ&KRC&ICo's attorneys appealed the injunction, they had little expectation of victory. The problem was their own success in promoting riparian rights. In 1909 the California Supreme Court strongly supported the rights of riparian owners in Miller & Lux's suit against the Madera Canal Company: a riparian was entitled to the full flow of the stream, even its floodwaters, against upstream appropriators. This decision, welcomed by Miller & Lux as a key to preserving its rights, also protected Stevinson's riparian property. Consequently, the SJ&KRC&ICo in 1909 initiated a new effort to perfect its rights through eminent domain. Relying on section 1238 of the civil code, which devolved the power of eminent domain onto public irrigation companies,[25] the SJ&KRC&ICo filed to seize 500 cubic feet per second of water against the entitlement of Stevinson's riparian land.

The firm's attorneys believed that Stevinson was the only downstream landowner who posed any threat to the canal company's right, and they reasoned that an eminent domain taking, or condemnation, would provide a more direct and potentially less expensive way of "completing the canal company's water rights" than the existing complex of lawsuits. Eminent domain was an "affirmative procedure" that would offset the multiple suits Stevinson had filed.[26] After the supreme court upheld the Stevinson injunction in 1912,[27] the eminent domain suit became the main battlefield for the two riparians. As Miller & Lux confronted timid jurists and hostile juries, its new strategy proved far from easy, however, belying notions that eminent domain furnished an easy tool for transferring private property to new enterprises.

The SJ&KRC&ICo's attorneys were highly conscious of the dangers posed by local antagonisms and prejudices but found them difficult to overcome. To mitigate their threat, Frank H. Short and Edward F. Treadwell decided to eliminate as many issues as possible from the eminent domain suit. Rather than demonstrate that the canal company was entitled to employ eminent domain, they filed a simple complaint that assumed that the SJ&KRC&ICo was a public utility and asked the court merely to determine the value of Stevinson's right and to set the appropriate compensation for his loss.[28] This effort at simplification was unsuccessful. After the SJ&KRC&ICo spent three weeks presenting its case, Stevinson's attorney, James Peck, moved for a dismissal. The SJ&KRC&ICo, Peck argued, had not established that it supplied a public use. Despite the ongoing protest against his ruling in the *East Side* case, which granted Stevinson 281 cfs of water, Judge Rector was hearing the eminent domain case. Short had rejected suggestions of bringing in an outside jurist; Rector, he argued, was familiar with the issues and was honest and willing to consider the law from an independent, open-minded perspective—a rare asset, given the emotions that water disputes raised in these communities.[29] To Short's dismay, however, Rector granted Peck's motion. Adopting a literal interpretation of the statute in question, Rector reasoned that, under the definition of public irrigation companies as those serving "farming neighborhoods," such companies were required to furnish water to all the residents of a county, a standard the SJ&KRC&ICo did not meet.

The canal company appealed the ruling, arguing this case in the same session of the state supreme court as its *East Side* protest. Again it confronted the uncertainty and unpredicability of litigation. Before the supreme court, Short and Treadwell stressed the implications of Rector's interpretation of the civil code for the future of public service companies. Because geography precluded most enterprises from serving every resident of a given county, there would be no way under Rector's interpretation for any irrigation company to obtain riparian rights by eminent domain. Recalcitrant landowners could hold up future water projects to the detriment of the state's development. The canal company's argument, Short felt, was "fortunate to be along that line with which this court had usually agreed," since Peck had "littered the case with all sorts of haphazard and psychological arguments."[30] In 1912, the state supreme court granted the SJ&KRC&ICo its right to a hearing. The decision, Short judged, was "clear and strong and possesse[d] the exceptional merit of covering and deciding every point clearly and fully in our favor." Yet a dissent from Judge M. C. Sloss underscored the problems of relying on judicial interpretation of policy issues. While Short had believed Sloss to be the justice most likely to support the SJ&KRC&ICo's position, Sloss had adopted Rector's literal interpretation of the statute.[31]

Having won the right to sue, Nickel hesitated momentarily. Eminent domain had not simplified anything, and he doubted that it was really in Miller & Lux's interest to increase the SJ&KRC&ICo's entitlement. Every cubic foot of water the canal company legally acquired was a foot of water Miller & Lux could not use. But the "public" that the company claimed to represent forced continuing action. When the water users threatened to form an irrigation district to acquire additional water and to seize control of the canals, Nickel moved ahead.[32] Allying itself with its customers and their demands, the SJ&KRC&ICo filed another eminent domain action in 1913. Once again appearing in Rector's court, the SJ&KRC&ICo stressed the importance of the canal and the benefits it provided, linking the future growth and continuing prosperity of the entire west side to the expansion of its services.[33]

Stevinson's attorney, James Peck, put on an aggressive defense that also catered to popular concerns. To counter the paean of praise from west side residents, he played upon the distrust of Miller & Lux and upon the increasing national and local concern for the conservation of resources. Unable to deny that the SJ&KRC&ICo serviced a large area, Peck instead asserted that the canal company did not need Stevinson's water; it could solve its problems by operating more efficiently and more fairly. Miller & Lux, Peck argued, had abused its control of the SJ&KRC&ICo, using it in a manner that deprived the public of water. He produced former SJ&KRC&ICo superintendents then in Stevinson's employ who insisted that Miller & Lux could have productively irrigated its ranches with only a third of the water it took if it had not freely and wastefully flooded its grass and alkali lands.[34] He pointed to the swamps, duck ponds, and hunting preserves created by water discharged through the SJ&KRC&ICo's waste gates. Covering 50,000 acres of cattle company land and used mainly by recreational hunters, these swamps seemed to mock the claims of water shortage.[35] While some of the same wetland habitats are now protected as ecological preserves, they did not meet the then commonplace, reformist view that water existed to promote economic activity. In Peck's picture, the needs of west side farmers could have been met "if the waters of the canal had been distributed to supply the demand rather than to serve the private use of Miller & Lux."[36] Those were the identical practices cited by the state's conservation reformers to prove the absurdity of California's acceptance of riparian rights.

Stevinson extended this attack on wasteful practices into a criticism of the canals themselves that mirrored some of the complaints in the ongoing rate controversy. The SJ&KRC&ICo's unlined earthen canals had been built in the 1870s and 1890s. Although some efforts had been made to control water losses—for example, digging new channel when the Main Canal ran through a band of extremely porous soil—the system experienced considerable seepage. With the flow restricted to 760 cfs by Stevinson's injunction, only 41 of every 100 cfs taken from the San Joaquin River at Mendota reached irrigators at the end of the line in Stanislaus County. In other words, 59 percent of the water diverted was lost through seepage. Such a volume of water, Peck argued, would irrigate 71,680 acres if it were conserved. He proposed that the SJ&KRC&ICo be required to replace its existing canals with a single concrete-lined channel. By cutting losses in this manner, the canal company could irrigate more land with the 760 cfs of water it already possessed than with the full 1,260 cfs it was seeking. Conservation, Peck insisted, must be encouraged if the state were to receive full benefit from its streams.[37]

Short and Treadwell scrambled to counter the image of corruption and inefficiency conjured by this defense. Although they insisted that Miller & Lux's use of water was irrelevant since it had an independent entitlement as a riparian owner,[38] they recognized that the perception of waste prejudiced their case. They had to explain and justify the cattle company's operations. A variety of ranchers, including Isaac Bird, manager of the Scottish-owned California Pastoral and Agricultural Company, and Henry Miller himself, were trotted out to testify that the practice of swamping land was both economical and beneficial. Swamping required little building of levees and it yielded a good crop of natural grasses at a lower cost than any other method.[39]

While such testimony might be dismissed as self-serving, Treadwell and Short answered the criticism with an appeal to the seeming neutrality of statistics and empirical evidence when they put W. C. Hammatt, chief engineer of both Miller & Lux and the SJ&KRC&ICo, on the stand. Presented as an expert witness, Hammatt was a West Point–trained civil engineer who had had no experience with water measurement or canal operations until hired by Miller & Lux in 1907. He testified that the canals' seemingly high losses to seepage were caused not by poor design or construction, but rather by the low volume flowing in the system under the current injunction. If the SJ&KRC&ICo's diversion were increased by the 500 cfs it sought, its water losses would decrease to 45 percent, a level comparable to that of other canals in the area—in fact, lower than that from Stevinson's own East Side Canal.[40] Conceding that concrete linings would eliminate seepage, Hammatt argued that they would be of little benefit to the west side of the San Joaquin because all the water that permeated the canal walls served to wet the surrounding lands and to reduce the amount required for irrigation.[41]

When the trial moved to consider the issue of compensation, the SJ&KRC&ICo's hope that eminent domain would be an easy alternative in their fight with Stevinson was again confounded by Peck's ability to conjure up images of embattled small farmers. When drawing up the complaint, Short and Treadwell had identified what they considered to be all of Stevinson's riparian property, in total 2,407 acres of unimproved and undeveloped land. They estimated that this property was worth $20 per acre, the average price received for similar tracts in the region, and posited an upper limit for compensation at $50,000, the purchase price of the entire tract. However, in an amended answer to the complaint, Stevinson introduced an additional 7,400 acres that he insisted were entitled to water.[42] Although this acreage was far from the river, Judge Rector allowed Peck to present a hypothetical reclamation scheme in which water would be delivered through the East Side Canal and land would be subdivided and sold to settlers. Stevinson proposed that the reclaimed land would be worth $300 an acre to family farmers and asserted a claim to damages of $275 per acre, or almost $2.7 million.[43]

As a matter of law, the issue of compensation was to be determined by the jury, a circumstance that presented Miller & Lux with a "very undesirable and vexatious problem."[44] Peck had successfully challenged all potential jurors from the west side, where most people were customers of the SJ&KRC&ICo or tenants of Miller & Lux. The jury was thus composed exclusively of residents of the east side of the San Joaquin, who traditionally saw themselves as economic and political rivals of those living west of the river. Local bias was buttressed by popular antimonopoly sentiments, which often led juries to favor individuals over large corporations. Throughout the valley, Miller & Lux was seen as a land monopolist, a perception intensified by its ongoing stiff opposition to the state water commission bill and other efforts at water reform promoted by local legislators and boosters. Repeatedly, hostility to the firm presented difficulties in even simple cases: juries seemed to find little wrong with stealing from Miller & Lux and frequently refused to convict notorious neighborhood cattle thieves. Economic rivalry and class hostility generated notions of justice that could override legal formalities.[45]

The problems were compounded by the instructions given the jury. Short and Treadwell had drafted some two hundred pages of jury instructions, but most of these were not utilized by the judge. Instead, Rector authorized the jury to decide what, to Miller & Lux, were crucial issues of law that lay outside the jury's province. Although the state supreme court had earlier ruled that the SJ&KRC&ICo was a public service corporation,[46] Rector directed the jury to determine both whether the proposed use of water was a public use and whether the condemnation was necessary. Jurors were told that there would be no need to condemn Stevinson's water if the seepage losses from the SJ&KRC&ICo canals were excessive, if the losses could be eliminated by repairing the canals, or if the canal company could supply its customers by conserving water "in a practical manner."[47]

Given those options, the results were not surprising. Although the trial had lasted two and a half months and had included vast amounts of technical and complicated engineering information, the jury deliberated only a few hours before returning a decision in favor of Stevinson. While nine jurors felt the condemnation would serve a public use, all twelve agreed that it was unnecessary. Miller & Lux and the canal company would get nothing.[48]

For the third time, the SJ&KRC&ICo challenged a decision from Rector's court. Rector, it protested, had abdicated his duties in this case: the court, not the jury, should have determined the questions of public use and necessity on which the verdict had hinged. Not only that, but he had improperly admitted vast amounts of testimony that prejudiced the outcome. While the public nature of the use depended only on who consumed the water, Rector had entertained evidence on Miller & Lux's ownership of the canal company and had allowed Peck to imply that Miller & Lux manipulated the utility, but he had not permitted the canal company to demonstrate how decisions were actually made. These improprieties had created a distorted and false impression that clouded the essential issues of law, the canal company argued. Similarly, testimony on the hypothetical reclamation project allowed for a great deal of cost manipulation that artificially inflated the extent of damages.[49]

The canal company's deeper objections concerned the admission of evidence on the cementing scheme and the linkage that had been made between entitlement and efficiency. The technology employed by the SJ&KRC&ICo, Treadwell stressed, should not be considered in evaluating its needs. Its earthen canals had been built by an adequate method, one still in common use. While new technologies might offer some advantages, they could not be imposed on irrigation companies as a prerequisite for employing the power of eminent domain. In essence, Treadwell suggested, a decision that the SJ&KRC&ICo must replace its earthern canals with one lined with concrete would be as inappropriate as a ruling that land could no longer be condemned to build railroads because "flying machines have come into vogue."[50]

The strident calls for water conservation that permeated California politics gave the cementing issue its importance. Progressive water reformers were urging courts and legislatures to adopt more rigorous standards of reasonable and economical use. Rulings in this direction could transform the pattern of water development just as *Charles River Bridge* had affected internal improvements in the nineteenth century.[51] By 1914, when this appeal was argued, some western courts had asserted the power to impose new technology and standards on irrigators. In Oregon, for example, the state supreme court had ruled that early settlers must change their methods of water use as demand increased, even if the change imposed great costs.[52] It was "the policy of the law," the Oregon court later added, "that the best methods be used."[53] For Miller & Lux, new standards threatened not only additional expenses but the loss of water to more efficient users, as irrigation agriculture with its greater dollar yields expanded along the borders of its ranches.[54]

Although Miller & Lux found frequent success in the higher courts, there was no guarantee. In this case, settlement of the issue was plagued by the vagaries of judicial behavior. After delivering his oral argument before the state's appellate court, Treadwell lamented that "questions of such importance" had to be submitted to the panel of judges then sitting. There was no predicting what would happen or why: the remarks of the presiding judge "were nothing short of imbecile" and it was clear that "his mind [was] gone completely." In 1915 the appeals court granted the SJ&KRC&ICo's request for a new trial, but the opinion accompanying the ruling was as unsatisfactory as Treadwell had feared. Some of the issues were decided quickly and easily in favor of the canal company: The trial court should have determined whether there was a public use, and testimony on the reclamation scheme should not have been admitted.[55] However, more complex issues—the necessity of the taking and the cementing proposal—were decided unfavorably, underscoring the difficulties that conservation posed for the judiciary. The appellate court conceded a "persuasive force" in the canal company's argument that, under the civil code, the judge must decide the question of necessity, yet it instead followed a set of early supreme court decisions that left the question for the jury.

The cementing scheme itself generated a rambling discussion of the value of conservation that disconcerted Miller & Lux's attorneys. Although remarking that the SJ&KRC&ICo's canals were probably "reasonably fit," the appellate court suggested that the law did not permit "extravagant waste" and in some circumstances might require that irrigation canals be sealed "in order that water might be utilized to the fullest extent."[56] The issue, the appellate court proposed, should be settled by a study of comparative costs that balanced the availability of water and its value to Stevinson against the cost of reconstructing the SJ&KRC&ICo's system.[57] If the burden on the utility were great compared with Stevinson's loss, "this improvement should be deferred until the advancing necessities and the increased and increasing appropriation of water make such a demand reasonable and just."[58] Although the court had implied that Stevinson's request was at that point unreasonable, any protection afforded was temporary, open to reconsideration as requests to use the river increased. Under the appellate court ruling, water rights were subject to technological advances, new uses of the river, and the whims of the juries evaluating them—the very situation Miller & Lux wanted to avoid.

Such a ruling and its implications could not be ignored. The SJ& KRC&ICo petitioned for a rehearing and, when it was denied, appealed to the state supreme court. Arguing that the decision of the appellate court would "cause embarrassment and uncertainty" in a succeeding trial, the SJ&KRC&ICo questioned the appellate court's extensive discussion of the cementing issue and requested the state supreme court to declare earthen canals acceptable and eligible to increase their water supply through eminent domain. It also renewed its argument that the issue of the necessity of a taking should be decided by the court, not the jury. When there was a public use and a demand for the water, the canal company insisted, "the conditions and character of the canals and the [water] loss therein is [*sic*] immaterial."[59]

This bid by the canal company was more successful. Although the state supreme court declined to hear the case, it issued a statement modifying the appellate court's decision as the canal company had sought. The question of necessity—in fact, all questions in an eminent domain case except that of compensation—was for the trial judge to determine. The supreme court chastised the appellate judges for even discussing the cementing scheme. As in *California Pastoral and Agricultural Company* v. *Madera*,[60] the supreme court sided with the irrigation company, ruling that "no unreasonable expense should be imposed on the public service company."[61] Although the issue of necessity was still left to the lower court, the burden of proof would be on Stevinson and, by implication, on any conservationist opponents, not on the canal company. The supreme court's willingness to support public utilities, which had hindered Miller & Lux's quest to shut down the Madera Canal and Irrigation Company, seemed to favor Miller & Lux's use of water through the SJ&KRC&ICo.

When the suit returned to the local courts, the main difficulty became one of finding a jury that was not hostile to the SJ&KRC&ICo and Miller & Lux. In 1915, in the third trial held in Merced County, Rector granted the canal company the right to take 500 cfs of water and directed the jury to determine only the level of compensation. The jury, however, again favored Stevinson, awarding him $425,000, or more than $175 per acre for swamplands that could be purchased on the open market for only $25 an acre. Rector threw out the verdict and granted a new trial and a change of venue to Mariposa County.[62] In upholding the change of venue, the state supreme court expressed its hope that the Mariposa jurors might not be "affected by those problems and prejudices that arise and persist where large corporations operate in the control of water."[63]

This hope was not realized. Peck again appealed to the predisposition of small farmers to favor the smaller operator against the larger corporation, labeling the canal company and Miller & Lux tax dodgers who controlled the Merced County assessor; he also appealed to the anti-German hysteria of the First World War period by continually referring to Miller's German birth.[64] At one point as the trial heated up, Peck and Treadwell "came to blows in the courtroom" and both were fined for contempt.[65] Although Miller & Lux had supplied eight witnesses, one a former member of the state railroad commission, who assigned values of $7 to $35 an acre to Stevinson's land, the jury granted Stevinson $200,000 (more than $80 per acre), a sum that the canal company also found unacceptable. Rumors abounded about jury tampering and bribes offered by Stevinson's forces. The verdict, like that in Merced County, was thrown out, and the case continued to move in and out of the superior and appellate courts until 1928, when an out-of-court settlement was reached. Under this agreement, the canal company paid Stevinson $90,000 for the rights to the 500 cfs of water it had been seeking.[66]

Eminent domain proceedings, initiated to forestall the growing volumes of litigation with the Stevinson interests, had proven to be a lengthy, expensive, and unsatisfactory method for securing water rights. Such complexities had been anticipated by both water reformers and opponents of Miller & Lux. The conservation commission and the attorneys for the Madera Canal and Irrigation Company had both pointed out the need to attenuate the hold of riparian rights on the state if irrigation development was to be carried out by private companies. Without some reform, they had argued, the expense of condemning riparian rights would force costs so high as to eliminate profits. This argument was rejected out of hand by Miller & Lux's attorneys in the litigation against the Madera Canal and Irrigation Company, but it was clearly central to the conflict with Stevinson, as well as in the rate litigation with the water users. Eminent domain had been devolved upon private enterprises throughout the West to encourage economic growth, but in this case it offered little to ease the process of expansion. While the public customers of the SJ&KRC&ICo were the main beneficiaries of the eminent domain suit, Miller & Lux's ownership of the canal company was always dominant. Fears of monopoly and of exploitation by utility companies had a stronger hold on the minds of the populace than abstract support for development.[67] The jury, an entity central to American law as a tool for protecting property against unjust seizure, prevented eminent domain from serving as a simple expedient for securing the SJ&KRC&ICo's water right.

The conflict between Stevinson and Miller & Lux was only one of the challenges presented by rival riparians. In some ways it was the least threatening; located downstream, Stevinson's claims did not directly interfere with Miller

& Lux's riparian irrigation. But even as they fought Stevinson, Miller & Lux and the SJ&KRC&ICo were also involved in a battle against an upstream landowner, Jefferson G. James, whose use of water in fact diminished the flow to both companies. Like Miller, James was a cattleman, reputedly the fourth largest "cattle king" in the state, with a wholesale meat business in San Francisco; but like Stevinson, James had decided to sell his 70,000-acre ranch in the form of small irrigated plots.[68] In 1898 James excavated the Enterprise Canal upstream from the SJ&KRC&ICo's headgates and above the bulk of Miller & Lux's property. Since none of James's land bordered the main channel of the San Joaquin, Miller & Lux treated his new canal as a mere appropriation. As it had so many times before, Miller & Lux filed suits in both federal and state courts, and it quickly won temporary injunctions that shut down James's diversion. James, however, asserted that he was not a mere appropriator; rather, he claimed riparian rights to the San Joaquin by virtue of owning land along Fresno Slough, which linked the Kings River in the south with the San Joaquin. Judge J. R. Webb of the Fresno superior court rejected this contention, but his elected successor, George Church, granted James's request for a new trial. Miller & Lux appealed this order without success. While the state supreme court upheld the initial injunction, it also accepted the order granting a new trial on the issues.[69]

Owning land along the San Joaquin in four counties, Miller & Lux exploited its size and influence to find a more sympathetic forum and to limit the issues before the court. Using the name of a neighbor whose land it sometimes leased, Miller & Lux filed a new suit in Rector's Merced County court that tested James's claim to be a riparian owner. Argument focused on the legal meaning of riverine geography. Fresno Slough had been carved by the natural force of the Kings River as it flowed into the San Joaquin; yet when the level of the Kings River fell, the waters of the San Joaquin filled what had originally been its tributary. James based his claim to the San Joaquin on the presence of its waters in Fresno Slough, a condition increasingly common as southern irrigation development exhausted the flow of the Kings.[70] Miller & Lux, on the other hand, insisted that Fresno Slough be considered a part of the river that had created it. In 1906, Judge Rector accepted Miller & Lux's position and ruled that James's land had no right to the waters of the San Joaquin; on appeal, however, the state supreme court rejected the notion that the origins of the stream bed determined the issue of rights. While the flow of the Kings might have created the slough, the waters of the San Joaquin filled it for much of the year, especially during the dry months, when water was most needed. This fact, the supreme court ruled, gave James a legitimate riparian claim on the San Joaquin itself.[71]

The declaration that James was indeed a riparian owner forced Miller & Lux and the SJ&KRC&ICo into a more complicated legal dilemma. As a riparian, James had a right to use the San Joaquin equal and concurrent with that of Miller & Lux. Miller & Lux could not deny this right without harming its own claims. As in its conflict with Stevinson, it had to find a course of action that did not undermine the very legal doctrine on which it depended. Focusing on the location of James's Enterprise Canal—which took water from a point above Miller & Lux's east side ranches, long before it could have reached Fresno Slough—Miller & Lux pointed out that James's riparian entitlement did not begin until water reached his land.

Although its argument was relatively simple and straightforward, Miller & Lux lost the first round of this challenge. In Fresno, Judge George Church refused to enjoin the Enterprise Canal. He presented a curious argument that claimed to encourage economic growth yet stripped improved land of property rights in water. In the broadest terms, Church ruled that James could take water from the upstream location because it was more "convenient" for him to do so and because his diversion encouraged the development and settlement of the region. More specifically, he denied that Miller & Lux's intervening property was riparian because the firm had deepened, dammed, and otherwise modified the sloughs that had naturally watered the area. In other words, because it had improved its land, Miller & Lux had lost its riparian rights; it had become a mere appropriator, whose rights were inferior to those of the riparian James.[72]

Once again Miller & Lux took its case to the state supreme court, and again it won on the grounds that a local decision imperiled vested property rights. Finding that Miller & Lux's improved land had not lost its riparian character, the supreme court rejected Judge Church's notion that the convenience of one property owner took precedence over the rights of another. Church had cited the rhetoric of *Fresno Flume*[73] that encouraged courts to modify the common law as circumstances dictated, but the supreme court rejected his modifications as being too radical. If James were allowed to take water without the permission of intervening riparian owners, the result would be "interminable confusion and litigation in the scrambling efforts of every riparian owner to go as far upstream as possible to get water."[74] The chaos would undermine property values and the sense of security necessary if irrigation systems were to be developed. As in *Lux* v. *Haggin* and many of the other water conflicts in which Miller & Lux was involved, the California Supreme Court held the protection and stabilization of property values to be paramount, while the local courts seemed willing to favor newer developers and interests.

Protecting the SJ&KRC&ICo's diversion was more complicated, however, since the canal company was an appropriator, whose rights were by law inferior to those of most riparian owners. Although Miller & Lux had enjoined the Enterprise Canal, James was allowed to take water from Fresno Slough, an activity that injured the SJ&KRC&ICo and its customers as much as the original scheme. The most direct response was to acquire more property, as Miller & Lux occasionally did to eliminate obstacles to its control of water. In 1908, for example, Miller & Lux had bought the Borland ranch, which also bordered Fresno Slough; Judge Church had ruled that the ranch was riparian to the San Joaquin River and had granted it an injunction limiting the SJ&KRC&ICo's diversion to 900 cfs.[75] Similarly, the cattle company had purchased riparian land from Thomas Rickey, a California cattleman, to gain control of the Walker River, which fed its main Nevada ranches.[76] Facing James's threat to the SJ&KRC&ICo, Miller & Lux offered to buy 40,000 acres of his land for $2.5 million.[77]

This effort failed, however, and Miller & Lux rejected the other option for acquiring James's property—an eminent domain condemnation of the water rights themselves. As the litigation with Stevinson had shown, an eminent domain suit raised as many problems as it solved. Such a suit would open Miller & Lux's affairs to the scrutiny of both another jury and the broader public; yet it could not end the threat posed by others upstream and, by publicly airing James's claims, might inspire them to demand compensation. Instead, the firm's attorneys developed a complex sequence of arguments that both asserted the primacy of public use and undertook to demonstrate the superiority of the canal company's right to this particular riparian claimant.

As in the eminent domain litigation, Short and Treadwell ventured into new territory when they asserted the claims of the public against a private riparian use. At this point, they proposed a judicial modification of the law to restrict upstream users in favor of the SJ&KRC&ICo. While Miller & Lux's name had become synonymous with riparian rights, its attorneys proclaimed that the traditional rule allowing no prescriptive titles to mature against upstream proprietors had worked a "great hardship" and had produced much "inequity" and "injustice."[78] Although there was some basis for this rule in cases involving private appropriators, public service companies like the SJ&KRC&ICo, they suggested, presented an entirely different set of circumstances; since the California court had never explicitly applied the rule against such users, the court could resolve the question in favor of the irrigating public.[79] Reasoning that such companies could use the power of eminent domain to seize upstream rights, Treadwell argued that if upstream riparian owners had never protested a public use, they should be viewed as having dedicated their rights to the public through implied consent. The situation in the San Joaquin Valley was a case in point: the SJ&KRC&ICo had been serving irrigators there for over forty years, while James had made no use of water that diminished the flow in the river; to hold against the canal company in this circumstance was "contrary to justice."[80] As in many cases involving railroad and utility rights-of-way, such a property owner should be limited to a claim for damages and not be allowed to enjoin the public use.[81]

At the same time, Short and Treadwell wanted to leave the supreme court a way to favor the SJ&KRC&ICo without asserting the absolute priority of the public use. They doubted that the court would change the law and worried that if it did, the change might harm Miller & Lux's private claims against the Madera irrigators and against the SJ&KRC&ICo itself. Thus, while raising the broad issue, they carefully stressed the uniqueness of their case against James. The largest portion of the brief, the section written with the most care, dealt with the physical and hydrological relationships among the headgates of the canal, the flow of water into Fresno Slough, and James's land. The canal company tried to prove by a variety of methods that its diversion had created an actionable interference with James's use of water. It argued that James was a downstream, not an upstream, owner, presenting elaborate maps and diagrams to show that water flowing from the San Joaquin into Fresno Slough passed the headgate of the canal before it reached James's ranch. The canal company also asserted that its dam had at times flooded parts of James's land and at other times had either drawn water away from it or diminished the flow of water to it. If any of these positions were accepted, the supreme court could find that James's inaction had given the canal company a prescriptive right, and it could thus enjoin his use without deciding the larger question of the priority of the public use.[82] It could protect the

SJ&KRC&ICo without weakening the traditional protections given property rights in water.

The state supreme court initially rejected this elaborate construction of the SJ&KRC&ICo's rights, brushing aside both the assertion of a public right and the notion that the canal company had acquired a prescriptive entitlement. Frank Short found the decision convincing, logical, and forceful and counseled Miller & Lux to settle with James.[83] As in the Stevinson litigation, however, the SJ&KRC&ICo's customers forced continued action. Eager to expand access to water and having no affection for riparianism, the Water Users' Association petitioned for a rehearing. The water users' attorney, J. P. Langhorne, boldly proclaimed the rights of the irrigators, insisting that riparians were duty-bound to "stop, look, and listen" when the public made use of water.[84] The SJ&KRC&ICo joined the appeal but filed its own memo for a rehearing. Giving credit to the enthusiasm with which Langhorne put forth his views, Treadwell himself now placed "little confidence in the argument of public policy" and had little hope that the state supreme court would adopt such reasoning. He still wanted to give the court "something tangible to act upon" and repeated his efforts to show that this specific riparian owner had had the opportunity to object to the canal company's diversion.[85]

These petitions were rewarded. In 1914, the supreme court granted a rehearing to take additional argument on the question of the rights of the public,[86] and in 1915 it found for the canal company, enjoining James from diverting any water that would interfere with a flow of 760 cfs to the canal company. Although it had restricted reargument to broad policy issues, the supreme court grounded the 1915 decision in the particular geography of the case. The court stated that in general terms a downstream user could not establish any priority of use against an upstream riparian proprietor; it summarized the arguments for recognizing a public use. Then, however, despite all the debate, it dodged the question of the broad rights of the public, declaring that the issue need not be considered in this case. Instead the supreme court decided that the SJ&KRC&ICo's dam had harmed James and that, by failing to protest the injury, he had consented to the SJ&KRC&ICo's diversion and could not interfere with it at that point. James had effectually "dedicated to a public use the riparian rights pertaining to . . . [his] land."[87] While refusing to set broad limits on private property, the supreme court pointed to its *Madera* decisions to assert that public utilities should be given a wide benefit of the doubt. As a result of this decision, and later rulings in Rector's court that expanded the canal company's right to 1,360 cfs, James and subsequent developers of his ranch had no choice but to rely primarily on wells for irrigation.[88]

Because the decision in *Enterprise* was a narrow one, the SJ&KRC&ICo found itself still vulnerable to other upstream riparian users. The threat they posed had intensified by 1912. For years only a few ranchers had bothered to use available, but expensive, gasoline-powered pumps to lift water over the steep banks of the upper San Joaquin, but the recent introduction of cheap hydroelectric power in the region made such irrigation economically feasible. More important, the recurrence of serious drought made it essential. Drought seared the valley in the winter of 1911–12: only 2 inches of rain fell from September 1911 to March 1912, compared with a normal seasonal average of over 6½ inches. Stockmen, desperate after a second year of little rain and unable to feed more than 200,000 head of cattle and sheep, in March 1913 began petitioning for permission to graze stock in Yosemite National Park. Increasingly, the *Fresno Morning Republican* reported, farmers were buying pumps and drilling wells in efforts to save their crops and their herds.[89]

By that time, Miller & Lux, whose lands were generally well watered, was complaining of the poor condition of its San Joaquin Valley property. Its ranches had almost exhausted their supplies of hay and, having been forced to allow ewes and cattle to graze longer than usual in the alfalfa fields as grasslands dried up, superintendents predicted poor hay crops in the next season. The lack of water, combined with alternating periods of extreme cold and searing heat, forced Miller & Lux not only to search out feed for sale and pasturelands for rent, but also to sell cattle as early as possible and to send more livestock than usual to its Nevada ranges. In March 1913, the firm began probing the causes of what seemed, even for a dry year, to be an abnormally low level of water in the river. Nickel ordered that a "competent man" be sent up the river to report on existing pumping plants and on any land that might be developed for irrigation in the future. He also suspected that Southern California Edison might be holding back water that should have been released into the river under the terms of the earlier contracts.[90]

In 1913, as it petitioned for a rehearing in the James case, the SJ& KRC&ICo initiated a suit in Rector's court challenging W. H. Worswick and other upstream riparian landowners who had recently begun irrigating their land. In 1914, Miller & Lux filed an additional suit against this group in an attempt to protect the Chowchilla Canal. Although surmising that the California court would not adopt his position, Treadwell again raised the priority of the SJ&KRC&ICo's public use and insisted that the upstream claimants bear the burden of defending their rights. Since the upstream landowners had never protested the SJ&KRC&ICo's diversion and since they had not filed claims for compensation when the canal company expanded its sales of water, Miller & Lux asserted that they had consented to the diversion and had dedicated their riparian rights to the public.[91] Again Miller & Lux hoped to elevate the claims of the utility that irrigated its own lands over the property rights of other riparian owners; again it fought to gain control of the waters of the San Joaquin without the difficulties and expenses of eminent domain and compensation.

As in the James litigation, Treadwell also tried to particularize the complaint. Following a line of reasoning endorsed by the Oregon Supreme Court, he presented an elaborate exegesis of federal land law intended to show that the defendants had no riparian rights, at least none superior to the canal company's diversion. The canal company had made its first appropriation in the 1870s on land acquired under the Swamp Land Act of 1850. Because the federal government had retained formal title to this land until 1896, Treadwell argued, the diversion had occurred on public land and, under the federal mining law of 1866, was valid against the riparian rights of all other federal land. Because the defendants had generally purchased their property after the diversion was made, they had no water rights superior to those of the canal company. Treadwell went on to assert that the Desert Land Act of 1877 had dedicated the water rights of all federal land to the public, thus stripping land purchased after 1877 of water rights.[92] Ironically, Miller & Lux in *Lux* v. *Haggin,* had successfully argued against these very propositions in its attempt to protect its own riparian claims.

Miller & Lux and the SJ&KRC&ICo had intended to use the mere filing of the Worswick suits to force a settlement from the upstream pumpers; many of the arguments were clearly not helpful to the cattle company. External pressures, however, again intervened to determine Miller & Lux's legal actions. In 1918, when some of the canal company's customers began organizing an irrigation district to take over the SJ&KRC&ICo, the firm decided to take the suit to trial. Treadwell reported a "fair" hope that the firm would win the case, and even an adverse judicial decision would be better, he felt, than to be subjected to public criticism for negotiating away water needed by the utility.[93]

However, victory was not to be his. In 1919, Rector ruled in favor of the riparian defendants—the upstream pumpers—and in 1922 the supreme court affirmed his decision. In *SJ&KRC&ICo* v. *Worswick,*[94] the supreme court declared, as it had almost forty years earlier in *Lux* v. *Haggin,* that swamplands were private property even before the final patent was issued. Equitable title rested with the private owner even if legal title did not, and thus an appropriation made on this land was not good against the government's water rights. Similarly, the Desert Land Act specifically provided for the sale and irrigation of desert lands; it did not broadly separate water rights from all government land. In this decision, as in *Lux* v. *Haggin,* the supreme court was concerned that no private property rights be suddenly removed.

In *Worswick* the California supreme court explicitly rejected the argument of implied dedication to a public use that it had ignored in *Enterprise.* Rector had found that Worswick and the other defendants had no legal knowledge of the SJ&KRC&ICo's diversion and thus had not consented to it. The supreme court agreed with this view and curtly rejected the notion of implied consent. Speaking for a unanimous court, Chief Justice Lucien Shaw reiterated the traditional interpretation of the relationship between upper and lower riparians: since an upstream owner could not prevent a downstream diversion, the downstream use did not limit his rights. This was a rule of property, and the canal company's status as a public utility gave it no rights greater than those of other water users. The decision reflected the philosophy of law outlined in Shaw's article of the same year, "The Development of the Law of Waters in the West." There he answered those who viewed riparianism as inimical to sound public policy and who attacked the court for upholding the doctrine. Such complaints, Shaw insisted, should have been made to the legislature before it adopted the common law in 1850. After that action, "riparian rights became vested, and thereupon the much more important public policy of protecting the right of private property, became paramount and controlling."[95] When the U.S. Supreme Court refused to accept the appeal of the *Worswick* decision,[96] the canal company and Miller & Lux were denied judicial relief from a decreasing water supply, except through the lengthy and expensive process of eminent domain.

Its vulnerability made Miller & Lux increasingly dependent on its alliance with Southern California Edison and placed it in the shadows of one of the great show trials of western riparianism—*Herminghaus* v. *Southern California Edison*.[97] In the mid-1920s, the heirs of Gustave Herminghaus, a cattleman of Henry Miller's generation, filed suit against Southern California Edison's Big Creek reservoir. Represented by Peck, the Herminghauses followed the tradition of much of Miller & Lux's earlier litigation in asserting that storage had injured their riparian property by diminishing the volume of the San Joaquin River. They claimed a right to the unencumbered flow of the river which at its highest stage flooded and irrigated their ranch. Miller & Lux, the long-term tenant of the ranch, had alerted the heirs to its litigious potential by trying to enlist them in an action against irrigators in Madera County. However, Miller & Lux opposed the Herminghaus suit against the power company. It had long since resolved its conflicts with Southern California Edison, and under contracts between the two firms, Miller & Lux was one of the main beneficiaries of the utility's challenged reservoirs, which retained and released water according to a schedule that conformed to the cattle company's needs.

Represented by Edward F. Treadwell, who had left Miller & Lux's employ in 1922, Southern California Edison offered a complex defense that confounded Miller & Lux. Hoping to avoid paying compensation for interfering with the river's annual floods, Southern California Edison argued that the Herminghauses' reliance on natural overflow was unreasonable and wasteful; the power company reservoirs, by contrast, both conserved water and met the public need for electricity. Although Miller & Lux had often fought efforts to impose reasonable use on riparians, it supported the electrical power company in this case, providing Treadwell with the witnesses needed to validate his criticisms of the Herminghauses. On Miller & Lux's part, J. Leroy Nickel had long ago reconciled himself to the realities of reasonable use and had already installed the types of improvements the power company demanded of Herminghaus.

Southern California Edison, however, also asserted that it was itself a riparian proprietor, both as the agent of Miller & Lux and by virtue of owning land at the headwaters of the river, and that as such it had a *riparian* right to store water.[98] The latter claim called for a radical expansion of the common-law doctrine of riparianism and provoked a fury of opposition from public and private irrigation agencies.[99] Despite its alliance with Southern California Edison, Miller & Lux also balked at the implications of this assertion. In its dealings with other irrigators, the cattle company had avowed its own right to store riparian waters and its absolute claim to the water released by the power company. Yet judicial acceptance of the utility's argument threatened to undermine Miller & Lux's control of the river. If Southern California Edison acquired an independent right to store water, the contracts guaranteeing the flow to Miller & Lux's land would be unenforceable. Unable to support Southern California Edison's claim and unwilling to oppose the power company, Miller & Lux entered no brief in a case that clearly affected its rights; unwilling to do anything to harm its ally, it refused even to answer press inquiries on the case.[100]

In 1926, the supreme court rejected Southern California Edison's riparian claims. In a strongly worded opinion, it ruled that the utility was a mere appropriator and reiterated its support for the property rights of riparian landowners. It repeated the principles stated in *Lux* v. *Haggin* and more forcefully in *Miller & Lux* v. *Madera:* Water used by riparian owners was not limited by the conditions of reasonable use and could not be subjected to any standards of efficiency in suits brought by nonriparian claimants. Any such restriction would divest the riparian owner of "his most precious right of ownership." [101] Improvements in irrigation techniques, whether as sought by conservation reformers after 1910 or by private companies citing the public's needs, would not be imposed on the holders of riparian rights by the California Supreme Court.[102]

Although critics denounced riparianism as a static doctrine that fixed the control of water in the hands of the few, in these conflicts it took on a more democratic cast, allowing new entrepreneurs and small landowners to irrigate and retain claims of water even when challenged by wealthy and powerful opponents such as Miller & Lux. The judiciary's acceptance of riparian rights as property rights bolstered Miller & Lux, furnishing the legal weapons for gathering up water and for winning key concessions from nonriparians, but riparian rights as a legal doctrine entailed more than the linkage of water to land. Riparian rights were correlative, giving every riparian an equal entitlement to use water at any time. The judiciary's embrace of riparianism thus allowed Worswick and others to divert from the San Joaquin just as it allowed Miller & Lux to irrigate its fields.

As the demand for irrigated crops and the availability of low-cost electricity increased, so did the threat to Miller & Lux's monopoly, and so did the legal dilemma posed by the doctrine that was the basis of its power. The SJ&KRC&ICo's customers forced Miller & Lux to act against riparian challengers, and ownership of the SJ&KRC&ICo allowed Miller & Lux to assert the public need for water as a palliative. But these efforts met with only limited success. Eminent domain actions subjected the firm to hostile public scrutiny, and efforts to persuade the court itself to limit upstream riparians were unsuccessful. The very property-centeredness that made the California Supreme Court an ally in most of Miller & Lux's litigation precluded the court from stripping the firm's riparian rivals of their claims. Miller & Lux possessed legal power because its arguments coincided with the ideology of judges, not because of direct influence. In the contest with other riparians, neither the firm's physical possession of land, water, and wealth nor the legal doctrine that armed it against appropriators could guarantee it a favorable resolution of competing claims.

4

The Political Battle over Water Rights

While Miller & Lux pursued its claims in the courts, the opponents of riparianism flocked to the legislatures of the West. There self-interested parties hoping to gain water the courts had denied them joined social reformers who saw riparian rights as hostile to irrigation and its promised benefits. At the turn of the century, irrigation had captured the imagination of the nation, and water law reform emerged as a panacea for both private and public ills. Irrigation agriculture would force land monopolists to subdivide their estates, and large, undeveloped ranches would be replaced by small, densely settled farming communities where cooperation and family values would predominate over destructive individualism. Irrigation would likewise promote economic opportunity, encourage the growth of the middle class, and eliminate extremes of wealth and poverty. It would stimulate immigration and economic growth and, since it was more efficient, would increase productivity and lead to more diversified farming. Employing a Jeffersonian rejection of judicial decision making as undemocratic, these critics demanded that legislatures change the laws governing water to reflect the needs and desires of the people for irrigation.

Miller & Lux mounted a regular, vocal opposition to efforts to modify the laws defining its property. In Oregon, where it owned a number of ranches, it fought a holding action against reform that it could not stop. In California, where its vast size gave it greater political influence, Miller & Lux fought more aggressively to prevent the implementation of changes perceived to be hostile to its interests. Ultimately, however, the efforts at water reform forced Miller & Lux to reconsider its rights and eventually to modify its canal systems. It invested increasing amounts of capital to develop the advantages of its water resources and to protect its legal claims, investments that would have long-term consequences for the financial viability of the firm.

In California, the first legislative attack on riparian rights came on the heels of the 1886 ruling in *Lux* v. *Haggin*. In this instance, self-interest capitalized on the reformist rhetoric of the period as James B. Haggin and William Carr funded and organized a mass antiriparian movement. Recruiting its support from petty speculators who hoped to benefit from the rising land prices irrigation would bring, the antiriparian group denounced riparian rights as an anachronism that hindered economic growth and prosperity. Insisting that prior appropriation was the more progressive, more efficient doctrine, they pressured the governor into calling a special session of the legislature to deal with the problems created by what they called a reactionary court. In this session, their proposals to remove Judge Elisha W. McKinstry and the others who had accepted riparianism floundered when their opponents rallied to defend the independence of the judiciary. In 1887, however, the legislature rescinded section 1422 of the civil code, which protected riparian rights. To meet the demands of the irrigation interests, California legislators also adopted the Wright Act, which allowed the formation of irrigation districts, political bodies to construct delivery systems. The districts could seize water rights and existing canals by means of eminent domain, could issue bonds, and could tax all land within their boundaries, regardless of benefit. They were to be locally and popularly governed, with all eligible voters in the district entitled to participate in all elections.[1] The demand that the public should glean the benefits of irrigation had attained an organizational outlet.

The elimination of section 1422 and the passage of the Wright Act, however, had little more than symbolic significance in the immediate period. The common law was still the rule of decision in California, affording protection to riparian rights even without statutory recognition, and within a few years section 1422 was reinacted. While farmers throughout the state rushed to form irrigation districts, few districts were initially successful, struggling as they did with court challenges and repeated difficulties in financing their bonds. Miller & Lux itself challenged the constitutionality of the Wright

Act when an irrigation district taking in some of its land was formed near Madera. This case centered on the power of the legislature to create irrigation districts, not on water rights, but the litigation duplicated many of the earlier conflicts. In addition to its usual attorneys, Miller & Lux hired E. W. McKinstry, who as a member of the state supreme court had written the decision in *Lux* v. *Haggin;* the Madera Irrigation District hired C. C. Wright, author of the Wright Act, to defend its position. Although the cattle company lost the case on appeal, the costs and delays that litigation engendered were successful in preventing the functioning of the Madera Irrigation District for this period.[2]

The more radical innovations in the law of waters came from the Rocky Mountain states, not from California, where riparianism enjoyed the support of many leading lawyers and law teachers.[3] Colorado, which had never accepted riparian rights, pioneered a code based on the doctrine of appropriation. There and in Nevada and other states that followed the Colorado doctrine,[4] legislatures and courts rejected the reasoning adopted in *Lux* v. *Haggin* that the property rights of public land must be acknowledged and recognized as transferable. Instead they asserted that the state had absolute control over natural water resources within its borders. Arguing on the basis of the needs of an arid region, these states recognized only prior appropriation, and they set up procedures, like those of California, that required water claimants to post proper notices and to construct ditches in a timely manner.[5]

In 1889–90 Wyoming established an effective system of state supervision over water. When the Wyoming constitution was written, careful attention was given to the problems that beset its neighbors, especially the incoherent method of establishing rights in Colorado, where claims far in excess of the actual flow of rivers had been recognized by the courts. A committee of politicians, lawyers, and engineers drafted provisions that declared streams to be the property of the state under the supervision of an appointed board of control. All water rights were to be appropriative and would be recognized only after state experts evaluated the need for a project and the actual availability of water. Embodying the increasing faith in scientific expertise and bureaucratic control that characterized the Progressive era, the water board withstood court challenges and was copied throughout the West.[6]

While reform efforts of this sort were repeatedly frustrated in California, where bills proposing the Wyoming system were defeated in both 1901 and

1909,[7] other states in which Miller & Lux owned land succeeded in adopting such changes. For example, in a 1903 effort to encourage federal reclamation projects, the Nevada legislature reiterated earlier court rulings that water belonged to the public, and it set up a modified version of the Wyoming system. Rather than a water board, Nevada created an office of state engineer, empowered to prepare a list of water rights for each stream, to conduct the hydrographic studies needed to determine what water was unappropriated, and to issue certificates of appropriation. Court challenges eventually forced the modification of the system, increasing the role of the judiciary and limiting the power of the state engineer in the final adjudication of property rights.[8]

Miller & Lux's numerous ranches in Nevada held water rights under the doctrine of appropriation, and the firm did not challenge the water reforms in that state. The important role given the judiciary accommodated its views; the firm filed suits as needed to apportion streams and it utilized the office of the state engineer.[9] Miller & Lux followed a different course, however, in Oregon, where it owned a number of small stock ranches that claimed riparian rights, and in California, the center of its landholdings, wealth, and power. With good reason, Miller & Lux viewed reform in those states as hostile to its interests and as a tool of its rivals.

Oregon adopted the administrative control of water in 1909. The state Grange, drylands settlers, and the U.S. Reclamation Service had all lobbied for a system that would regularize water titles, encourage investment in irrigation utilities, and place scientific expertise and efficiency at the center of water development. Modeled on the Wyoming system and written with the aid of Wyoming's influential state engineer, Elwood Mead, the Oregon code created a state water board with responsibility to determine the water rights of a stream upon the petition of any private claimant; it empowered the state engineer to investigate the actual flow of the state's rivers and the volume historically diverted from them. The statute also modified the state's water code. Earlier, Oregon had followed the California doctrine of riparianism, and the 1909 code recognized existing riparian rights.[10] But the new statute proclaimed that in the future only appropriative claims could be acquired.

In the same year the Oregon Supreme Court acted to limit riparianism. In *Hough* v. *Porter*, the Oregon court found that the federal Desert Land Act of 1877 had nullified riparian rights on the public domain. The Desert Land Act offered settlers up to 640 acres of arid land at $1.25 an acre on the condition that they irrigate at least one-eighth of it within three years. At the time of purchase, settlers need pay only $0.25 per acre, with the remaining $1.00 due when the final patent was issued. More important for *Hough*, the federal law stated that the right to water depended on a valid appropriation and that all water not so used was to be held for appropriation and use by the public. This language had generally been accorded no significance in states that accepted riparian rights. Following *Lux* v. *Haggin*, courts had viewed it as a mere restatement of the sections of the federal mining law of 1866 that acknowledged valid appropriations made on public lands. Purchasers of public land were considered to have acquired all its common-law property rights, including the right to riparian waters not previously appropriated. However, in 1909 the Oregon court rejected this interpretation and declared that riparian rights did not fall to those patenting public land after 1877; instead, all the water rights of public land were made available to appropriators and were to be governed by the doctrine of beneficial use.[11]

In 1911, Miller & Lux came face to face with the new Oregon system in a dispute concerning the rights to the Silvies River, which watered the main Oregon ranch of its subsidiary the Pacific Live Stock Company (PLSCo). Miller & Lux had previously become involved in a long-running fight for control of this river with another large rancher, William Hanley. Both faced challenges from farmers who, inspired by talk of a federal reclamation project in the region, had begun homesteading the sagebrush lands upstream of the ranchers. The group of farmers had earlier tried forming a company to develop land and water under the Carey Act,[12] an effort Miller & Lux had moved to block before the state land board.[13] In 1912, some of the dryland farmers petitioned the water board to distribute the waters of the Silvies, claiming the surplus for the irrigation of their land.

At that time, the state water board was new and relatively untested, but as part of the reforms of 1909 it threatened to undermine the value of Miller & Lux's Oregon ranches. In its first actions, the water board had recognized the rights of riparians to irrigate and had granted such users up to 3 acre-feet of water a year for overflowed land, an amount many felt was adequate for irrigation if improvements were made to deliver and spread the water effectively. While such a finding might protect the portions of the PLSCo ranch that were already ditched, the company owned a great deal of fertile land bordering the river that was not naturally flooded and for which irrigation facilities did not yet exist. Earlier, riparianism had protected claims to the entire flow of the river and had allowed for future development, but such a view was unlikely to be adopted by the new agency. Instead, any surplus over that actually applied to land (by both riparians and appropriators) would probably be awarded to others requesting it.[14]

Viewing the water board as an ally of the dryland farmers it was fighting, Miller & Lux hoped to remove consideration of its rights from this new forum and to keep them before the courts for as long as possible. It requested that the federal court remove consideration of its rights from the Oregon water board on the grounds of diversity of jurisdiction; when that request was denied, it petitioned for its claims to be removed to the federal courts because of the preexisting and ongoing litigation with the rancher Hanley; then, after reluctantly filing its claims with the water board, it protested that the required fees created an unjust tax on property that invalidated the entire statute. Even if this litigation were unsuccessful, Miller & Lux's attorneys reasoned, the delay it created would buy additional time to put water on the PLSCo land and thus protect the firm's claims.[15]

At the core of Miller & Lux's complaint was its assertion that the 1909 statute violated provisions of both the state and federal constitutions that protected property and established the separation of powers. On the advice of Samuel Wiel, who in 1911 had published a massive treatise on western water law, Edward Treadwell conceded that a water board might conduct an investigation and might even determine the nature of beneficial use, but Treadwell insisted that such an agency could not determine water rights. Because such a determination would transfer property, it was a function of the courts and required that property owners be accorded both the form and the substance of due process. Distrusting rival claimants, elected officials, and experts like the state engineer, Miller & Lux protested that the water board based its findings on unsworn personal statements and hearsay evidence. Moreover, the 1909 statute declared such statements by self-interested parties to be prima facie evidence of rights; challengers were required to disprove such claims rather than claimants to demonstrate their assertions. While the law provided for a final court hearing, water users were bound by the findings of the water board for the duration, subject to criminal penalties for using water—even that customarily relied upon—if such use violated a water board ruling.[16]

The water board itself and the U.S. Reclamation Service, which entered the case in support of the Oregon statute, argued for the rationality and regularity of the board's procedures. Adopting arguments used earlier to defend the Wyoming board, Oregon maintained that its water board did not exercise judicial functions but was merely an administrative agency similar to the U.S. Land Office and a variety of newer administrative agencies. The Oregon law, counsel for the Reclamation Service argued, was well within the powers of the legislature to promote the public good and had established a "scientific and modern system for water legislation." The law provided an effective response to the continual delays and appeals that had historically dominated water rights litigation and that made it impossible to market commercial irrigation bonds. According to the state, water issues were primarily issues of engineering and physics, and the statute made it possible to handle such questions scientifically and to provide stable titles to water that would satisfy private investors' demands for security.[17]

While the PLSCo would ultimately fare well before the state water board,[18] its effort to restrict the power of the agency was unsuccessful. The circuit court rejected its argument in 1914; two years later, the U.S. Supreme Court rejected its plea as well. Dismissing Treadwell's technical arguments as ridiculous, the Supreme Court described the Oregon process as a continuum that began with an administrative investigation and ended with a hearing before a court. As such, it fulfilled all the constitutional requirements of due process. In its ruling, the Supreme Court called attention to a 1914 decision of the Oregon Supreme Court that underscored the danger impelling Miller & Lux's opposition to the water board's procedure. Following a water board examination of the claims to another eastern Oregon stream, the Oregon Supreme Court had limited riparian rights as Treadwell had anticipated. The court had recognized riparian rights to the water necessary to irrigate overflow land but had rejected claims to the full flow of the river. Such claims, it ruled, had not created vested rights within Oregon. The wetting of overflow lands created a beneficial use that was recognized, but natural flooding was condemned as wasteful. Water had to be conserved to be more profitably exploited, and a riparian was allowed only enough water to irrigate by modern, efficient methods; all the rest could be distributed to other claimants along the stream.[19] Reflecting the capitalist view of nature, the Oregon Supreme Court saw water and water rights as productive assets valuable primarily as a means to convert land into cash profits.

As Miller & Lux confronted the new Oregon law in the courts, it also faced a reinvigorated campaign for water reform in California, where reformist

political crusaders joined with the economically motivated farm entrepreneurs of the Central Valley to challenge Miller & Lux's control of water.
Hiram Johnson, who in 1910 was elected governor on the platform of throw-
ing the railroad out of state government, made water conservation one of
the "ten commandments" of his first administration.[20] In 1911, the legislature, filled with recently elected antimachine Republicans, established a
conservation commission "to investigate and survey the natural resources
of the state" and to propose legislation to conserve them.[21] Former Governor George Pardee, who had supported earlier attempts at conservation
reform, was appointed chairman of the commission, and its technical work
was delegated to specialists such as Frank Adams of the U.S. Department
of Agriculture's Office of Irrigation Investigations.[22]

On the whole, the members of the conservation commission identified
themselves with the doctrines of Gifford Pinchot and Theodore Roosevelt,
that conservation should serve development.[23] In the commission's view, the
problem confronting California was the inefficient and often wasteful use of
natural resources. The land, forests, and water of the nation had originally
been placed in private hands so they would not lie fallow but would stimulate
economic development. The private control of timber and water, however,
had led to their being held in "private cold storage."[24] At the same time, the
commission asserted that unregulated privatization had resulted in waste and
destruction as the owners tried to "get rich quick." Consequently, the public
enjoyed only limited use of its own resources and had been compelled to
pay exorbitant prices for what little it did get. Reflecting the negative view of
human nature held by many Progressives, the commission placed responsibility for this problem not on heinous crimes but on the "very natural human
greed" of those who had been given ownership of the water and forests. Only
new law and a system of administrative control could remedy the situation.[25]

The conservation commission particularly criticized the impact of riparianism on the state. Riparian rules of title, the commissioners asserted, were
opposed by all "who desire to see the water resources of California developed and used for the benefit of the people."[26] Riparianism encouraged the
waste of water while allowing water to damage land and other resources as
it flooded to the sea. Although never named in the commission's report,
Miller & Lux provided the commission's example of riparianism at its worst.
Two photographs included in the report were identified as depictions of
land swamped by wastewater in the Los Banos area—the same area cited by

Stevinson's attorney, James Peck, to prove his accusation of waste in the eminent domain suit. Claiming that riparianism was an issue only because water had been squandered under its rule, the California conservation commission described an example of an inferior and unnecessary use of water—a large riparian proprietor who "flood[ed] his almost limitless cattle pastures with unnecessarily enormous quantities of water, and d[id] not permit even the excess to be used on the irrigable lands of others, where it would be of great value to those others and therefore to the state." [27] As result of this "waste," unmistakably that of Miller & Lux, large amounts of fertile, irrigable land could not be brought into production. That was the problem to be remedied. Water should be productive, generating hydroelectric power, irrigating land, fulfilling the domestic needs of cities. Allowing it to flow over one's land and unused into the sea or preserving it only for its natural beauty was not an appropriate option to the commission; water should be used rationally and efficiently to produce the greatest value possible from the soil.

The conservation commission reported that it would not be easy to force riparian owners to cease wasting water because riparian rights were vested property rights. However, the commission expressed the hope that the state supreme court would modify its support for riparianism. Relying on Samuel C. Wiel's article "Public Policy in Water Decisions," the commission pointed to the decisions in *Fresno Flume* [28] and in *Gallatin* v. *Corning Irrigation Company* [29] as illustrating a trend away from the protection of riparian rights. Dicta in *Fresno Flume* implied that common-law doctrines that worked a hardship on the state would be ignored by the court. Given the commission's view of riparianism as harmful and even destructive, it seemed to require but one more step by the court to prevent waste by riparian owners.[30] If the judiciary did not modify riparian doctrine, the commission suggested that the state seize riparian rights under eminent domain, paying compensation where due, thus freeing the water for beneficial use and appropriation. The state, the commission argued, could afford to condemn riparian rights since the action would create vast amounts of new wealth. At a minimum, the commission proposed using the state's police powers to increase access to water; the legislature could "so regulate the enjoyment of it [water] by its present owners that it will be as little as possible provocative of public distress or inconvenience" [31]—a plan no more amenable than seizure to riparian owners such as Miller & Lux.

The concrete application of this reformist zeal fell somewhat short of its rhetoric in attacking riparianism. The conservation commission proposed legislation to establish a water commission in California, similar to Oregon's, to rationalize the appropriation of water. By removing water rights issues from local county governments and placing them under the control of a centralized administrative agency, the bill would eliminate the overclaiming of rivers that had plagued the state under the old code. The water commission was to investigate the uses of water on an entire watershed and then to issue both certificates confirming existing rights and permits for new appropriations that reflected the realities of water availability. The bill would establish annual fees for hydroelectric plants, limit hydroelectric company licenses to twenty years, set time limits for the development of allocated resources, and prohibit capitalization of water rights.[32]

The water commission bill offered a statutory answer to the California Supreme Court's 1909 ruling in *Madera*[33] that riparian owners were not limited by the concept of reasonable use. Section 11 of the water commission bill declared that any riparian waters not put to "beneficial use" for a period of ten consecutive years were forfeit; "not needed" by riparian users, such waters were made available for appropriation.[34] While "beneficial use" was a term subject to interpretation, the practice of allowing water to naturally overflow riparian land did not fit the accepted standards. In fact, the bill defined as wasteful the application of more than 2½ acre-feet of water per year to uncultivated lands. Although Miller & Lux irrigated large units of cultivated land, even more of its irrigated land was native pasture; it also flooded large areas of alkaline land in an effort to flush them of salts and increase their production of livestock feed. These practices were central to the cattle company's operations, thus making the restrictive definition of "beneficial" one of the most threatening portions of the bill.

While the water commission bill won the endorsement of a wide range of water reformers, many considered it at best a weak compromise. Frank Adams, who had done much of the technical work for the conservation commission, privately criticized the lack of enforcement provisions and the failure to strengthen the office of the state engineer. Elwood Mead, who had pioneered the movement for the administrative control of water, believed the bill left entirely too much power to the courts. It would allow water rights cases to be initiated in local courts, bypassing the commission altogether, and would subject the commission's decisions to appeal and judicial review. The treatise writer Samuel Wiel noted that it would have been "proper and feasible" for the bill to have regulated riparians just as it had appropriators. However, all those arguing for change in the state's water code publicly accepted the bill as an unavoidable compromise, the first step in the direction of reform.[35]

Similarly, although some of the opponents of Miller & Lux distrusted George Pardee, chairman of the conservation commission,[36] reformist interests within the San Joaquin Valley galvanized around the San Joaquin Valley Water Problems Association to give qualified support to the water commission bill. The Water Problems Association was formed in January 1913, during a period of drought and water shortage in the valley, to develop a comprehensive plan for irrigation, drainage, reclamation, and water conservation in a twelve-county area. It was an organization of organizations; all water companies and irrigation districts, groups interested in water reform, and municipal and county governments were invited to join, with each member organization having one vote. Although the association included private irrigation companies, it was dominated by local lawyers and politicians associated with Progressivism and Wright Act irrigation districts.[37] Its president, John Fairweather, was a Progressive newspaper editor and director of the Alta Irrigation District; its secretary, A. L. Cowell, was the attorney for numerous irrigation districts in the region; both Robert Hargrove and L. L. Dennett, who sat on the executive board, had represented irrigators opposing Miller & Lux, and both would run for the legislature as Progressives and water reformers. Hargrove was typical of many of the activists in the association. He opened its first meeting with a stinging attack on Miller & Lux for depriving the farmers of Madera County of water, championed the storage of floodwaters to expand agriculture, and was the first person in Madera County to become a lifetime member in the California Raisin Exchange. In his view and that of others throughout the valley, reformism, opposition to Miller & Lux, and economic self-interest were inextricably linked.[38]

In February 1913, the Water Problems Association voted to endorse the general principles of the water commission bill. The greatest support for the bill, not surprisingly, came from those in the San Joaquin Valley who lacked adequate water supplies, while it was opposed by private water companies, riparian owners, and established irrigators. Yet like the technocratic reformers, many members of the Water Problems Association protested that the bill fell short of what was needed. They particularly criticized what they saw as the bill's protection of riparian rights: it initially allowed riparian owners five years in which to develop the water flowing through their lands before this water was made available to others. Viewing the bill as only one step on the road to reform, the Water Problems Association called on the state to move further to stimulate local development by at least providing financial guarantees for irrigation bonds.[39]

Weak as it was, the water commission bill aroused the well-financed opposition of both Miller & Lux and the state's hydroelectric companies. In Oregon, Miller & Lux's lack of political influence had forced it to stand by while the legislature undermined riparian rights. In California, however, it had the connections and the will to fight politically. Miller & Lux's attorneys, Frank H. Short and Edward F. Treadwell, had lamented the state of California politics since 1911. To them, Governor Johnson and the legislature appeared willing to accept even "hopelessly bad arguments" if made by an "alleged friend of the people." The water commission bill was seen as one of the "bad" proposals. In fact, Short wondered how a "civilized people" aware of the conditions in California could even consider such a law. While Short felt that a commission of limited powers might help stabilize water development, the one proposed would harm all legitimate enterprises.[40] He and Treadwell lumped the water commission bill with two other proposals they found pernicious—the single tax and the eight-hour workday[41]—and resolved to organize an opposition.

In December 1912, Short and Treadwell set out to entice local chambers of commerce and irrigation companies to lobby against the water commission bill.[42] They wanted to isolate Pardee from others in the Johnson administration and to get "the small fellow worked up" in opposition to the proposed bill.[43] To this end, they attended meetings and forums scheduled by the Water Problems Association to debate the issue. In these debates Treadwell moderated the rigid defense of riparian rights that characterized his legal briefs. He asserted that the interests he represented were eager to see floodwaters conserved and put to proper use, a portrayal that few in the valley could accept. The state, Treadwell proposed, should conduct a survey to determine the facts of the water problem and to study storage possibilities, but it should not impose the proposed scheme of administrative control. Earlier efforts to institute a water commission had failed because of fear that it would erode local power,[44] and Treadwell resolved that the best tactic to defeat the new bill was to evoke the same fear of losing control. He opportunistically pointed out that the Pardee bill would take the control of water away from local courts and juries and transfer it to an arbitrary board and the state supreme court, to which all appeals would go. Miller & Lux, of course, had repeatedly relied on the supreme court to overturn the unfavorable decisions of local superior courts, but the delays and expenses of appeals, as well as the proriparian stand of the high court, had led most irrigation forces to fear it as an enemy, a fear Treadwell hoped would work in his favor. As an alternative to the new legislation, he pointed to the constructive role that riparian rights had played in the development of the San Joaquin Valley and asserted that "his interests" would cooperate with a movement to resolve water problems if it were carried out in the "right spirit."[45]

Frank Short, who represented the privately owned Fresno Canal and Irrigation Company and various other utilities, as well as Miller & Lux, urged that legislation to regulate the use of water be framed carefully so as not to hamper legitimate enterprises. In the case of riparian rights, he argued, it would be less expensive to condemn or purchase them than to try to take them without compensation, through the legislative fiat that many in the Water Problems Association seemed to advocate. Compensation in such cases should be based on the value of the water to the owner, not the potential value to someone else.[46] The problems inherent in Short's proposal, however, had been made clear by the SJ&KRC&ICo's ongoing efforts to condemn James Stevinson's water rights. Eminent domain was a lengthy procedure, and the basis on which compensation was to be paid had not been settled. The value set by an irrigation company on its works and, more important, on its water right could stymie any assumption of public control by a local group.

Miller & Lux also moved to develop a legislative campaign. While contemporary supporters of the water commission bill such as Franklin Hichborn attributed the organized opposition to the bill to a "Power Trust" that feared the fees and regulations proposed for hydroelectric companies,[47] it was Miller & Lux's attorneys who galvanized the resistance. In February 1913, Treadwell wrote to Short of the need for a "campaign" to defeat the bill by creating the appearance of popular opposition. "The present legislature," wrote Treadwell, who had frequently lobbied on behalf of Miller & Lux, "must be handled quite differently from any previous one." It was concerned primarily with the "popularity" of legislation and would not listen to property owners. The only way to approach it was to use "the same tactics [as] the other side" to prove that the water commission bill did not have the support of the people. To accomplish this, he proposed a public meeting in Sacramento at which the "proper persons," those "persons actually interested in vested water rights," would be present. Treadwell and Short would stay in the background while the meeting discussed the serious objections to the bill. The next step would be to work through the press to widen the popular opposition to the bill.[48]

By March, the plan was in place. The Northern California Water Association was formed to front the opposition; George O. Perry and N. C. Ray were hired as spokespersons for the fight; and Miller & Lux and other large companies, including the Kern County Land Company, Stevinson, and power companies such as the San Joaquin Light and Power Company and Pacific Gas and Electric, pledged to furnish the necessary monies. At the meeting in Sacramento (to which people who were "programmed properly" had been invited), Perry and L.A. Nares, manager of the Fresno Canal and Irrigation Company "convincingly" argued the opposition point of view before the legislature.[49] The publicity campaign was initiated with a pamphlet, "Confiscation not Conservation," which stressed the lack of protection for water users against the "unlimited discretion" of the water commissioners. It also pointed out the lack of "provision in the act for the enforcement of an economical use of the water, for the storage and regulation of stream flows or for the preserving of watersheds."[50]

This campaign, which attempted to exploit the conservationists' own goals to defeat their proposed bill, met with some success, as letters opposing the water commission bill began to flow into Sacramento. As a result, the bill, which was initially assumed to be without opposition, was temporarily defeated. Not until June, after numerous delays as its proponents and Governor Johnson desperately tried to assemble the necessary votes, did the legislature enact the bill, and then by only a narrow margin.[51]

With its property rights at stake, Miller & Lux did not give up the fight even then. Instead it capitalized on new Progressive electoral reforms, which Short had earlier denounced as being among the "fallacies of Populism,"[52] to launch a referendum campaign against the water commission bill. That campaign, too, was led by the Northern California Water Association, and financing came from the same group of water and power companies that had bankrolled the previous effort. Solicitors were hired to gather signatures on the petition to repeal the law, often recruited through a network of attorneys friendly to Short and Treadwell,[53] and the organizers again printed flyers attacking the bill. To win the votes of small farmers and the urban workingclass, Miller & Lux labeled the water commission a threat that would involve all water users in endless litigation, "take the water from small users, and accumulate it in the hands of large companies," and jeopardize the water rights of cities such as Los Angeles and San Francisco.[54] It would rob irrigators of their water and taxpayers of their money. The Farmers Protective League, an organization formed after the Wheatland hop strike to fight organized labor and the eight-hour workday movement, was enlisted in the campaign. The *Farmers News*, mouthpiece of the antilabor group, printed two lengthy critiques of the water commission bill urging its rejection; the Northern California Water Association paid the costs of both.[55] Actions against the single tax, which Miller & Lux was also subsidizing, against the eight-hour workday, and against the water commission were seen as part of a "three-cornered fight" that Treadwell hoped would develop "into a general opposition to the Johnson administration."[56]

As the referendum campaign got underway, the debate became personal and vehement. Despite Miller & Lux's attempts to keep its role hidden, it was eventually exposed, and the referendum itself was denounced as a misuse of electoral reforms that were intended to serve the people.[57] Miller & Lux's enemies labeled it a "water octopus . . . in a position to bleed them [irrigators] dry" if the water commission failed, evoking the fear of strangulation that had been so successful in Hiram Johnson's earlier campaign against the Southern Pacific's political power.[58] Fairweather cited Miller & Lux as the very reason the law was needed. When opponents of the water commission bill pointed out that current law prohibited the hoarding of water, Fairweather retorted that it was not the practice of the "water-hog" to follow the law. As he put it, "Do Miller & Lux allow Madera county residents to use any water out of the San Joaquin river, even when thousands of second feet of water are doing them a positive damage and plenty is going to sea? No, never."[59] The water commission bill, he argued, would give local farmers the water they craved. From the other side, Treadwell and Short attempted to impugn the motives of Fairweather and Pardee. The motives of the reformers, the Miller & Lux attorneys asserted, were selfish and venal: they simply wanted to secure positions on the water commission at the proposed salary of $5,000 a year.[60]

The fear of monopoly and the arguments of the reformers proved more powerful. While Miller & Lux acquired enough signatures to place the referendum on the ballot, the majority of them came from urban centers. Almost 23,000 of the 37,000 who signed the petition were from San Francisco, Alameda, and Los Angeles counties; Sacramento and Santa Clara counties provided another 5,500 signatures. Little support for the drive was forthcoming in the region where Miller & Lux owned land and water.[61] In Madera County, the site of the bitter battle between Miller & Lux and the Madera Canal Company, only twenty-five people signed the referendum petition. Miller & Lux superintendents found it difficult to garner support for the repeal effort anywhere in the San Joaquin Valley. In some towns they could not find solicitors to circulate the petition, reporting that "the people in this community look with much suspicion upon anything pertaining to water issues that is urged by Miller & Lux or the canal company."[62] Ultimately the repeal effort failed. The water commission bill became law in December 1914, delayed, but not stopped, by the efforts of Miller & Lux and the large water and hydroelectric companies allied with them.

The attack on riparian rights continued during the next session of the legislature. Farmers and reformers from the San Joaquin Valley continued to criticize the water commission bill for being too generous to riparians, since in its final form it granted a ten-year period in which to develop riparian claims. Flush with their recent victory over Miller & Lux, they wanted immediate access to riparian water for their own proposed and imagined developments. In 1915, legislators from valley communities thus introduced new legislation to further "remedy the great wrongs" created by the riparian monopoly of water.[63] In April, the judiciary committee recommended passage of Assembly Bill 328, which, according to the *Fresno Morning Republic*, struck "at the very foundation of the water monopoly of Miller & Lux."[64] Introduced by Fresno Assemblyman Henry Hawson, AB 328 would allow appropriators challenged by a riparian owner to demand that the riparian prove damages. If the injury was slight, the court could not grant an injunction but could only require that the appropriator post bond to guarantee against any losses that might result from the project at issue. Edward Ellis of Livingston and L. L. Dennett, a Progressive organizer of the San Joaquin Valley Water Problems Association, introduced companion bills that would have further limited riparians. Ellis's proposal called for riparian waters not then in beneficial use to be considered abandoned and available for appropriation. Dennett proposed that the statute of limitations for riparian challenges to upstream diversions be reduced from five years to three months. Dennett, who also introduced a constitutional amendment to eliminate riparian rights, argued that the proposed modification of the Code of Civil Procedure would itself effectively end riparian rights.[65]

While AB 328 passed the assembly, none of these bills was enacted during session.[66] The momentum for legislative change in the water code seemed to be lost. The water commission bill had been saved from defeat in 1913 only by the concerted efforts of Hiram Johnson. By 1915, the Progressive movement was in disarray, split by ideological differences over U.S. involvement in World War I and by personal conflicts among its leading spokesmen. Johnson, after declaring that the goals of the Progressive movement had been met, went on to focus on the national internecine rivalries that ultimately destroyed the Progressive party.[67] Without the support of the broader movement, the Central Valley reformers lacked the votes to further modify the state's water code. They could not overcome the powerful interests and the pattern of inertia that supported vested riparian rights.

Instead, the legislature established yet another committee, the State Water Problems Conference, which was charged with recommending a unified state policy on irrigation, storage, and other water issues. Treadwell briefly contemplated working with this group. He presented J. Leroy Nickel, then president of Miller & Lux, with a scheme to settle all the rights to a river through an in rem procedure. In lieu of their traditional claims, riparians would receive the first priority to divert a specified volume of water per acre or, if they refused to settle, would receive just compensation for the expropriation of all water rights above this volume. This procedure, Treadwell later explained, would allow for the expansion of irrigation that reformers desired while keeping water out of the hands of mere speculators by requiring compensation. He hinted at this plan in his arguments against the Oregon water commission, but it was never put before the public in California. Once the sixteen members of the conference group were appointed, Nickel and Treadwell decided cooperation was impossible.[68] The majority of those appointed were state officials connected with water regulation who had Progressive credentials.[69] They included such opponents of Miller & Lux as L. L. Dennett and L. J. Maddux. Maddux, then chairman of the state senate's committee on irrigation, had been the district attorney of Stanislaus County during much of the battle over the SJ&KRC&ICo's rates.[70]

Like the conservation commission, the water problems conference valued water for its potential to generate profits, and it found the doctrine of riparian rights to be "foremost among the problems" confronting the state. The water problems conference ignored the development of canal systems and exploitation of water by riparians like Miller & Lux and Jefferson G. James to repeat the standard rhetoric of the western antiriparian movement: Riparian rights "retarded progress toward the fullest utilization of the water resources for all or any of the most valuable purposes."[71] The conference recommended Ellis's and Dennett's earlier proposals for restricting the power of riparian owners to enjoin upstream developments and for radically limiting the statute of limitations governing when such actions could be brought. (Bills to this effect were again introduced in 1917.[72]) To speed up water litigation, the conference also proposed curbing the use of so-called experts. Expert testimony, it recommended, should be restricted to that of engineers appointed by the state or the courts, since their evaluations would be objective and nonpartisan.[73] Most important, the conference recommended the strict application of reasonable and beneficial use as a remedy for the damage caused by riparianism. While riparian rights were property rights and could not be eliminated by legislative fiat, the members of the water problems conference concluded that strict definitions of reasonable use could be established that would be found constitutional by the courts.

The law of water rights was in fact couched in terms of reasonable and beneficial use, a situation that both politicians and their allies among the technocratic reformers hoped to exploit. The interpretation of "reasonable" varied according to local custom and the attitudes of judges and juries, a factor clearly important in the conflicts between Miller & Lux and rivals such as the Madera Canal and Irrigation Company, Fresno Flume, and James Stevinson. Frank Adams of the Office of Irrigation Investigations proposed a method by which the definition of beneficial use might constrain older, less efficient users of water. In a 1914 article in the *California Law Review*, Adams outlined the standards of water usage set at the U.S. Reclamation Service's Conference of Irrigation Managers in November 1913. Accepting water as an asset to be exploited, this conference emphasized efficiency. "Reasonable" use, Adams reported, required that an irrigator take all steps necessary to minimize the amount of water used, including proper methods of applying water, careful preparation and cultivation of land, and adequate maintenance of ditches and other structures.[74] While the volume of water reasonably necessary to irrigate would be protected as a right, the emphasis was not upon the entitlements of water users but on their responsibilities to the community and on the limits to be set on water usage by the community (and by implication the courts).

In fact, Adams and the Conference of Irrigation Managers proposed adopting a stricter standard of economical use, which made explicit the exploitative paradigm of many water reformers. Economical use measured the financial outcome of irrigation, the profits generated rather than the yield per acre, to determine the merit of a use. It implied that the community could dictate not only the method of water delivery but even what crops could be planted. Adams urged irrigators, courts, and administrative agencies to adopt the new standard. The doctrine of economical use, he argued, coincided with the public interest, "with the general welfare of society as a whole," while the theory of beneficial use looked only to the welfare of the individual irrigator.[75] In fact, Adams focused his research for the Office of Experiment Stations and the California Department of Engineering on measuring the volume of water required to raise various crops economically. The solution to water shortage, he contended, lay in better training and selection of settlers and, above all, in the establishment of the new standards of economical use.[76]

California's water commissioners and some western courts seemed willing to take on this assignment. Although still limited in its powers, the water commission quoted Adams's goal as its own in its 1917 report. The objective of the new irrigation laws, wrote Commissioner A. E. Chandler, was "efficiency" in the development of water.[77] In the view of the technocratic reformers of the Progressive conservation movement, new rules favoring the most advanced users and developers of resources had to be imposed on society. Similarly, some courts had begun adopting the newer goals. In Oregon, the state supreme court had stated in 1909 and again in 1912 that when the demand for water increased, earlier settlers would have to modernize and adopt efficient methods of using water, even if such changes put an irrigator to considerable expense.[78] By 1915, the agitation of Adams and others had so disturbed any earlier consensus on the meaning of a beneficial use that Samuel Wiel worried in the *California Law Review* lest the changes go so far as to replace government by law with government by men.[79]

Although much of the legislation to restrict riparian rights was defeated in California, the passage of the water commission bill and the continuing political assault on riparian rights were unsettling evidence of the erosion of Miller & Lux's influence throughout the San Joaquin Valley. That Miller &

Lux took the attack seriously is clear from the energy Treadwell and Short expended in opposing the water commission bill itself. While the firm had once been able to dominate, if not control, many local politicians, it now feared at each election that its opponents would coalesce and put their own candidates into office. Henry Miller doubted that the firm could continue to rely on the law to protect its rights and anticipated increasing problems with local irrigators and officials when they learned that Miller & Lux was the beneficiary of Southern California Edison's new reservoirs. As the ideological struggle continued, even Nickel began to worry about what he called the "moral" position of the firm.[80]

The Progressive campaign for water reform coincided with other challenges to Miller & Lux's control of water, particularly the rate conflict with the SJ&KRC&ICo's customers, who allied themselves with the reformers, and the litigation with Stevinson. While Stevinson had been able to enjoin the SJ&KRC&ICo's diversion, E. S. Wangenheim and other irrigators were pressing for an extension of the canals to the north, and customers within the existing service area were cultivating new acreage that expanded their need for irrigation. All of this growth threatened Miller & Lux's ability to deliver water to its own lands, especially to its nonriparian pastures, and intensified legal concerns about its relationship with the canal company. The contracts granting Miller & Lux water at no charge were fairly clear, specifying the source as "wastewater," that is, water not needed by other customers. As such, Treadwell explained in 1913, the supply was "not a right of a permanent nature." The limits on the SJ&KRC&ICo's diversion meant that Miller & Lux would gradually lose the ability to irrigate vast areas. Even the contracts granting Miller & Lux special low rates suddenly seemed open to attack. They protected only enough water for 33,333 acres and, in Treadwell's view, might be invalidated on technical grounds because the two firms had been reorganized in Nevada.[81] When combined with the political power of the reformers, these threats impelled Nickel to consider more carefully the nature of his claims to water and the means to protect them.

During the decade preceding the water commission bill, Miller & Lux had excavated a number of small canals to direct waters from the SJ&KRC&ICo's canals over its ranchlands. One of them, the San Luis, ran along a ridge between the San Joaquin River and the Main Canal of the SJ&KRC&ICo to the west. Nickel had contemplated transferring the San Luis Canal to the SJ&KRC&ICo to simplify the administration of water to his land, but the new pressures on his claims to water forced him to reconsider. In 1913, he decided to expand the San Luis into an independent irrigation system. Despite Treadwell's misgivings that such a project might be viewed as an admission that Miller & Lux had never been entitled to water from the SJ&KRC&ICo, Nickel commissioned the excavation of the Helm Canal, which ran parallel to the SJ&KRC&ICo's Main Canal for seven miles and then delivered water to the expanded San Luis.[82]

Behind Nickel's decision was the water commission act. Much of the acreage served by the San Luis was grassland that could not be easily or quickly put into cultivation. The water commission law required that riparian rights be put to use and also limited the amount of water that could be used on native grasses to 2 ½ acre-feet per year. By expanding the San Luis system, Nickel hoped to avoid the increasing interference of the Railroad Commission and the SJ&KRC&ICo's customers in his affairs, as well as the limits set on the riparian use of water. While the referendum campaign delayed application of the law, Nickel expanded his irrigation system. Once it was in place, he reasoned, Miller & Lux's claims would be protected since the law could not be applied retroactively to water already utilized.[83] At the end of 1914, he filed to appropriate water to irrigate additional nonriparian land through the San Luis system. There was some risk that this appropriation would be opposed by other riparians, but Nickel decided it was a risk that had to be taken. A year earlier Nickel had refused a proposed settlement of the eminent domain suit against Stevinson because it did not include water for nonriparian land; Treadwell had rejected as suicidal any discussion of nonriparian irrigation because it would increase Stevinson's resistance.[84] Given the popularity of the reform movement, Nickel felt that the courts would uphold nonriparian uses that did not damage riparian claims. The passage of the water commission act would influence them to be liberal toward appropriators and "to refuse to let flood waters remain unused in the channel and be lost in the Bay."[85] With his faith in riparianism waning, Nickel in 1918 decided not to buy some river frontage because "riparian rights have not the value . . . that they formerly had."[86]

Yet although Nickel acknowledged that the law was changing, he refused to recognize the authority of the water commission as an institution. His superintendents and lawyers were directed to avoid any actions that would bring the firm before the water commission, and in 1919 Miller & Lux went to court to challenge the commission's power to regulate appropriations. In

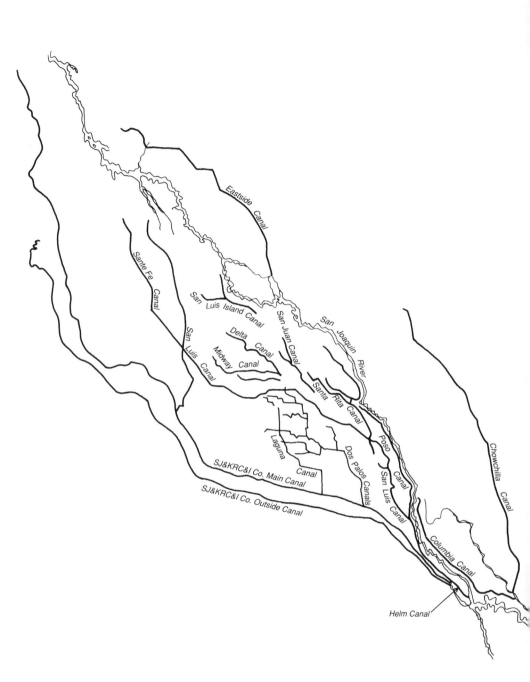

Map 4: Miller & Lux's canal systems along the San Joaquin, ca. 1916. Drawn from Miller & Lux Inc., Map of portion of the San Joaquin Valley showing lands of Miller & Lux and others, compiled by Charles B. Gleaves (1916), Bancroft Library, University of California, Berkeley.

1915 Miller & Lux had filed to appropriate the surplus waters of the Kern River in the name of the Tulare Water Company. The district attorney of Kern County protested the application, charging that Miller & Lux and the Kern County Land Company already had a near-monopoly on the river and should not be granted any more of its flow. After investigating the river, the water commission rejected Miller & Lux's application, stating that there was not enough water regularly available to supply the request. Miller & Lux applied for a writ of mandamus to force the commission to recognize its appropriation. It charged that the commission could not deny any application to appropriate that was properly prepared and filed. In 1921, in *Tulare Water Company* v. *State Water Commission,* the supreme court accepted this reasoning, ruling that the water commission could reject applications only for procedural errors, not on substantive grounds—greatly circumscribing its ability to administer or supervise claims to the state's rivers.[87] Miller & Lux again reaped the benefits of taking its claims to the courts, with their history of protecting property rights, rather than resting its case before political institutions that seemed to harbor its opponents.

The water commission bill alone had little direct impact on the operations and interests of Miller & Lux. The law's restrictions on riparian use were never applied against the firm. In 1911, Wiel had predicted that section 11, which required that riparian waters be used if they were not to be lost, would be found unconstitutional; similar laws had been rejected in other states.[88] Miller & Lux declined to test the law, preferring instead to quietly expand its diversion, and section 11 was never raised in a case where the requirement of ten years of nonuse was invoked. But in the 1920s and 1930s, the California Supreme Court found section 11 to be invalid because it attempted to remove vested property rights.[89] In *Herminghaus* v. *Southern California Edison,*[90] the state supreme court not only rejected section 11 but reasserted the position it had taken in *Miller & Lux* v. *Madera:* An upstream appropriator could not hold a riparian owner to the standards of reasonable or economical use, and extensive improvements to provide water for others could not be required. In other cases raising section 11, the court implied that the statute had gone beyond the legitimate uses of police power, thus rejecting the line of reasoning that Adams and the conservation commission had seen in the court's earlier decisions.

The *Herminghaus* decision, however, sparked another effort at limiting riparian rights, one in which Miller & Lux played a conspicuously minor role compared with its activities against the earlier water commission act. In 1927, a referendum was placed on the ballot to restrict riparian owners to a reasonable use of water. Proponents of this amendment had hoped to include language that would clearly oust riparian rights from its preeminent position in California water law. The legislature, however, adopted a mild version of the proposal that declared conservation of water and elimination of waste to be state goals. All water users were to be limited to that water "reasonably necessary for the beneficial use to be served," but they were assured in turn that any water reasonably used or legally appropriated would be protected.[91] In 1928, the proposal, which was generally perceived as restricting riparians and easing the development of water storage systems, was adopted by popular vote.[92]

In this instance Miller & Lux mounted no opposition. In fact, Treadwell and others linked to large riparian interests cooperated with reformers such as Frank Adams in the initial discussions of this proposal. Adams attributed this to a post-*Herminghaus* "recogni[tion] . . . that something had to be done"[93] about excessive riparian claims. Although Miller & Lux saw the amendment as hostile to its interests, it limited its response to a recommendation that "its people" vote against the proposal.[94] By that time, Miller & Lux was involved in a complicated effort to set up a water storage district, which circumscribed its activities. Beset by new financial problems that limited its expansion projects, Miller & Lux had embarked on a venture that hoped to use reformist inventions such as irrigation districts to its own advantage.

5

Retreat from the Courtrooms:
The Formation of Water Storage Districts

As J. Leroy Nickel's legal views changed, so did both his responsibilities and Miller & Lux's financial and economic options. In 1913 Henry Miller set up a trust and transferred control and management of the firm to his daughter, Nellie Miller Nickel, and her husband, J. Leroy. Miller himself had a knowledge of ranching that had created its own myths. Stories abounded about his ability to judge the weight and value of herds of cattle at a glance, about his influence over other men, and about his prodigious memory for detail. He had run the ranches through personal contact and knowledge of his employees, instructing his foremen, superintendents, and housekeepers in the minutiae of ranching, farming, cooking, and cleaning on frequent, unscheduled visits to the ranches. Nickel was less savvy. Although he had run Miller & Lux's affairs in San Francisco for many years, he had little experience in the country; another failing, according to some former Miller & Lux employees, was that, unlike Miller, Nickel was a poor judge of character. For whatever reason, Nickel's assumption of leadership was not smooth, and he clashed with many of the firm's older superintendents. With little personal knowledge of the daily affairs of ranching, Nickel wanted to run operations scientifically and so consulted various experts; the older managers, in his opinion, did not run ranches efficiently or economically.[1]

Nickel had little time to master the firm's daily operations before confronting major economic problems. The winters of 1911–12 and 1912–13 had been extremely dry, forcing the firm to spend unusually high amounts on feed, rent, and freight. In 1913, the tariff on beef was lifted and the price of cattle fell dramatically after Australian chilled beef had arrived in San Francisco in good condition. As a result, Miller & Lux could no longer control the supply or price of meat in the region. The immediate loss of income forced the firm to halt the excavation of new canals that the water commission bill had encouraged. Dredges that had been operating twenty-four hours a day were cut back to one ten-hour shift; operators who had been working eight-hour shifts were expected to work ten hours for the same pay. Complaining about rapidly increasing expenses and demanding retrenchment at all ranches, Nickel laid off large numbers of employees. Although his ranching supervisors resisted these orders and tried to complete the plowing and planting of fields, the cutback was so rapid and so dramatic that it produced near-panic in some rural communities. Miller & Lux's managers feared a run on the banks the company owned because depositors had lost faith the firm's credit.[2]

Throughout the rest of the decade, Nickel continued to press his managers to restrain development work and worried about the large number of men employed on the ranches. He lamented that he had been "reckless" in his earlier call for rapid expansion. In 1909 the firm had spent $140,000 on improvements; in 1912, $355,000; and in 1913, $595,000—more than the total spent in 1909, 1910, and 1911 combined; taxes in 1913 were 38 percent higher than in 1909 as well. Although construction of the San Luis system was to proceed with "due diligence" to protect the appropriation, Nickel insisted that no other new projects be undertaken; he even proposed selling the firm's horses to prevent superintendents from ditching, checking, or plowing new fields without prior approval, and he again cut wages.[3] After Miller died in November 1916, federal and state demands for millions of dollars in inheritance taxes put additional pressure on the firm. Although the heirs successfully fought these claims, the battle lasted until the mid-1920s and forced the firm to borrow additional money to stop the seizure of its property in the meantime.[4]

The expansion of the San Luis system continued, but high wages during World War I took a heavy toll. The firm had previously depended on cheap labor to modify sloughs and to ditch and check fields for the profitable irrigation of alfalfa and pasturelands. Much of the firm's earlier expansion had taken place during the depressions of the late 1870s and the 1890s; when jobs were hard to find, Miller & Lux was able to hire laborers for as little as $0.75 a day. Generally, Miller paid for land improvements from earnings and typically waited for the low wages of the winter season or general downturns to embark upon long-planned projects.[5] However, the rapid escalation of wages during World War I undermined this policy. Although cattle prices also increased, the size of the firm's herds was limited by difficulties in harvesting the hay and grain to feed them. Initially unwilling to raise pay scales, Miller & Lux in 1917 lost part of its hay crop when both its skilled and unskilled workers flocked to jobs paying two and three times as much. In 1918, the firm had difficulty hiring farm carpenters at wages of $45 per month plus found; by way of comparison, in 1917 the federal government had paid carpenters $5.50 a day for an eight-hour day. Forced to concede on wages and to try to recruit laborers from Mexico, Miller & Lux postponed most development work and contracted out its harvesting.[6]

In the postwar period, falling commodity prices and rising taxes continued to constrain the firm's expansion projects. In 1921, low prices for wool, hides, sheep, and cattle gave the firm its lowest earnings in years. As he again cut wages, Nickel lamented the "reckless practice" that had grown up on the ranches. In his view, superintendents hired too many men who did too little work; they ditched and plowed new fields without permission or consideration of the costs and benefits of such operations. Although he had been selling bonds to pay for the continuing development of the irrigation system, Nickel at that point felt it unwise to continue borrowing, given the weak markets for land and agricultural products.[7]

Miller & Lux also confronted renewed efforts to organize irrigation districts in both Oregon and California. Spurred on by the booming markets of World War I, farmers demanded more water to exploit their property. With the support of new state water commissions, farmers proposed to appropriate surplus waters, relying on eminent domain to set loose the resources they needed, backed up by legislation that limited riparian owners to a reasonable use. The irrigation districts not only sought water claimed by Miller & Lux, but often included large parcels of its land that would be assessed to pay for the new reservoirs and canals.

Traditionally, Miller & Lux had gone to court to oppose such efforts. With confidence in the law, its attorneys, and its money, the cattle company simply initiated litigation that exhausted the opposition. After World War I, however, the firm began exploring alternatives to simple litigation. Given its money troubles and the pressures to sell some of its land, the firm began to experiment with irrigation districts, ultimately attempting to mold and use them to its own advantage. If an irrigation district could be controlled, it offered a new way to fund canal construction while pacifying and containing the demands of rival farmers. The experiment, however, was less than successful. As Miller & Lux's rivals manipulated the law and engineering concepts to their own advantage, the firm's effort to capitalize on irrigation districts brought to the fore conflicts over the nature and value of property in water that had often been masked by the legal rhetoric of earlier litigation.

Where Miller & Lux had the support of other property owners, it found the formation of an irrigation district to be a simple and effective strategy for freezing out new interests. That was the case in Harney County, Oregon, where the tactic was used to protect the water rights of the Miller & Lux affiliate Pacific Live Stock Company (PLSCo) from homesteaders moving onto the sagebrush lands above the Silvies River. The farmers were led by C. B. McConnell, an attorney employed by the Oregon & Washington Railroad & Navigation Company (OWRN), which planned to open a rail line through the region. In 1912 McConnell filed notice to build a reservoir on the Silvies. The PLSCo, a major riparian owner on the stream, offered to cooperate with this effort if McConnell would provide it the water it had always enjoyed. While the PLSCo initiative followed the model developed in dealing with power companies such as Southern California Edison, it was somewhat disingenuous. The firm had blocked other appropriations by court actions that found there was no surplus water in the Silvies. In fact, the Bureau of Reclamation had already explored and abandoned a project on this stream because of its limited flow.

McConnell, himself an opportunist with political connections, rejected the offer of cooperation. Instead, he contested the rights of the PLSCo and more than a hundred other landowners before the recently formed state water board, which at that time was chaired by another attorney working for the OWRN. When Miller & Lux delayed this adjudication by denying the jurisdiction of the water board, McConnell induced the state attorney general to file an action to recover some of the firm's riparian lands, which he alleged had been acquired fraudulently. This lawsuit was ultimately settled out of court; Miller & Lux admitted no guilt but agreed to pay a $25,000 fine and sell some of the disputed acres.[8]

While he pressed for prosecution of the land suit, McConnell formed an irrigation district in Harney County. Made up primarily of drylands, this district included property belonging to the PLSCo and to William Hanley, a cattleman and riparian owner who had long challenged PLSCo for the domination of the Silvies and the adjoining range.[9] Oregon's irrigation district law, modeled on the Wright Act, gave each landowner one vote regardless of the amount of land owned. Both PLSCo and Hanley opposed the McConnell district, rightfully foreseeing that it would be controlled by settlers hungry for the water the cattlemen depended on. By their numerical strength, the newcomers could pledge the good lands of the two firms as security for the bonds needed to improve poor lands, using "one man's property against his will for the benefit of another."[10] Confronted with this greater enemy, the PLSCo settled long-standing differences with Hanley and used him as a front in the attack on the district. The PLSCo and Hanley subsidized propaganda and later shut down the county's pro-McConnell newspaper. Both protested the inclusion of their lands in the district, and Hanley filed suit challenging the legitimacy of the district itself. This suit was successful, and in 1919 McConnell's district was temporarily defeated.[11]

With the McConnell forces regrouping, PLSCo business manager A. R. Olsen proposed that the firm itself form an irrigation district and use this reformist instrument to co-opt the opposition. Many landowners were disenchanted with McConnell, he noted, but they lacked leadership and looked to the big companies for guidance. In 1919, while it continued to oppose dryland districts in neighboring counties, the PLSCo met with Hanley and other influencial landowners to organize their own Harney County district. Mainly encompassing already irrigated lands, the district would allow those with established water rights to control reservoir development and would be dominated by the two big companies. Along with the petition to form the district, the majority of farmers signed an agreement allowing Hanley and the PLSCo each to designate one of the three directors of the district. The third director and an advisory committee would be chosen at large. With Olsen furnishing transportation to the polls, the voters endorsed the district in January 1920, and Hanley and Olsen were elected to the board of directors. McConnell challenged the legality of the district, charging among other things election fraud, but he was unsuccessful.[12]

In forming a district they could control, Hanley and Miller & Lux hoped to protect themselves "against unreasonable extravagance." They thus directed

Olsen to hire an engineer who could make a "disinterested" and "cold-blooded" report on the prospects for developing the river. To ensure that the report would not be "unduly favorable," the engineer was informed in advance that he would not be further employed by the district. The engineering study indicated that a reservoir would provide only 110,000 acre-feet of water at a cost exceeding $30 per acre. Regarding this supply as inadequate, Miller & Lux directed Olsen to eliminate the few drylands from the district and to establish clear priorities along the river.[13]

Despite such problems, the irrigation district played an important ideological and economic role. It not only contained the local opposition, but it also increased the superficial attractiveness of the region. In the compromise of the land fraud suit, Miller & Lux had agreed to subdivide some of its Harney County property, but with its Oregon ranches showing losses, it was unwilling to spend money to ditch and check the land for easier sale in small units.[14] To encourage farmers to buy such tracts, which they would then have to prepare for irrigation, the district hinted at a regulated, secure, and popularly controlled source of water. In 1921, although doubts about the adequacy of the water supply continued to be raised, some $2 million worth of bonds were issued to finance reservoir construction.[15]

The fortunes of the Oregon irrigation district, however, were of minor concern to Miller & Lux, which was preoccupied with the control and utilization of the California rivers feeding its main ranches. Miller & Lux tried to duplicate the Oregon experience to exploit irrigation district laws in California, but there the effort proved much more difficult. Where farmers in Harney County welcomed the firm's direction, those in California's Central Valley had a long history of hostility to Miller & Lux as a land and water monopoly. The presence of experienced local and state leaders within this opposition severely complicated attempts to manipulate irrigation district laws. Yet the importance of the region and expanding financial difficulties goaded Miller & Lux to exploit the money-raising potential of such public bodies.

The first abortive efforts at cooperation between Miller & Lux and irrigation interests along the San Joaquin began in 1916, when a group of Madera County boosters approached Frank Short, the attorney who had frequently represented Miller & Lux. Planning to form an irrigation district and construct a reservoir, the Madera forces hoped Short could arrange a settlement with the cattle company, which had repeatedly thwarted their ambitions. Short proposed to Miller & Lux's attorney, E. F. Treadwell, that Miller & Lux treat with the group as it had with Southern California Edison. Short and Treadwell worked together to devise a contract that would protect Miller & Lux's rights yet allow the Madera district to proceed. The negotiations, however, were particularly difficult because irrigation, unlike electricity generation, consumed water. Fearing the loss of the winter waters that greened its rangelands, Miller & Lux's ranching superintendents lobbied against any real concessions. Even as a contract was drafted, tensions between Miller & Lux and the Madera Irrigation District (MID) mounted. The MID included a great deal of Miller & Lux's land, and its promoters requested money from the firm to complete the initial surveys. Foreseeing the high cost of the reservoir scheme and the damaging taxes that would pay for it, Miller & Lux president, J. Leroy Nickel, curtly demanded that his property be excluded from the district.[16]

In 1918, Miller & Lux's concern about the MID was temporarily over-shadowed by rumors that farmers in Stanislaus County were forming an irrigation district. Water had been in short supply that year, and the farmers proposed to build a reservoir that would irrigate a larger territory for a longer season than did the SJ&KRC&ICo. The proposed district was huge, stretching from Mendota to Westley on the west side and incorporating the Stevinson colony on the east side of the San Joaquin. It embraced the entire area served by the SJ&KRC&ICo, taking in much of Miller & Lux's most productive land, and it united two groups long hostile to the firm's claims to water. To call an election, organizers needed the signatures of five hundred residents, including the owners of 20 percent of the land in terms of dollar value. Given its size and composition, the district might well succeed, and Miller & Lux had to focus attention on defeating it.[17]

In planning the firm's response to this new challenge, Nickel rejected Treadwell's suggestion that further cooperation with the MID could block a west side project by freezing water rights. The tax burden imposed by the MID was more palpable to Nickel than this hypothetical benefit. Instead he relied on a report from J. F. Clyne, superintendent of the SJ&KRC&ICo, that farmers served by the canal company would oppose the large district if they could get good water service without it. With the petition drive under way, Clyne mobilized the vague antidistrict sentiments and encouraged the divisiveness among irrigators that the firm had manipulated in the rate fight. To simulate an independent opposition, he recruited local farmers to speak at public meetings while he stayed away. The SJ&KRC&ICo, Clyne and his friends argued, provided the cheapest water in the state, while an irrigation district would lead to higher rates and place a lien on all land within its borders. This appeal to pecuniary interests prevailed: the number of established irrigators who agreed not to sign the petition or to withdraw their signatures was great enough to prevent the establishment of the district.[18]

When the legislature met in 1919, many of the San Joaquin concerns moved to Sacramento as landowners sought legislative favors. Lobbyists roamed the corridors and water-related bills were churned out amid accusations of corruption and bribery. Miller & Lux opposed limitations on riparian rights while unsuccessfully pushing an ordinance that would give private canals the right to condemn land. This proposal, though couched in the language of the public interest, was directed at the Pope & Talbot Company, which refused to allow Miller & Lux to cut a canal through its land and even planned to booby-trap the site to prevent construction.[19]

Among the most debated issues during the legislative session was the "Irwin bill," which purported to "democratize" the Wright Act by lowering the proportion of votes necessary to form a district from two-thirds to a simple majority of the resident landowners. The Irwin bill was supported by long-time opponents of Miller & Lux such as James Peck and A. L. Cowell of the California State Irrigation District Association and by the Crocker interests, which wanted to transfer an unprofitable canal system to landowners reluctant to accept the burden.[20] State Engineer W. F. McClure and Elwood Mead opposed the measure, fearing it would allow the formation of unpopular districts and erode the already weak market for irrigation district bonds. The bill, however, passed and survived efforts to induce the governor to veto it. At the same time, the legislature quietly adopted the California Irrigation District Act, which provided for alternative irrigation districts governed on an acreage basis.[21]

With the passage of the Irwin bill, popularly controlled districts again threatened Miller & Lux's command of water. Activities around the MID were reinvigoraged, calls for a dryland district on the west side of the San Joaquin resurfaced, and new organizing began in Kern County. None of these endeavors could be ignored. "The formation of these districts," attorney Treadwell warned, "is likely to ruin the company. They can be formed without the company, and when formed will be governed irrespective of it." Miller & Lux's rights and canals would be expropriated; compensation would be set by juries, which historically were unfriendly to the firm; and the bonds to finance the confiscation would then become a lien on the firm's land.[22]

Eschewing particularistic tactics that required the wooing of local farmers, the firm adopted the strategy it had used in Oregon and embarked upon a project of creating irrigation districts it could control and manipulate. In doing so, it capitalized on the California Irrigation District Act, which provided for water districts in which political power was based on the acreage owned. By August 1919, Miller & Lux had submitted a petition for a "California district" in Kern County, just in time "to make us safe" against a Wright Act district.[23] Ultimately, five small California districts were formed in Madera County and another on the west side of the San Joaquin, each drawn to include little more than Miller & Lux's property. While the firm hoped to use some of these districts to improve water delivery, the main goal was obstruction. Miller & Lux argued that land in one of its districts could not later be included in a Wright Act district, which by definition served the same purpose.[24]

Having fabricated this defense, Miller & Lux broke off all negotiations with the Madera Irrigation District and publicly announced its "emphatic opposition" to the MID project. The breakup shocked many who had hoped for a reconciliation. According to W. M. Conley, attorney for the MID, the announcement came "like a bombshell." Resolute in his belief that Madera County needed an irrigation district, he concluded that "the cause of the people (which is the cause of development and progress) will ultimately triumph over the opposition of the few, who seek a monopoly in the natural resources of the State." Animosity was fueled when real estate agents dealing in Miller & Lux's lands reportedly advertised that this land was part of the MID, even as the firm obstructed the organization of the district. Whatever friendly feeling toward Miller & Lux had been generated by the earlier discussions evaporated.[25]

The battle lines were drawn, and the Madera District recruited allies in the state regulatory agencies. In May the U.S. Department of Agriculture's Division of Irrigation issued a report condemning Miller & Lux's districts and endorsing the broader MID plan. Miller & Lux's Madera County districts relied entirely on groundwater, which, the report stated, would not provide an adequate supply for irrigation agriculture.[26] In June the state water commission agreed to conduct hydrographic studies to determine how much of the flow of the San Joaquin was available for appropriation. Although the Madera District was to contribute $9,000 to the cost of the work, the commission's intervention greatly eased the burden it faced in preparing for future eminent domain proceedings. Treadwell tried unsuccessfully to prevent the agreement, arguing that it made the state a tool of private interests out to destroy Miller & Lux's rights. W. A. Johnstone, chairman of the water commission, curtly invited Miller & Lux to participate. Insisting that the commission was unbiased, he asserted that cooperation with the MID served the general public by encouraging the "greater use of the San Joaquin."[27]

The formation of Miller & Lux's California irrigation district on the west side also drove some of the firm's allies in Fresno and Merced counties into the opposition camp. Those irrigators, "formerly friends of the canal company," who had stood with Miller & Lux against the drylands district and against the Irwin bill, were unwilling to enter an irrigation district controlled by the firm. The partnership between the farmers and the cattle company had always been uneasy. Distrust arising from the water rate conflict and fed by general antimonopoly sentiments simmered just below the surface. While respect for Henry Miller had tempered such attitudes during his lifetime, Nickel, who now headed the firm, was disliked within the valley communities.[28] Nickel, in turn, displayed a repeated insensitivity to the popular mood: in 1918, as Clyne scrambled to defeat the drylands district, Nickel had suggested that the SJ&KRC&ICo increase water rates. With the cattle company continuing to expand its private canal system and preparing to defend its rights against the Madera District, the SJ&KRC&ICo's customers feared they would lose water. The irrigators thus filed their own applications to appropriate and store water and to establish a separate, smaller Wright Act district.[29] Their proposed West Joaquin district excluded enough of Miller & Lux's property to make it possible to secure the signatures of the owners of 20 percent of the land value.

In August 1920, the state supreme court declared the California Irrigation District Act unconstitutional, scuttling all of the Miller & Lux–controlled districts.[30] The elimination of the districts, however, was not enough to stymie the West Joaquin district that the firm's actions had provoked. The expansion of irrigation and Miller & Lux's sales of land to small farmers had permanently changed the complexion of interests along the river, increasing the number of people whose financial success depended on exploiting the water that Miller & Lux claimed. That much had been made clear in the earlier conflict over water rates. Aggravating the opposition, the firm's attempt to manipulate irrigation districts had given economic rivalries a political form that could not be easily contained. As Nickel put it, the people of the west side had "tasted blood" and were unlikely to be as tractable as in the past.[31]

Nickel rejected suggestions that Miller & Lux set up its own Wright Act districts along the San Joaquin and fell back on the firm's traditional weapon—litigation. When the Madera Irrigation District took the first step toward implementing its plans—buying a gravel pit for use in constructing a reservoir—the cattle company moved to enjoin the district as a threat to its riparian rights.[32] The action was the same type it had used against the Madera Canal & Irrigation Company, against Fresno Flume, and that it held over the heads of upstream users such as Southern California Edison. Ultimately, twenty-odd suits were initiated challenging the MID or its assessment of Miller & Lux's land, suits that Treadwell said would keep the district's attorneys "busy for fifty years."[33]

At the same time, the cattle company temporarily restrained the organizers of the West Joaquin district from filing their petition, hoping to use the time gained to defeat the movement. The firm attempted once again to convince local landowners to withdraw from the irrigation district by raising the specter of cost. As Nickel put it, the petitioners should be shown "that their actions will produce expensive and endless litigation which their lands will have to bear."[34] Treadwell meanwhile contrived legal arguments against the West Joaquin district, including the novel claim that the owners of already irrigated land could not petition to form an irrigation district because such a district would not serve a public purpose: it would not reclaim or improve land by making it habitable, by increasing its population, or by enhancing its value, as the Wright Act required.[35]

However, the litigation that Miller & Lux threatened was a double-edged sword. When Miller & Lux filed its suit against the Madera Irrigation District, the district counterfiled to condemn enough of the cattle company's riparian rights to complete its project. Miller & Lux had been forewarned of this serious challenge, but went forward anyway, with what might be called an expensive game of "chicken." To meet an eminent domain suit, the company had to prove both the extent of its use of water and the value of this right. In spite of all its previous litigation, Miller & Lux had never been forced to quantify its rights. In fact, it had carefully avoided doing so, as defining its rights would be equivalent to limiting them. In the earlier suits against upstream diversions, Miller & Lux had been required only to demonstrate that it possessed riparian property. It usually did so by presenting maps that were colored to indicate its riparian lands; Treadwell would then aver that he could provide the court with the requisite deeds and plats if desired.[36] Such a tactic, however, would be inadequate to defend against an eminent domain suit.

The possibility that the West Joaquin district would seek to condemn the SJ&KRC&ICo provoked additional concerns, since such an eminent domain suit would delve into the relationship between the canal company and Miller & Lux. In particular, Nickel worried about how such a suit would treat Miller & Lux's claim to own the canal company's surplus water and wastewaters. In the earlier rate litigation, the cattle company had struggled to convince the courts that those waters should be treated as its property. Given popular attitudes about land and water monopoly, it would have even more difficulty convincing a jury such as the one that would set its compensation during an eminent domain proceeding. At the same time, the cattle company could not demonstrate clearly which of its lands had been irrigated from the canal company, or when. The merging of the office staff and management of Miller & Lux and the SJ&KRC&ICo had led to careless recordkeeping, and the firm now faced the problem of reconstructing the irrigation history of its ranches on a plat-by-plat basis. By July 1920 Nickel had a bookkeeper working on this task sixteen hours a day.[37]

The company's recordkeeping problems were further complicated by the casual treatment accorded to water released from Southern California Edison's reservoirs. Miller & Lux considered such water to be a part of its riparian rights, to which neither the canal company nor its customers had a claim. Since 1913 it had been developing the San Luis system to deliver such water independently of the SJ&KRC&ICo. A material accommodation to legal change, this construction was prompted in part by the Water Commission Act's command that all riparian rights be put to beneficial use. By creating a wholly private system, the firm also hoped to escape court-imposed limits on the SJ&KRC&ICo's diversion and to minimize scrutiny by the Railroad Commission. However, because the San Luis system was incomplete, throughout the 1920s Miller & Lux continued to use the SJ&KRC&ICo canals as conduits to its own system. Miller & Lux viewed water transported through the San Luis system as its private property, stored for its benefit by Southern California Edison, and it subtracted from the total delivered to its land by the SJ&KRC&ICo the volume released from the power company's reservoirs. This practice dramatically reduced Miller & Lux's irrigation bill, but the ledgers showing the adjustment of accounts proved to be an embarrassment. In fact, Nickel wanted no evidence of the water released from power generation to appear on the canal company's books. In February 1921 Nickel was alarmed to learn that Miller & Lux's water bill included charges for all water delivered to the cattle company through the SJ&KRC&ICo's canals; an improperly supervised bookkeeper had neglected to subtract the water supplied by the reservoirs. Nickel abruptly postponed the annual meeting of the SJ&KRC&ICo's board of directors until the error could be corrected. For "obvious reasons," Miller & Lux's account was not to be credited for this water; instead the SJ&KRC&ICo's books were to be expunged of any record of the reservoired water, a solution that protected against accusations of fraud and that might preclude other irrigators from claiming such water as part of their entitlement.[38]

With litigation looming, Miller & Lux began to flirt with the west side landowners. In 1919 Clyne had attempted to subvert the organization of the large drylands district by meeting with its Stanislaus County organizers and promising that the SJ&KRC&ICo would help build a new canal to irrigate their lands. This effort was dropped when Miller & Lux formed its own districts under the California Irrigation District Act.[39] In 1920–21 similar negotiations were broached with the proponents of the West Joaquin district. Using Treadwell and A. L. Cowell, attorney for the West Joaquin district, as intermediaries, Nickel proposed that Miller & Lux facilitate the organizers' goal of storing water for late-summer irrigation, offering to pay half the costs of the necessary investigations; the firm promised to join in a district of some sort if storage proved feasible. In return, Nickel demanded that all activity to organize under the Wright Act be stopped. This condition was a test of sincerity to Nickel, who suspected that the true aim of the district's advocates was to seize control of the SJ&KRC&ICo and improve its water rights against those of the cattle company.[40]

Instead of a Wright Act district, Miller & Lux proposed forming a water storage district under the legislation enacted in 1921. This statute, which Treadwell pronounced to be "remarkably well-drawn," provided for large districts that could handle irrigation, drainage, water storage, and the de-

velopment of hydroelectric power. Such districts had to be approved by the
state engineer, a provision that troubled the firm even though Treadwell believed it might be unconstitutional. More important, however, voting rights
were based on the value of property owned. While every resident in a Wright
Act district had an equal voice in its decisions, landowners in a water storage
district got one vote for every $100 of assessed value, and assessments were
apportioned according to the benefits to be received.[41] Storage districts were
not democratic organizations but business entities governed by wealth and
stock ownership. Given its massive holdings on the west side, Miller & Lux
would be able to call the shots in a water storage district.

The West Joaquin district, however, was not easily dismissed, especially
in negotiations with Cowell, who was ideologically committed to the Wright
Act. While Cowell and his clients were willing to collaborate with Miller
& Lux, they insisted on forming a Wright Act district. Such an organization would provide a mechanism for collective action, giving small farmers a
voice and protecting their interests within any larger enterprise. The result
was a series of proposals and counterproposals. The promoters of the West
Joaquin district redrew its boundaries to exclude cities and towns, hoping
to answer Nickel's charge that urban voters would be "only interested in the
expenditure of large sums of money to make 'times good.' "[42] Cowell even
suggested that the district's leading proponents enter a "gentlemen's agreement" as to its goals and its officers to assure Miller & Lux that the district
would respect the cattle company's interests.[43]

Nickel, however, was adamant that no Wright Act district be formed and
that local irrigators accept Miller & Lux's leadership. In return, he offered
elaborate arrangements for selecting the storage district's directors and for
casting Miller & Lux's votes, arrangements that he claimed would protect
the interests of smaller farmers and demonstrate the sincerity of the firm.[44]
At one point Cowell demanded that Miller & Lux complete all pending litigation and guarantee the canal company's water rights before the formation
of a storage district. With suits pending against upstream users such as the
MID and with the eminent domain suit against Stevinson still unsettled,
Nickel lashed out at the irrigators: the west side landowners, he charged,
had never given the SJ&KRC&ICo adequate assistance in its litigation; they
must now support Miller & Lux or risk losing everything to the MID.[45]

Yet despite his reluctance to make any concessions, by 1921 Nickel desperately wanted to form a storage district for the infusion of capital it promised. The firm had suffered another bad year in 1920; wages had remained high while prices for meat and byproducts plummeted. In the spring of 1921, the Miller & Lux payroll had to be trimmed to meet interest and tax charges. While committed to developing canals, as a means both to improve his lands and to lock in his control of water, Nickel stopped all work on such "betterments." He was determined not to increase the firm's floating indebtedness for permanent improvements. Instead, further improvements must await the formation of irrigation districts, which could issue bonds to finance construction.[46]

Sensing that Cowell could not "properly present . . . the necessity of joining with us in an effort to defeat the Madera Irrigation District," Nickel directed Clyne to recruit prominent local landowners to promote the storage district scheme. Nickel was encouraged by Clyne's evaluation that most on the west side of the San Joaquin were neutral both to the Wright Act district and to Miller & Lux. Again Miller & Lux appealed to the pocketbooks of the small farmers, arguing that the formation of both a Wright Act district and a storage district would lead to duplication and "useless expenditure." A storage district organizing committee was fabricated, although Nickel concluded that Miller & Lux would have to do the bulk of the work if the district was to be realized. Recognizing that promotion of a storage district would "require a great deal of patience and hard work to educate these farmers to a proper realization of the true condition" in the valley, Miller & Lux hired an organizer, W. F. Hume, "a good talker who could write as well." Hume scheduled meetings in local communities to promote the new scheme and spent at least part of his time issuing polemics against the Madera Irrigation District.[47] By January 1922 a petition for the West Side Storage District was being circulated.

But even as the petition was being prepared, Miller & Lux trod a narrow line in trying to accommodate all elements on the west side. Clyne attempted to build an alliance with other large landowners as the firm had done earlier in Oregon. The 1922 petition encompassed a relatively large amount of unirrigated land, and the storage district promised to take in additional drylands when the claims of the Madera Irrigation District were defeated. Clyne had drawn the boundaries to win the support of E. S. Wangenheim, manager of the Simon Newman Company, who had been active in the earlier water rate conflicts and in the efforts to form the large Wright Act district. By 1922 Wangenheim was promoting a Wright Act district to serve the drylands north of the SJ&KRC&ICo canals, the West Stanislaus District, which had considered joining with the MID to build a reservoir.[48]

Nickel and attorney Treadwell, however, distrusted Wangenheim and suspected that Wangenheim's promotion of the drylands was part of an MID plot that included State Engineer McClure. The formation of any water storage district, required approval from the state engineer and Nickel wanted the boundaries of his district drawn narrowly so that McClure would have "no shadow of a basis for holding up or rejecting the petition."[49] While Clyne counseled that Miller & Lux must proceed "on the assumption that the state engineer is going to be just and reasonable," Treadwell warned of conspiracy.[50] McClure had already committed himself to the MID and the validity of its water right. The inclusion of large amounts of dry land in the West Side Storage District might give him an excuse to kill it or force it to merge with the MID under the assertion that the MID's water rights were superior to the claims of the Stanislaus County lands. The suspicions at Miller & Lux increased with the announcement of a conference to plan a superdistrict that would include the MID and land on both sides of the San Joaquin to Patterson in northern Stanislaus County. That summer paranoia reached its height during hearings on the West Side Storage District. There Treadwell publicly accused McClure of colluding with the MID to defeat the West Side District, an outburst for which Clyne later apologized although Treadwell would not retract the accusation.[51]

Notwithstanding Nickel's apprehension, rapprochement was the theme of 1922. At various times Nickel, Treadwell, Clyne, and Wangenheim met with the MID to work out a compromise between the MID and the West Side Storage District, and between the MID and Miller & Lux as the largest single landholder within the MID's boundaries. Others, including the attorney Frank Short, the San Francisco bankers Frank B. Anderson and Frank G. Drum, and Secretary of Commerce Herbert Hoover were drawn into the effort, and in July 1922 the MID signed a secret contract to pay Tom F. Saunders and P. H. Bottoms to mediate a settlement. Although the arrangement with Saunders and Bottoms backfired—the exposure of the secret contract provoked a deceived and insulted Nickel to cancel all dealings with the MID until its board of directors was replaced and the contract abrogated—in September 1922 the negotiations paid off: Miller &

Lux, the West Side Storage District, and the MID signed a "memorandum of agreement."[52]

Under the terms of this agreement, the MID and the West Side Storage District were to be dissolved and replaced by the larger San Joaquin River Water Storage District; all litigation and all efforts to perfect the Madera district's appropriation were to be suspended. The San Joaquin storage district would then accommodate the needs of all landowners, and thus eliminate the bitter rivalries that had divided the region, by purchasing Miller & Lux's water rights and by constructing a reservoir at Friant. Advocated for years, the Friant reservoir was the material basis for a reconciliation. Engineering and technology would increase the size of pie to be divided, making it possible to furnish water to Miller & Lux and to the customers of the SJ&KRC&ICo according to their existing priorities, while at the same time distributing enough additional water to irrigate thousands of dry acres both in Madera County and on the west side of the San Joaquin.[53]

The contract set up an administrative apparatus that protected each major interest group by guaranteeing its representation in the decision-making process. Miller & Lux was to appoint four members of the board of directors; the remaining landowners, divided into districts on the east and west sides of the San Joaquin, were to elect four others; and the eight in turn would choose a ninth. To assure the directors of the MID a voice during the planning period, Miller & Lux agreed to give them proxies for part of its lands in Madera County. Preliminary engineering work was consigned to Harry Barnes, then engineer for the MID, and to W. C. Hammatt, for years employed by Miller & Lux. In addition, the contract set a time limit to guard against filibuster: any party could withdraw from the agreement unless all plans were carried out within one year.[54]

With the accord finalized, a rush to organize the water storage district began. Nickel was selected president of the initial organizing group; Milton T. Farmer, whose firm represented the MID, was appointed attorney; and petitions were drawn up embracing more than 900,000 acres of land, half of which had never been irrigated. By December 1922, having secured the requisite signatures, the directors asked State Engineer McClure to certify the formation of a district without delay. Quick approval, however, was not forthcoming. Stating that he must be certain "that both the state and the Madera Irrigation District shall be adequately and properly protected," McClure insisted that the proposed district submit detailed engineering studies before he would sanction it. In addition, he asserted a right to exclude land nominated if the proposed district exceeded the area that could be feasibly served by the available water.[55]

This posture reflected not only partisanship but also a more general effort by McClure and his adviser S. T. Harding to expand the role of the state engineer and of expertise in water development. The California Supreme Court was then reviewing the constitutionality of the water storage act, which had been challenged partly because it did not provide for an appeal from the decisions of the state engineer. McClure and Harding responded that the law, in fact, had not given the state engineer enough discretionary power. The failure of early irrigation districts demonstrated the need for supervision; the engineer must protect the public, not by simply aiding individual districts, but by safeguarding investments in land and in storage district bonds. The engineer's approval of a district, McClure argued, should signify that both the district and the lands within it could bear the expenses of development. Such certification required a comprehensive investigation that considered the dependability and availability of water, the cost of the project (including the cost of preparing land for irrigation), the benefits to be derived, and such general factors as soil, climate, and the availability of transportation. The engineer should use this information to mold the character of the district. Interests not willing to submit to such supervision could simply use "older methods of organization,"[56] which would lack the warrant of his office and expertise.

McClure's position disturbed the promoters of the storage district. Nickel greatly feared delay; he wanted to consummate the marriage of fractious interests and secure the dissolution of the Wright Act districts before beginning the potentially disruptive investigations of water rights.[57] Milton T. Farmer, who represented the MID, was no less perturbed by what he saw as a premature request for engineering studies. He wrote McClure that the development of the region had been hindered in the past "because of a lack of water rights and of a machinery harmonious and elastic enough to put those rights upon the lands adapted for their use." The current prospects of cooperation should not be held back by unnecessary technicalities. Not only were McClure's demands inexpedient, but they were unconstitutional under recent decisions of the California Supreme Court. The state engineer had no authority to modify district boundaries, but should trust "in the good sense of the petitioners" and approve all proposals not "entirely impractical."[58] These sentiments were echoed by Treadwell. Since his victory in *Tulare Water Co.* v. *State Water Commission*,[59] he had repeatedly argued that water districts could be formed without the approval of state regulatory agencies.[60] Ironically when McClure formally rejected the petition for the district in June 1923, he acknowledged that this action did not legally prevent the organizers from continuing their efforts.[61] McClure's disapproval, however, when coupled with his uninterrupted promotion of the Madera Irrigation District, presented a serious obstacle to the Miller & Lux–endorsed project.

By 1923 Nickel's early animus toward McClure's insistence on excluding lands had turned to relieved approval, a change impelled by a concern for dollars and cents. In condemning the storage district, McClure had pointed out that 233,000 of the 933,000 acres within it were hardpan lands, unfit for extensive cultivation and unlikely to benefit from irrigation. It was this land he sought to exclude. Miller & Lux owned at least 100,000 acres of hardpan lands, much of it marginally improved riparian pasture. As the cost of the preliminary investigations began to exceed estimates, Nickel worried that, given the poor state of the livestock industry, such ranges could not bear even the minimum assessment necessary to pay the district's administrative and interest charges. Much of the inferior land was in Madera County, where a similar worry over expenses had driven Nickel's earlier, vigorous opposition to the MID. At this point he asked his staff to consider ways to lessen the cost of the San Joaquin storage district to Miller & Lux, including schemes of retaining water rights or removing land from the storage district altogether.[62]

Clyne at first dismissed the problem of costs. He and Treadwell were more concerned with the broader consequences of Nickel's new proposals. Trusting the assessors to be fair, Clyne argued that the taxes on parcels that received few benefits would be negligible; it was the firm's more fertile but undeveloped property that would suffer. He cautioned that if the firm removed its hardpan and alkaline lands from the district without finding a way to retain their water rights, it would forfeit 80 percent of their value.[63] Treadwell was equally circumspect. Nickel's proposed schemes would violate the terms of the 1922 agreement in which Miller & Lux had pledged both to put its land in the storage district and to transfer all its water rights to the district. Treadwell also feared that the exclusion of such tracts might appear to be an admission that they had no water rights.[64]

The ultimate solution was to yield to McClure. In 1923 the state supreme court found the water storage district act constitutional in *Tarpey* v. *McClure*, [65] but the decision did not clearly settle the state engineer's role. The court refused to define the nature of the investigations that the state engineer could require; concluded that he could not prevent the establishment of any district, even if it was not "feasible"; and stated that he could exclude only property that was "not susceptible of irrigation from the same system." This decision mimicked earlier arguments made by Miller & Lux to restrict the power of the water commission and other state regulatory agencies. However, the firm in this case decided to ignore the limitation on the state engineer. While not wanting to enlarge his powers, Nickel decided that the engineer could exclude tracts that would not benefit from irrigation, as long as the owners did not protest.[66] By doing so, Nickel could limit the cost to Miller & Lux's less fertile lands. The only other options, either petitioning for a new, redefined district or circulating special petitions to withdraw land, were rejected because they might expose the directors to public criticism.[67] With this decision, Miller & Lux's ranch and farm superintendents began drawing up lists of its inferior parcels. Concluding that the lists should be as extensive as possible, Clyne directed that "all lands . . . that are not sufficiently fertile to grow some crop that will keep a family on a fifty-acre tract" be considered for withdrawal from the district.[68] In the end, Miller & Lux eliminated an area exceeding that specified in McClure's objection.[69]

In November 1923 McClure approved the formation of the scaled-down district; an organizational election was scheduled for early 1924. Facing no opposition, the district was accepted and a board of directors was selected according to the 1922 accord. Nickel remained president, and Miller & Lux placed three other representatives on the nine-member board of directors.[70] However, it is unclear whether this reflected the approbation of the majority of landowners within its boundaries or simply their indifference and skepticism toward the scheme. Slightly more than five thousand landowners were eligible to cast more than 168,000 votes, based upon the valuations of their land. With its vast holdings, Miller & Lux held one-third of the ballots; fewer than 1 percent of the landowners controlled a majority. Although notices were posted throughout the region and proxies were received, 70 percent of the non–Miller & Lux votes were not cast. More than 60 percent of the 87,339 votes polled came from the cattle company.[71]

Miller & Lux had succeeded in setting up the water district it wanted, an achievement that Nickel hoped would trump the claims of the firm's rivals and ease the financing of water development. Yet this very success initiated a new phase of conflict over water, law, and power in the valley. The contract linking the competing groups was full of abstractions that had to be made concrete; legal constructs had to be defined in the real terms of productive, exploitable resources. Not only did the storage district have to settle its boundaries, but it had to devise a detailed plan for the transference of water rights and the development of the river. The seasonal flow of the river had to be determined, and the existing water rights had to be agreed upon, measured, linked to specific parcels of land, and assigned priorities. All the water rights to be transferred to the storage district had to be valued, as did the various canals, weirs, and rights-of-way that would pass to the district. Plans for the reservoir, for the canal system promised to Madera County, and for both new irrigation and drainage works on the west side had to be prepared. The cost of this new work had to be calculated. Finally, all the land in the district had to be assessed, a task that required an appraisal of the specific dollar value of the benefits accruing to each unit. These activities forced Miller & Lux to confront issues it had carefully avoided in all its earlier litigation—in particular, the legal meaning of property rights in water. They also gave engineers and state officials increasing power over the firm's property.

From the beginning, Miller & Lux's suspicions and fears had circumscribed the engineering research entailed in the district's planning. By late 1922, Barnes and Hammatt had initiated investigations needed to draw up a storage district plan. Harding had also embarked on a separate study of the river at the behest of McClure and the state water commission. Cooperation among the engineers might have promoted efficiency, but it was rejected because it presaged loss of control and threatened the value of the firm's property. While the various engineers often portrayed themselves as objective professionals interested in serving a broad public, Miller & Lux more accurately regarded engineering work as value-laden and partisan, especially since water rights involved questions of both law and fact.[72] Conflict, competition, and concern about future litigation would dominate the engineering work, as became clear when the state water commission proposed to measure the height of the water table.

As a result of years of irrigation and swamping of grasslands, drainage was a serious problem in the irrigated sections of the San Joaquin Valley; on some of Miller & Lux's lands the water table was within inches of the surface. Hoping to solve the problem by opening up clogged drainage channels and by drying up canals not in use, Miller & Lux refused to let the water commission sink test wells on its property. A water commission study of the water table would make the drainage problem a matter of public record and could do long-term damage to efforts to sell land.[73] Both the legal and engineering departments of Miller & Lux warned against such a study. Cooperation with the state engineer and with the MID would give its enemies information they were not normally privy to, information that could be used to compare "a working irrigation system in the normal course of development" with a "paper project." Judges, jurors, and commissioners, not seeing such a comparison for what it was, might be influenced unduly by an ideal, though chimerical, project.[74]

In such a case, measurements of the water table were important since waterlogging often indicated waste of water, and waste was a legal justification for limiting actual water rights. In fact, this argument had been used by Miller & Lux in its efforts to restrict the appropriations of the Madera Canal & Irrigation Company and by Stevinson in his attempt to block the SJ&KRC&ICo's eminent domain suit. Treadwell counseled that the cattle firm take its own measurements of the flow of the river. The water commission, he reminded, had been created to restrict riparian rights; it was generally hostile to Miller & Lux and in 1922 had entered into "an unjust contract" supporting the MID. In the future, when Miller & Lux might again be "at arm's length with the Madera Irrigation District," it would need its own figures to prove its claims. To cooperate with the water commission early in the game would "give them standing and merely strengthen their condition to hurt us."[75]

The heed paid legal issues also hindered the essential task of classifying water rights. Here again Miller & Lux saw law as both reflecting and determining its control of productive forces. In 1922 Miller & Lux retrieved a list of its rights and priorities that Hammatt had furnished Harding, on the grounds that the claims were "subject to litigation."[76] In 1923 protests from the firm's attorneys forced Nickel to cancel his request that Hammatt and Barnes inventory the cattle company's water rights. Treadwell, who had recently left the firm's employ, argued that such an inventory "would be very dangerous" because many of Miller & Lux's rights were uncertain. The matter should wait until negotiations for the district's takeover of riparian rights were underway. T. P. Wittschen, the firm's new attorney, agreed that "the time is not right." The company needed a "private and confidential appraisement" of its water rights so that it could decide what compensation to demand. For Barnes and Hammatt to take an inventory would only "stir up agitation and discussion" and provide an opportunity for the public to settle on a low figure. In fact, since the nature of the water rights would be an issue only if the district was later challenged by a third party, Wittschen asserted, Miller & Lux need never define its rights but could simply sell them "all" to the district.[77]

As a result of these concerns, the storage district's governing board subdivided rather than consolidated the engineering work it faced. The directors instructed Hammatt and Barnes to inventory only the physical properties involved (primarily the canals of the SJ&KRC&ICo, of Miller & Lux, and of the Madera Canal & Irrigation Company) and to determine the amount of water in fact appropriated and beneficially used. Another engineer, A. J. Wiley, was hired to develop plans for the proposed Friant reservoir and to analyze its costs. Miller & Lux was to draw up the list of its water rights, and attorneys Farmer and Wittschen were directed to "attempt to agree on any debatable legal claims involved."[78] By the fall of 1924, Hammatt and Barnes were working on the "setup" for the district, a plan detailing what water rights the district would buy, how they would be distributed, and what irrigation works needed to be built. Barnes was to do the field work, including planning and estimating the costs of the new irrigation system for Madera County. Miller & Lux, after some debate, assigned Hammatt to prepare historical data on water rights, to assemble the diversion rights of the various canals, and to determine the yield of each of its rights and the land to which each was attached.[79]

Hammatt's task was by far the most difficult and, to Miller & Lux, the most important, for it involved a determination of which water rights Miller & Lux would sell the district and which it would retain for its future needs. Miller & Lux had created an intricate mosaic of rights for its lands. Individual plots were often served by more than one canal, and as such might have complex claims to water—at the same time riparian, prescriptive, and appropriative—that required a determination of how and when they had been irrigated. This system was most labrinthine on the west side, where land not only had riparian rights from a variety of sloughs of the San Joaquin

but was also served by the SJ&KRC&ICo (whose appropriation dated to the
1870s), by the San Luis system (appropriation initiated in September 1913),
and by the Firebaugh system (begun during World War I), as well as being
irrigated by water stored in the hydroelectric company reservoirs.[80] The task
of segregating these overlapping water rights, complicated by the poor state
of recordkeeping, was made even more difficult by Nickel's efforts to ensure
the firm the best water rights at the lowest price.

Nickel's manipulations were particularly intricate in the region served by
the SJ&KRC&ICo, where notions of law directly affected the economics of
cost. Land under the canal company had two different types of water rights.
The first, the so-called cropland right, attached to land that had purchased
water from the canal company. Those tracts would have the first claim on
the river, up to the SJ&KRC&ICo's maximum diversion of 1,360 cfs, and
because they would not use the proposed reservoir, they would have one of
the lowest assessments in the district. The second type, the grassland right,
attached to the thousands of acres that Miller & Lux flooded from the canal
company's wastewaters. Since the firm was selling this right to the district,
these parcels would suffer a much larger assessment to pay for the new storage
facility. Obsessed with reducing future costs and intent on retaining cheap
water for all his best lands, Nickel began to increase the area entitled to a
cropland right, in some cases demanding and paying for additional deliveries
from the SJ&KRC&ICo. Each adjustment, however, lowered the value of the
grassland right, and thus the compensation Miller & Lux would receive from
its sale to the district.[81] In 1924–25, as these factors were weighed, the status
of the firm's land was frequently redesignated, each time forcing Hammatt
to recalculate the yields and values essential to setting up the district plan.

The creation of the setup also demanded consensus on the legal standing
of many of Miller & Lux's claims to water. In general, the persistence of the
firm's attorneys and its seeming willingness to withdraw from the cooperative effort allowed Miller & Lux to impose its views. By November 1924
the storage district had recognized the canal company's surplus waters as
Miller & Lux's property, paving the way for their sale to the district. The
storage district's attorney, Milton Farmer, also conceded that the grasslands
had additional rights separate from those of the canal company and that any
water flowing through the SJ&KRC&ICo's system above 1,360 cfs belonged
to Miller & Lux. The cattle company would have had to prove such major
issues of law and fact in litigation seeking to condemn its property, and there

was no guarantee that Miller & Lux would easily win its argument in court, where the ideology of judges came into play. As a case in point, the master in the rate cases had rejected the argument that the SJ&KRC&ICo's surplus waters belonged to Miller & Lux (although his decision was ultimately overturned on appeal), and the canal company's customers later intervened in the litigation with the MID to claim that all the water belonged to the public. In the negotiations, however, Miller & Lux's economic might, as proven in its victorious and costly litigation, helped extract legal concessions. By April 1925 the district had also abandoned claims to water stored by Southern California Edison, agreeing that Miller & Lux could retain this water for its San Luis and Firebaugh systems, even though such a property right had not yet been recognized by the California courts.[82]

Meanwhile two other engineers were hired, A. Kempkey by the district and Fred H. Tibbetts by Miller & Lux, to appraise the physical structures and water rights involved. Once again Miller & Lux rejected cooperative study. When Farmer suggested that Kempkey and Tibbetts "value such water rights as they thought would be in the best interests of the district to acquire," Miller & Lux attorney Wittschen testily and publicly instructed Tibbetts to act "as a partisan employed to see that the best value possible is placed on water rights consistent with fairness." The purchases to be made by the district and the prices it would pay were to be settled by negotiations between the interested parties, not by engineering consensus. Kempkey and Tibbets were not to duplicate the efforts of Hammatt and Barnes but were to place dollar values on all properties. They were allowed to consult with each other, but only after Tibbetts had reported his findings to Miller & Lux to ensure that the firm was not left "in the dark."[83] To the cattle company, engineering work remained partisan and adversarial.

As might have been foreseen, Kempkey and Tibbetts initially came to quite different conclusions, especially about the value of Miller & Lux's grassland rights. Kempkey appraised those rights at $2,605,000, or $6.97 per acre-foot; Tibbetts at $6,865,000, or $18.40 per acre-foot.[84] Early in January 1925 Wangenheim, who served on the district's governing board, proposed that the engineers prepare individual reports and let the directors set a compromise value. Nickel, president of both the district and Miller & Lux, objected to this procedure as potentially divisive, believing that the figures could be reconciled if Kempkey was properly educated. Kempkey, Nickel noted, wanted to be fair but was ignorant of the productiveness of

alkali lands and of the techniques of swampland irrigation. He had been misled by Wangenheim and others who consistently stressed the weak market
for such lands because it was in their interest for him to undervalue them.
Clyne was directed to introduce Kempkey to other cattlemen who were using
swampland irrigation and to show him the extensive improvements made on
the tracts in question.[85]

Whether or not these tutorials convinced him, Kempkey was persuaded
that the district required an agreement with Miller & Lux on the appraisal of
the grassland right. In his formal report, Kempkey set its value at $4,628,000
or $12.38 per acre-foot, a figure just under the numerical average of the two
earlier valuations. Since the per–acre-foot value was used to calculate other
water rights, the increase had a dramatic effect. Under Kempkey's original
appraisal, the canal company's water right was worth $1,355,000; under the
final figure, $2,421,000. In general, this compromise increased the value of
Miller & Lux's water rights by 80 percent.[86]

Although the priorities of the various diversions had not been established
and estimates of riparian damages were incomplete, in April 1925 the board
of directors began considering a composite plan submitted by the engineers.
The plan proposed a storage district of 549,000 acres, of which 370,000
acres would receive district water. The remaining land, much of it belonging to Miller & Lux, retained its own water rights or would be developed
later. Estimated costs ran to $34 million, including $13 million to purchase
property and water rights from Miller & Lux and almost $5 million to
build delivery canals in Madera County. The largest assessments would fall
in Madera County, where 167,000 acres would be served by district-built
canals, by the proposed reservoir, and by purchased water rights; the smallest, on Miller & Lux's holdings and on the 145,000 acres already irrigated
by the SJ&KRC&ICo.[87]

Although Harding warned them that the plan would not satisfy the state
engineer, the board of directors formally submitted it to McClure on May 22,
1925. On May 28, after at best a cursory examination, McClure rejected it.[88]
McClure and Harding, who had been early supporters of the MID, found
the storage district's plan vague, inconsistent, and often unsubstantiated.
In their view, the engineering work failed to provide adequate information
for judging the feasibility of the district and was furthermore plagued with
mathematical errors. The appraisals were too high and favored Miller & Lux,
an implication of bias and unprofessional behavior that drew an immediate,

angry response from Kempkey. Kempkey was chastised for appraising water rights without weighing their usefulness to the district and for valuing the physical properties according to the full cost of reproduction, "without consideration of the ability of the purchaser to pay"—procedures adopted, of course, at the behest of the storage district's directors.[89] Harding, in fact, believed that the SJ&KRC&ICo should be forced to accept a price well below even the inventory values of its properties. Aware of the compromises made with Tibbetts, McClure declared that the $4 million value assigned to the grassland right was unjustified. A district at such prices was economically unfeasible and could not be sanctioned. Likewise, he and Harding denounced the legal concessions made, especially the district's recognition of Miller & Lux's claim to the water stored by the power companies. The very presentation of this report, Harding later charged, was merely an effort to force through a scheme that served the interests of Miller & Lux while disregarding both the requirements of the law and the rights of the minority landowners.[90]

Similar sentiments quickly emerged in the valley itself. Within days of the submission of the plan, a meeting of the Los Banos Farm Center condemned both the storage district and Miller & Lux, charging that the firm was selling the district water rights that had cost it nothing. Miller & Lux's earlier court-won victories recognizing the monetary value of water rights had little popular appeal, especially among those who believed that water was common property for all to exploit. A few weeks later a hundred irrigators attending a meeting of the Los Banos Farm Bureau agreed that a district was desirable, but not "at the figures named in the Kempkey report." This group wanted a material reduction in the price the district (and thus their land) would pay for the properties of the SJ&KRC&ICo on which they depended. Thus came the division over valuation that Nickel had hoped to avoid.[91]

In the face of the opposition, the board of directors backed down from an earlier threat to seek a writ of mandamus to compel McClure to accept the plan. On June 5, it withdrew the proposal and resolved to accept McClure's offer of cooperation. Harding was assigned to review the plan and point out its defects so that they could be rectified. The resolution, Harding concluded, "marked the end of the plan dominated by Miller & Lux." From that point on, other landowners would increasingly assert "their interests and right to be heard."[92]

CHAPTER

6

Money and the Return to Litigation

After 1925 Miller & Lux entered a new relationship with San Joaquin River Water Storage District, one impelled, however, as much by the firm's own financial problems as by the actions of the state engineer. By late 1926 Miller & Lux had dissociated itself from the direct management and control of the district's affairs. These tasks fell to E. S. Wangenheim, who replaced J. Leroy Nickel as the storage district's president, and to the district's long-time engineer, Harry Barnes. The district assumed an independent existence, and the cattle company became one of a number of legally antagonistic interests: potential sellers of water rights. From 1926 through 1928, Miller & Lux, under new management and subject to questions about the legal premises of its water rights, compromised earlier principles as it negotiated to sell water rights for much-needed cash. Ultimately the district failed. When the fractious marriage of the Madera Irrigation District and Miller & Lux dissolved, the difficult partition of property, of the San Joaquin, moved back into the courtroom. Later the federal government took over the reservoir project. Despite the repeated claim that water storage would extract greater profits from both land and water, private capital had abandoned the venture as too expensive and too risky.

McClure's rejection of the storage district plan came at a time when Miller & Lux was most vulnerable. While many industries had recovered from the postwar depression of 1920–22, agriculture had not. Overproduction and falling international demand left agriculture in crisis. Though prices for some farm products rose slightly in the mid-1920s, wages, taxes, and the cost of goods farmers bought rose even faster. The number employed in agriculture declined, and land values dropped precipitously. More particularly, California cattlemen faced a series of ecological and environmental problems. Rainfall had been scarce since 1917, and in 1924 the state experienced profound drought. In 1923–24, Miller & Lux recorded only 3.65 inches of rain in Los Banos.[1] These difficulties were compounded by an epidemic of foot-and-mouth disease that broke out in early 1924. State and federal inspectors quarantined large parts of California and ordered the slaughter of millions of cattle, sheep, and hogs that had been exposed to the disease. While cattlemen desperately needed pasture, stock could not be moved out of the state or even from one area to another within it. In March, anticipating the closure of the San Francisco abbatoir for disinfection, Miller & Lux began slaughtering livestock as rapidly as possible. By June, still unable to move even uninfected cattle to its traditional pastures in Oregon and Nevada, the firm began to import feed to avoid starvation. For most of the year, California's agricultural products, from the meat, hides, and byproducts Miller & Lux traded in to the fruit, vegetables, and grains of smaller farmers, were embargoed by states and countries fearing the contagion. The generally low prices for meat continued to fall, and business activity within the state declined by 18 percent.[2]

With water shortage came the expected cries of misuse and misappropriation. Irrigators in Dos Palos Colony repeatedly requested water and in July filed a complaint with the Railroad Commission alleging that they had been denied water necessary to protect their investments, while the canal company continued to deliver water to Miller & Lux and its tenants in the Los Banos vicinity.[3] In a later, more bizarre incident, a number of canal company employees were arrested when George Fink of Stanislaus County charged them with extortion in connection with fines the company allegedly levied on those wasting water; the charges were quickly dismissed, however.[4] Throughout this period, the canal company insisted it was doing its best to provide water to those with the most to lose, at a time when only a fraction of the water needed was available.[5]

Miller & Lux in turn suspected that upstream users, including its erstwhile ally Southern California Edison, were using more than their allotted share, thus exacerbating the problems posed by nature.[6] Most of the firm's animus centered on the Tranquillity Irrigation District, which had succeeded to the James rights to pump from Fresno Slough. Publicly accusing the district of stealing water, Miller & Lux filed a contempt suit alleging that the district was violating court orders that limited pumping. Meanwhile, the canal company manipulated the level of the slough to keep the Tranquillity irrigators from getting water.[7] Nickel, president of Miller & Lux, eventually filed a damage suit against the district. Miller & Lux's attorney resisted filing the suit, warning Nickel that it might last for years, open up all the rights along the river, and raise the question of who owned the water stored by Southern California Edison. If Miller & Lux's claim to own the reservoir water were not accepted, the firm would be at a distinct disadvantage in its dealings with the storage district. These questions, in fact, were just the sort the firm had originally sought to avoid, but Nickel, uncompromising after years of litigation to protect his claims to the water, was determined to teach the district a lesson and doubted that the $7,300 fine imposed in the contempt proceeding was sufficient. As the suit was filed, the attorneys worked feverishly to effect a settlement and then to preclude any consideration of the stored water if the case were to go to trial.[8]

By the fall of 1924, Miller & Lux was in serious financial trouble. In April Nickel had announced that the drought and the foot-and-mouth disease epidemic were forcing the firm to exercise "the strictest economy possible." No ranch improvements were to be made except for building fences to stop the spread of disease. All men not engaged in producing crops, especially those tending lawns and ornamental gardens, were to be discharged.[9] These cutbacks were inadequate, and in October the firm found itself short of cash. Facing heavy expenditures for hay and corn at the same time as a commercial note came due, it delayed paying its assessment to the San Joaquin storage district, instead arranging for the district to borrow money if it were needed immediately.[10] While Miller & Lux had engaged in massive projects to build canals and check new land since 1913, in the fall of 1924 Nickel ordered that no money be spent on expansion "regardless of the prospect of good returns." The past development policy, he concluded, had resulted in "an enormous plant for which we cannot get satisfactory men to operate . . . and are in a constant state of worry and anxiety."[11] In November he ordered a 50 percent cutback in the payrolls of both Miller & Lux and the canal company. As president of the storage district, Nickel also insisted that Harry Barnes, the district's engineer, quickly complete his engineering work and discharge his fieldmen, an ultimatum that Barnes later said prevented him from making a complete and proper study of water rights.[12]

In 1925 Miller & Lux disclosed a major refinancing and reorganization of the firm. Cattlemen throughout the nation had increased their debt in the World War I era, and Miller & Lux was no exception. Its indebtedness had grown dramatically since 1910, when it had borrowed $5 million to settle finally with Charles Lux's heirs. In 1918 the debt was increased to $10 million and in 1920 to $15 million,[13] partly to pay federal and state taxes on Henry Miller's estate. In 1918 the firm paid $2.5 million to stop federal distraint procedures while it continued litigation protesting these taxes. Its property had been appraised at more than $40 million, but the postwar agricultural depression and its own reluctance to sell any but its poorest lands threatened the firm's liquidity.[14] Thus in 1925 bonds and notes totaling $25 million were issued, secured (as the earlier debt had been) by the firm's land and, more important for the history of the storage district, by the firm's water rights, "appraised by Tibbetts and Kempkey at $13,742,000."[15]

This time the financiers demanded a role in management. Frank B. Anderson of the Bank of California and Harry H. Fair and Charles R. Blyth, who represented the syndicate floating the bond issue, joined family members J. Leroy Nickel, J. Leroy Nickel, Jr., and George Bowles on the Miller & Lux board of directors. Nickel remained chairman of the board but resigned as president and general manager of the firm, replaced in this role by James E. Fickett, who also served as the seventh member of the board of directors. Miller & Lux announced that it was going to increase its production of cotton; begin a campaign to recruit settlers and subdivide its land "into small farms and plantations"; and "broaden" its policies toward water rights and its past reliance on litigation. In fact, the 1925 trust deed required the sale of land and specified that all monies from the sale of land and water rights be put into a sinking fund to retire the bonds. This would quickly become Fickett's major concern: where Nickel's correspondence had dealt with cattle, canal development, and litigation, Fickett's was dominated by land sales and then, as the agricultural crisis continued and deepened, by foreclosures. In 1930, having retired about 35 percent of its debt, this "oldest and largest of California livestock producers" sold its breeding herd and "HH" brand to a firm owned by the Swift interests. At that point, it became almost exclusively a real estate company capitalizing on the rent of land and water to other producers, not the active ranching enterprise that Henry Miller had led.[16]

The refinancing scheme, which demanded that Miller & Lux appear both vigorous and progressive if its bonds were to sell, impelled it to withdraw the 1925 plan for the San Joaquin River Water Storage District and to offer to cooperate with the state engineer, W. F. McClure. But although the storage district's leadership had declined to take legal action against McClure's rejection of its initial plan, it still hoped to win official sanction for the proposal without making substantive alterations. Nickel retained the presidency of the district until mid-1926, and his management style and hostility toward McClure in the interim did not change appreciably. With no hint of self-criticism concerning his actions as director of the district, Nickel blamed Harry Barnes and Miller & Lux engineer W. C. Hammatt for the inadequacies of the engineering studies and directed them to prepare the corrections and explanations required.[17] He rejected McClure's suggestion that S. T. Harding be allowed to reappraise the water rights. Distrusting Harding's "startling legal views," Nickel saw little hope of effecting a compromise through him unless the district were willing to accept his domination.[18] Instead, the district should aim to persuade the state bond commission to endorse its bonds even if McClure, a commission member, cast a negative vote. To do so, Nickel proposed that the district arrange for the earlier appraisals to be reviewed by a disinterested, respected engineer, one who could "command the confidence of the directors" and earn the approval of the attorney general.[19]

Ultimately three men, H. L. Haehl, B. A. Etcheverry, and F. C. Herrman, were hired to conduct this review. Finding the district's problems "increasingly intricate and difficult as we acquaint ourselves with their detail," this group pressed the directors to decide exactly what property they planned to acquire and to provide complete information on the yields and legal status of the water rights. But like Kempkey and Tibbetts before them, the latest experts were kept on a tight rein. When Etcheverry ventured to comment on the adequacy of the water rights, specifically that Miller & Lux's riparian lands would not be damaged by the district and thus need not be compensated, he was directed "to value the property to be acquired and not pass upon engineering matters or policies adopted by the Board of Trustees."[20] By January 1926 this board of review had completed its work. It valued the water rights and properties that the district planned to acquire at $8,332,000 (including $4,168,700 for water rights), some $4 million less than the value Kempkey and Tibbetts had placed on them.

The new assessment satisfied no one. While the new valuation was 35 percent lower than that proposed by Kempkey, many landowners within the storage district still felt it was too high. To those in Madera County facing costs of close to $70 an acre, the burden on land seemed unreasonable and impossible to sustain. In fact, some farmers who had purchased land during the war boom were facing unbearable levels of debt, often owing more than the current value of their property. Miller & Lux was well aware of the problem, as many of those who had bought land from the firm had made no payments since 1920–21; some had deserted their farms. With land prices falling, the firm was discounting the debt of the more reliable purchasers and repossessing the land of others.[21] Having made these concessions, however, the firm was in no mood to compromise on the price of its water rights, and it rejected the new appraisal as too low. In March 1926 Miller & Lux presented a "proposed asking price" of $10,905,000 for the SJ&KRC&ICo and for the rights to some 230,740 acre-feet of cattle company water. Even at this price, it argued, the cost of the district would be within the range of other similar projects.[22]

Opinions about the district, however, continued to diverge. In setting its asking price, Miller & Lux valued the canal company's water right at $1.9 million. While this was substantially less than the $2,421,000 appraisal in the Kempkey report, it stood in sharp contrast to the book value of $1 million, and even that value had been only grudgingly conceded by the master in the earlier, acrimonious rate conflict. Miller & Lux justified the larger figure by basing it on the canal company's latest adjudicated right to a flow of 1,360 cfs; during the rate litigation it had been limited to 760 cfs. Barnes, however, seeing himself more than ever as the independent champion of the storage district and the public, argued that an examination of the company's current and potential earnings placed a maximum value of $760,000 on its water right.[23] In March the opposition multiplied when the Stevinson interests filed suit against the district and Miller & Lux, challenging the appraisals and the potential purchase of Miller & Lux's water rights at those prices. The suit alleged a conspiracy led by Nickel to solve Miller & Lux's financial problems by selling the landowners something the cattle company did not own.[24] In June a group of irrigators under the SJ&KRC&ICo filed a protest with the Railroad Commission, complaining that the district's plan projected their annual costs at \$4 to \$5 an acre, whereas the SJ&KRC&ICo charged only \$1.25 to \$2.50. The irrigators claimed that the prices placed on the canal company's properties were "expensive, unreasonable, and greatly disproportionate"; that the transfer of the canal company to the district was unjustified; and that it would impose an unfair tax on their land.[25] No price for the whole package of rights was acceptable to all interest groups. The reevaluation scheme had produced dissonance, not euphony, and the affairs of the storage district had again reached a crisis.

While most of the disagreements were honest, the outcome of treating water as a legally vendable commodity and of engineering uncertainty, McClure and many in the valley saw them as products of Miller & Lux's venality and its corruption of the district. They demanded that Miller & Lux remove itself from a leadership position because its interests as the seller of water were clearly hostile to those of the district as purchaser. By September Miller & Lux, under Fickett's management, had conceded to the concern about conflict of interest, replacing Nickel and the other representatives of the cattle company on the board with directors mutually acceptable to the state engineer and the firm.[26] Wangenheim, as its new president, and Barnes, committed to an independent district, became the key figures in the storage district's ongoing activities.

In this role, Barnes mounted the podium to present the seemingly neutral solution: the storage district must review its entire plan "from a strictly economic standpoint and in accordance with the requirements of the state engineer."[27] Assuming that the district existed for "the mutual benefit" of all landowners, neither to profit Miller & Lux nor to get something for nothing, Barnes began preparing a new setup of water rights that would resolve the differences within the district and between the district and the state. In doing so, he used Hammatt's various studies of the yields of Miller & Lux's water rights as the basis for determining which rights best met the needs of the district. In addition, he suggested the exclusion of more land to reduce the amount (and cost) of water the district must buy, the acquisition of some power-stored water, and the generation and sale of hydroelectric power to defer part of the district's expenses.[28] However, the notion that disinterested expertise could solve the district's problems again proved misguided.

As before, the protean murkiness of the Miller & Lux records impeded the efforts to set up the water rights. Barnes was quickly frustrated with the mutability of Miller & Lux's claims, especially in the case of the San Luis

Canal. In his study of August 1925, Hammatt had established the volume of the San Luis right (without power-released water) at 203,886 acre-feet. Of this, the district proposed to buy the so-called "excluded right," which yielded 63,056 acre-feet. These calculations were later used in tentatively resolving the status of the SJ&KRC&ICo and the San Luis system to Harding's satisfaction. Barnes, however, requested that Hammatt separate this right into its monthly yields, a request that led Hammatt to conduct a "more exhaustive" investigation. According to this analysis, the San Luis right supplied 205,223 acre-feet; more important, the "excluded right" furnished 77,646 acre-feet of water—in other words, 14,590 acre-feet more than cited by Hammatt in August 1925. The discrepancy could not be ignored. It required recalculation of the yield of the SJ&KRC&ICo and the presentation of the new figures to Harding and to Miller & Lux, which might then raise its asking price.[29]

Even more unsettling, the new figures threatened efforts to find historical evidence that legally validated the claims. As Barnes lamented, "What assurance is there that additional facts may not be discovered that may later justify further revision?" In general, Barnes recognized that ultimately the foundation of these rights rested on "agreement and understanding." The paucity of the diversion records left too much to judgment for the situation to be otherwise. The problem, simply stated: "Who is to agree and who is to understand? And when the agreement and understanding is had, where is any evidence that anybody is going to follow it?"[30] At issue was not only the relationship between Miller & Lux and the rest of the district's landowners but also that between the storage district and the outside world. McClure and Harding, echoed by Barnes, insisted that the storage district's water rights be definite and certain, with the cattle company to specify exactly what water rights it was selling and what it was keeping, and that each claim have adequate support to establish a prescriptive or appropriative right that could withstand any challenge. Only then could a secure and stable district be formed.[31]

Harding, in fact, opposed both the legal premises of many of Miller & Lux's claims to water and the concessions underlying the district's plan. While not a lawyer, Harding was not shy about his views on water law. In the fall of 1925 he played a key role in organizing the opposition to Southern California Edison's assertion in the *Herminghaus* case of a riparian right to store water. He convinced the Irrigation District Association to enter the case against the power company, lobbied the Madera Irrigation District and the storage district to do the same, and wrote the first draft of the state's amicus curiae brief in the case. In reviewing the storage district plan, he objected to the delineation of the SJ&KRC&ICo's right, questioned the soundness of the rights of the San Luis and other Miller & Lux canals, and rejected the cattle company's claim to own both current and future power-stored water.[32]

Harding's queries about the SJ&KRC&ICo's title provoked little concern. This right had been repeatedly adjudicated, and though subject to a damage payment to Stevinson, was clearly and easily defensible. Even so Harding disputed its volume, insisting that it was limited to the average of past diversions, not to the court-recognized maximum. Miller & Lux simply responded that it had generously based the price to the district on the minimum yield of the adjudicated right. Since the canal company was a regulated utility, the Railroad Commission would ultimately rule on the definition of rights and their transfer to the storage district.[33]

The questioning of the San Luis right more quickly confounded the attorneys and engineers. The claim had never before been subjected to public scrutiny, and the precise use of water was poorly documented—its history, of course, having been the subject of repeated, oft-changing engineering studies. The original proposal treated the San Luis right as prescriptive and vendable, but after Harding's report, Milton Farmer, the district's attorney, began to worry about its validity against downstream riparian owners. A good deal of the land irrigated through this system was riparian, and since riparian owners possessed a common right to irrigate, such a use would not create a valid prescriptive title.[34] Although a notice of appropriation had been posted, Farmer doubted that this step was adequate to start the statute running. Not only should this water be segregated into riparian and appropriative components, he maintained, but before it was transferred, its title should be quieted at Miller & Lux's expense.[35]

Four months later Farmer had been persuaded that a landowner could have both appropriative and riparian rights to the same water. Though never adjudicated, the San Luis right was as secure as that of the SJ&KRC&ICo.[36] As Fickett later explained to the as-yet-unconvinced Barnes, the San Luis Canal Company had filed a notice of appropriation in 1913, then had constructed a dam and provided water "indiscriminately on riparian and non-riparian lands of Miller & Lux for beneficial uses." Since the San Luis company owned no land, such actions put downstream owners on notice that an adverse use was intended; because this usage had continued for more than five years, the title was complete.[37] Even so, studies of this right continued, with Miller & Lux engineer T. C. Mott later breaking it down into water used on land listed in the notice of appropriation, water used on nonriparian land not cited in the notice, and water used on unlisted riparian lands.[38] By mid-1927 the San Luis right was again divided into appropriative and riparian portions, with Miller & Lux retaining much of it for its own advantage.[39]

McClure and Harding also challenged the ownership of the power-stored water. In this case, competing interests confronted a gap in the law of waters. Stored water was indeed a material benefit of economic development, of capital invested in exploiting natural resources. But the investment at issue had preceded the creation of the legal rules and rights governing its products. While no one disputed the idea that stored water was a profit-generating commodity, the way in which it would be recognized as property became an important factor in the ongoing social and economic struggle between Miller & Lux and its rivals. Each marshaled a fine array of ideology and argument to fill the gap.

Miller & Lux dated its claim to the power-stored water from its first contracts with Eastwood and others involved with hydroelectric development. These contracts, sought by the developers to prevent litigation such as that directed against Fresno Flume, reserved the cattle company's riparian rights but stayed its opposition to the reservoirs if the hydroelectric companies observed specified flow schedules and released waters as Miller & Lux needed them. In the postwar period the stored waters, released during the driest parts of the year, became increasingly important to the development of the cattle company's land. In fact, the firm's acquiescence to the storage district was predicated partly on the power-released waters. By retaining control of this water as an independent source, the firm would both minimize the cost to its lands and maximize its autonomy.

The storage district had conceded Miller & Lux's claims to the power-stored water to prevent it from withdrawing from the project and opposing the construction of the reservoir at Friant. According to the legal theory adopted early in 1925, the power-released waters were part of the ordinary flow of the stream. As such, they could not be appropriated by the district over the objections of the riparian owners.[40] Miller & Lux, however, went beyond this assertion of riparian entitlement to insist that it had an exclusive right to the waters that was not shared by other riparian landowners.

Since those interests had not protested the construction of the reservoirs, they had lost all claim to the impounded waters. The water belonged to the power companies that had stored it and to Miller & Lux, whose title was impressed at the reservoir as a result of its contractual alliance. Both of these theories, however, were untested and had been challenged by the MID in a suit that had become abeyant under the 1922 accord forming the water storage district. But the storage district had accepted even this Miller & Lux claim to a separate, private water supply when drafting the contract to purchase water rights, and Milton Farmer, the districts' attorney, had joined the Miller & Lux attorneys in defending this position against the Tranquillity Irrigation District's averment of a riparian interest in the power-released waters.[41]

Harding challenged these claims and the district's acceptance of them with a legal theory adapted from the earlier MID suit. Relying on the 1918 state court decision in *Horst* v. *New Blue Point Mining Company*,[42] he argued that the power-stored waters were not a part of the natural flow of the stream to which riparian rights attached. *Horst* considered waters artifically added to a stream, specifically waters brought from another watershed, to be abandoned. Harding argued that it was "logical" that water stored by the power companies was likewise "foreign water" when it was returned to the stream. Since *Horst* "apparently decid[ed] definitely that riparian rights d[id] not attach to such foreign water," Harding maintained by analogy that such rights did not attach to the power-stored water. Rights to stored water had to be based on appropriation or prescription, but even then, because this water was wastewater, those appropriating it could not demand continued delivery from the power companies. On this basis, he recognized Miller & Lux as having a right to that portion of the currently stored water that it had used beneficially for at least five years; however, the firm had no claim to future storage. To Harding, the district was waiving a valid claim to a valuable source of water by conceding Miller & Lux's title to all power-stored water.[43] The legal issue was clearly one of dollar and cents.

For a year following the Harding report, Miller & Lux insisted on its exclusive right to power-released waters and on retaining them for its own use. But Barnes, infected by Harding's suspicions, repeatedly demanded engineering support and legal justifications for this position. In June 1926 Hammatt completed a study that segregated the power-released waters and documented their use by the cattle company. Miller & Lux had intended this study to reinforce its broad assertion of rights by showing that the stored water had been put to beneficial use. Instead, the weaknesses of the data undermined the earlier acceptance of this assertion. Hammatt had records of the river's flow, of the timing and volume of water released from the reservoirs, and of the actual diversions through some of the canals operating with formal appropriations. However, Miller & Lux had kept no records of the irrigation of its uncultivated grasslands, which were simply flooded in turn as water became available. Hammatt established by deduction that some 48,000 acre-feet of power-released water were used through canals such as the San Luis, but he had to assume the broader proposition that he was expected to demonstrate—that all the water had been used "in some manner" by Miller & Lux. Thus in his tabulations, he simply placed in a column labeled "Riparian" all power-released water beyond that going to the measured diversions.[44]

While Miller & Lux considered its claims to be "reinforced by prescription,"[45] Barnes believed that the record of use contradicted the allocation of power-released water to Miller & Lux in the original plan for the San Joaquin storage district. In another setback for the company, Farmer moved into the camp of the doubters. In 1925 Farmer had accepted the assertion that the power-released waters were riparian in nature, and as late as April 1926 he had assured Barnes that Miller & Lux's title was good, if not as a riparian right, then by prescription.[46] In August, however, after a number of conferences on the question, Farmer recanted his earlier position and joined Harding in arguing that once impounded, the waters lost their riparian character. Miller & Lux's rights could rest only on appropriation or prescription, and such a claim had been "considerably weakened" by the Hammatt report.[47] Bolstered by Farmer, Barnes reported to the district's board of directors that Miller & Lux's right to the power-released waters was limited to that used through its measured diversions. Unmeasured use on riparian lands had created no prescriptive right; all riparian owners had an equal claim to such water. His new setup recommended the purchase of the cattle company's prescriptive right to the stored waters.[48]

Barnes thought circumstances favored the district at that point. As a result of McClure's pressure, Nickel and the other Miller & Lux representatives had been removed from the storage district's board of directors. The district's new leadership, Barnes felt, could influence Miller & Lux president Fickett. As vice-president and then president of Miller & Lux, Nickel had

defended the firm's claims to water for decades; he was knowledgeable, con-
tentious, and stubbornly opposed to compromising with old adversaries. But
Fickett, Barnes wrote, was "not as fully advised as he might be concerning
the position of some of his own properties" and had to rely on others for
information.[49]

Barnes believed he could exploit Miller & Lux's seeming legal and financial weaknesses to persuade Fickett to accept the district's terms. Clearly
the district's proposal to acquire power-released waters was an obstacle to
agreement; Miller & Lux had claimed such waters as its property from the
beginning. But since the *Herminghaus* decision, Barnes suggested, the contracts with Southern California Edison had become "a bit of a boomerang":
unlike the Herminghauses, Miller & Lux could make no claim against the
reservoirs, yet its own title to the released waters was uncertain. By selling
the district its prescriptive rights, however, Miller & Lux could stabilize the
title, since the district would withdraw any claim to future power company
storage. Settlement with the district would also end the challenge from the
MID while leaving the cattle firm with both adequate water and access to
a new reservoir. Barnes argued that Miller & Lux's indebtedness also recommended settlement; there was no other buyer for more than a fraction
of the firm's water rights, which were mortgaged for $10 million, and the
water rights themselves could not generate enough income to pay the annual
interest on the debt. Similarly, the district's purchase of the SJ&KRC&ICo
and associated water rights would allow Miller & Lux to rid itself of a utility
that was "practically a white elephant," generating little income but earning
the constant scrutiny of the Railroad Commission. Earlier, the firm had been
"rich enough and powerful enough to crush the opposition or wear them
out"; this was no longer true. Miller & Lux's interests, Barnes concluded,
lay with the "peaceful solution of water rights questions" that the district
provided.[50]

Barnes was correct in his perception that Fickett would negotiate. Facing
an apathetic market for the firm's bonds, Fickett was willing to make some
concessions to arrange the sale. Following Hammatt's advice, he refused to
sell all of the firm's prescriptive claims to the power-released waters. Instead,
he proposed that Miller & Lux retain that portion of the power-released
waters necessary to irrigate a block of some 60,000 acres of croplands. This
water, however, would be treated as part of the measured diversions and
no longer segregated from the natural flow, a position Barnes and Farmer

regarded as legally sound. The prescriptive right to power-released waters in excess of this amount would be sold to the district. Fickett also conceded that the water rights of the district and Miller & Lux be set up according to a flow schedule that treated all power-released water as part of the natural stream (at least for the purposes of engineering). His concern was simply that the firm's lands "get as much water as they require and to the extent which they have received it in the past."[51] Legal principles were subordinated to pragmatic demands. In fact, Miller & Lux, increasingly uncertain about the fate of its legal theories, filed to appropriate the power-released waters in a move designed to "fortify its title." The storage district would likewise file to appropriate these waters, though promising to withdraw its filings if a contract with Miller & Lux was consummated.[52]

In December 1926 Farmer and Miller & Lux's latest attorney, J. E. Woolley,[53] began framing a new contract to reflect these concessions and Barnes's revised setup. The contract was to be supplemented with maps showing the various water rights and delineating the lands for which riparian claims were being waived, a narrative of the historical derivation of each entitlement, and a flow schedule allocating the water among the various rights. The entire contract depended on the resegregation of the land under the San Luis right and on negotiations with Chowchilla Farms, the East Side Canal Company, and the Tranquillity Irrigation District, interests which had additional, though smaller riparian claims.[54]

By April 1927 Woolley and Farmer had submitted a contract to the district's directors. Barnes, whom the lawyers had consulted on each preliminary draft of the proposed contract, quickly stepped in to interpret and evaluate its provisions for the board. His key criticism concerned the question of warranty on which he had been rebuffed by the attorneys. Miller & Lux refused to provide any warranty of title for its water rights beyond the assurance that its records were bona fide. Barnes warned that, in the absence of warranty, the directors should move cautiously and only after careful examination of the documents and the rights involved. Barnes's argument found a receptive audience. The board of directors, following his lead, demanded extra guarantees from Miller & Lux, including its written pledge to continue to defend and use its water rights in the period before their transfer to the district. The directors also requested the removal of a clause limiting the district's sale of water to land within the current district boundaries.[55]

Miller & Lux answered each of these requests with a resounding no. Bristling at the implication that the firm might not continue to defend property it had spend years acquiring and protecting through frequent courtroom battles, Woolley replied that the cattle company would offer no guarantee beyond that already provided in the contract. Miller & Lux also refused to allow water sales to land outside the current boundaries; such sales would increase the damage to the firm's riparian lands beyond the level at which it was being compensated, and they might allow the district to acquire rights to additional unappropriated and unceded waters. Following this rejection of unlimited expansion, the directors suggested that the storage district buy fewer of Miller & Lux's preferred water rights. The cattle company again refused any concession. It had priced and sold land on the assumption that the district would be purchasing an established portion of its water rights; the district must buy all the offered water or none of it.[56]

In March 1928, with the MID again raising concerns about costs, the storage district began negotiations on the price of the Miller & Lux properties. It offered to pay Miller & Lux the board of review value of $8,332,000 if Miller & Lux allowed it to annex more land to help defray the expense of buying all the preferred water rights. Miller & Lux in turn requested additional compensation for the riparian damage entailed by a larger district and for the power-released waters that the district would receive. Ultimately, the district accepted Miller & Lux's final price of $9,326,150, with the understanding that it was receiving all of Miller & Lux's interest in the unreserved power-released waters and would have a free hand in negotiating with Southern California Edison. By June Miller & Lux had signed a contract. It was turned over to W. A. Sutherland, the storage district's new attorney, to be executed when the flow schedule and other exhibits were completed.[57]

However, the signing of this contract did not realize the promise of the storage district. While a number of smaller riparian claimants, as well as the MID, had also settled with the district, negotiations with the riparian owner Chowchilla Farms, Inc. dragged on. Represented by the storage district's former attorney, Milton Farmer, Chowchilla Farms wanted the district to purchase its riparian rights and to provide it with an alternative source of water. At the same time, it demanded a share of the power-stored water from Southern California Edison and Miller & Lux.[58] Meanwhile, the district's acquisition of the SJ&KRC&ICo had been interrupted. Despite opposition from a large group of customers and from the ever-present Harding, in 1926 the Railroad Commission had approved the transfer in the spring of 1928 without deciding on the merits of the district's plan. Dissidents challenged this decision, and in July 1928 their appeal was pending before the state supreme court.[59] A new setup reflecting the district's enlarged boundaries had yet to be completed, and the annexation of the additional land awaited approval by the state engineer's office. Both the abstract of water rights titles, which had been consigned to Sutherland, and the final flow schedule had to be drafted.[60]

Miller & Lux insisted on the speedy resolution of these issues. In July 1928, complaining that people with no interest in the project were "resorting to dilatory tactics with great and irreparable injury to Miller & Lux," the cattle company repeated an earlier plea that the state engineer reappoint its representatives to the district's board of directors. Unsuccessful in this, the firm in August delivered an ultimatum: if the district had not completed its plans and submitted them to the state engineer by 31 December 1928, the contracts to sell water rights would be terminated. Fickett argued that the deadline allowed ample time for the completion of the plan if the storage district was really desired. If not, then "all parties concerned—including the general public—will be better off by knowing the true situation." In fact, Miller & Lux considered that there was only a remote chance that the district would become functional. The firm planned to reprice its lands according to its retention of water rights and had established mutual companies to administer the canals as its land was sold.[61] On 1 November 1928, Fickett repeated his demand that the district's plan be completed by year's end and requested that its bond issue be kept to $30 million. Neither of these conditions could be met. In December, the board of directors voted that the project could not be carried out. Only at this point were Miller & Lux's representatives placed back on the district's board of directors, now to supervise its final dissolution.[62]

Out of the demise of the storage district arose a tenuous agreement between Miller & Lux and the Madera Irrigation District. In January 1929 the MID resolved to purchase 329,200 acre-feet of water from the cattle company for $1.25 million. Miller & Lux cautiously embarked on the negotiations, warning the MID that any such sale would be subject to the requirements of Miller & Lux's croplands and would require a careful expression of the respective rights and obligations of each party. Miller & Lux offered the same guarantees it had provided the San Joaquin storage district and sought some assurance that the MID had the money to pay for its purchase if a formal contract were signed.[63]

Arrangements for this sale proceeded slowly. Since it had to negotiate with other riparian interests as well, the MID decided that all the rights along the San Joaquin River should be determined before it proceeded with the purchase of water rights. While Miller & Lux prepared petitions to have its land excluded from the district, Harry Barnes, once again employed as the MID's engineer, drew up and circulated a schedule of water rights "as they are claimed to be." Curiously, Miller & Lux objected that the initial schedule granted too much water to the SJ&KRC&ICo. In 1929 the SJ&KRC&ICo recorded the second smallest run-off in the history of the river, and the long-simmering conflict with the outside customers heated up as they demanded a share of the power-released waters being delivered to Miller & Lux. Uncertain of its continuing ownership and control of the canal company, Miller & Lux was unwilling to sacrifice any of its rights to this public.[64]

By February 1930 Barnes had prepared a plan for the MID. Stripped of Miller & Lux's land, the irrigation district consisted of a trim 200,000 acres. It would purchase the needed water rights, build distribution canals, and construct a dam, reservoir, and generating plant at Friant for $15,336,000. Ironically, the gross per-acre cost, $76.67, in fact exceeded that estimated for the Madera region under the proposed San Joaquin storage district. However, as in the case of the storage district, this cost of the MID was to be reduced to $49 per acre by selling electricity generated at Friant to the San Joaquin Light & Power Company (SJL&P).[65]

While the sale of electricity seemed essential to the MID's economic feasibility, it required even further concessions from Miller & Lux. The SJL&P's agreement with the MID hinged on being released from the restraint Miller & Lux had placed on its use of the river. Under a 1919 contract with the cattle company, San Joaquin Light & Power could store water for its Kerckhoff plant only when the flow of the San Joaquin exceeded 3,000 cfs. For much of the year, the company had to run water straight through its generating station, holding none back if it was to preserve the stream for Miller & Lux's irrigation. The power company wanted the flexibility of unrestricted storage so that it could vary electricity generation according to its customers' needs, slacking off on weekends and reserving water to meet peak weekday demand. In fact, during 1928 it had done just that and was consequently being sued for damages by Miller & Lux. SJL&P would pay generously for MID electricity only if it could gain the right to unrestricted storage from Miller & Lux.[66]

Always alert to Miller & Lux's financial weaknesses, Barnes saw this proposal as a sound one. Clearly advantageous to the irrigation district and the SJL&P, the proposal, he argued, would also benefit Miller & Lux by allowing it to sell some of its water rights for needed cash without disturbing the supply to its croplands. The SJL&P operated upstream of the proposed Friant reservoir and any fluctuation in the stream caused by the utility's less restrained storage could be minimized by releasing water at Friant. In addition, the small amount of water actually involved would come from the rights the MID was purchasing.[67]

Miller & Lux's engineers and superintendents were less sanguine about this scheme and about Barnes's plan in general. At issue was the relationship between legal doctrine and Miller & Lux's continuing control of property in water. The MID plan required Miller & Lux to accept a specific flow schedule and a rigid definition of the water requirements of its land. A. R. Olsen, then managing the firm's San Joaquin operations, worried that the flow schedule might not meet the firm's future needs. Having always based its rights "along broad lines," Miller & Lux was at that point being asked to specify and limit them. Yet acceptance of the limits would give no protection against later claims by the MID or other irrigation districts that Miller & Lux's use of water was unreasonable compared with the needs of their public.[68] Miller & Lux engineer K. Cameron had long been cynical about such cooperative efforts. Calling it "odd" that after six years of work on setups and demand curves, "the curve is still an approximation," he cautioned that a definition of rights in this manner had neither a legal nor a technical foundation. To accept the arrangement Barnes proposed at a time when the legal status of stored water was "in a haze of uncertainty" was to substitute "water rights based upon agreements between individuals for those based upon well-established, fundamental principles accepted by law."[69] Chief Engineer Thomas C. Mott added that San Joaquin Light & Power would reap great benefits from Miller & Lux while granting it no compensation, even for past damages. At the same time, Miller & Lux would have to place men upstream to monitor the river, as the SJL&P had already proven to be an unreliable ally. However, concern for the firm's changing economic position tempered Mott's evaluation; under the refinancing scheme, Miller & Lux had disposed of land and of its entire herd, and it was using less and less water. Thus, although Mott disliked the MID proposal, he exhorted Miller & Lux to act on it quickly, for by selling land "we are gradually losing strength in our title . . . [and] should bend every effort to dispose of it [surplus waters] before titles have become more clouded through non-use or sale of land."[70]

The sale to MID was never consummated. Heeding the warnings, Miller & Lux applied a number of conditions to the sale of water, including compensation for past and future damage by the SJL&P, the appointment of a water-master to control the reservoirs, and a guarantee that the MID would provide a minimum supply to the firm's croplands even if it had to reduce its own consumption.[71] Miller & Lux also demanded that the MID formally drop all litigation pending against its water rights. Under the 1922 accord, Woolley argued, these suits should have been dropped six years earlier, when the storage district was first established. Instead, they were being used as a club to force the firm to compromise its rights, and they had created "a cloud on the company's title." The MID refused this request, and in May 1930 negotiations ended. Each side vowed to go to court to protect its rights, and each hired additional attorneys to conduct the expected trials: Stephen W. Downey and Farmer for the MID, and Treadwell to join Woolley for Miller & Lux.[72] Miller & Lux would no longer postpone the reckoning when faced with the fading of its legal claims to water. Once again, the courtroom became the forum for resolving economic conflicts.

In July 1930 the MID reactivated its condemnation proceedings against Miller & Lux, but by October the suit was again on hold. Unable to sell bonds or negotiate a bank loan in this depression year, the MID could not raise the money to pay for the water rights it might win in court.[73] Instead, Miller & Lux prosecuted two suits against the MID, both actions to quiet title, one for its own water rights, the other for those of the SJ&KRC&ICo.[74] Such actions could lift the "cloud" hanging over property, but they required the plaintiff to positively assert its own rights. Miller & Lux thus had to specify its riparian and prescriptive rights and present its claim to exclusive property in the power-released waters.[75] In addition, it had to defend against a cross-complaint filed by a number of the SJ&KRC&ICo's customers who asserted even greater rights for the canal company than Miller & Lux would admit or fight for.[76]

In all, this was the very type of litigation the firm had been avoiding. But the pressure of ambitious development projects and poor management, of low cattle prices and high labor costs, had recast Henry Miller's original enterprise. With the bankers in control, the sale and leasing of land replaced ranching and farming, a transformation that endangered the firm's property in water. Miller & Lux had formed mutual companies to administer the water and the private canal systems serving the intensively farmed areas on the west side; however, the mutual companies were paper organizations that only hinted to purchasers of the firm's land that control over the water would eventually lie with them. When selling both irrigated farmland and less-developed tracts, Miller & Lux had reserved ownership of the corresponding water rights, anticipating their separate sale to the San Joaquin storage district. Yet after liquidating its herds in 1930, Miller & Lux had no need for the vast pastures produced on the grasslands by flood irrigation, and it faced the eventual forfeiture of this water. Prescriptive and appropriative rights depended on beneficial use, and even riparian rights might be subject to such a requirement; the 1928 constitutional amendment, adopted in the flurry of criticism following the *Heminghaus* decision, seemed to demand beneficial use of all water claimants alike. Moreover the reservation of water rights was itself of uncertain legality. Riparian rights attached to land and could not be severed from it, so that after the storage district had collapsed, the purchasers of Miller & Lux's land, not the firm itself, might prove to be the legal owners of such waters. The firm's then-mortgaged water rights had to be fixed before these liabilities turned into tangible losses.

The trials began in December 1930, before Judge Charles G. Haines, who had been recruited from the San Diego County bench in the hope of securing an unbiased magistrate.[77] The two suits against the MID, heard in tandem, with evidence being taken over a one-year period, provided a final forum for Miller & Lux to quash the doubts that had haunted its water rights since Harding's 1925 report. With the MID basing many of its arguments on Harding's criticism, Miller & Lux was determined that "every possible acre of riparian land be adjudicated." Although the MID agreed to stipulate that Miller & Lux owned the land in question, the firm had to establish the natural condition and flow of each slough, no matter how small, as it crossed each parcel of land. This process was crucial to establishing the riparian character of land, especially that on the west side of the San Joaquin, where natural conditions had been obscured by extensive development. Miller & Lux also needed to show the artificial addendums to these sloughs to prove the appropriative rights it claimed for the San Luis and other private canal systems. Woolley thus instructed Mott to carefully redraft the earlier maps and profiles, which given the firm's former coolness toward fixing its rights, had ignored numerous sloughs.[78] In the case of the SJ&KRC&ICo, Woolley had to counter Harding's allegation that its right was limited to the water that was in fact put to beneficial use. He directed Mott and Olsen to prepare the historical record of diversions and explanations of any discrepancies it contained; to interview alfalfa farmers who could testify to the actual duty of water in the region; and to utilize soil classifications to find the maximum area that could be planted in alfalfa and other water-guzzling crops. The goal was to secure enough water to optimize future development of the system within the 1,360-cfs right acknowledged by Miller & Lux.[79]

Not only did the firm have to demonstrate the physical reality of its claims, it also had to prove them in law. Key to its arguments, of course, was the general doctrine of riparian rights as applied between appropriators and riparian owners: a riparian was entitled to "the full, ordinary and usual flow of the stream" and could enjoin any upstream taking. An upstream appropriator acquired a right to water only after five years of adverse use, and the MID had at no time diverted any water. This precept of riparianism, which Miller & Lux had imprinted on the public consciousness in *Lux* v. *Haggin* and *Miller & Lux* v. *Madera Canal & Irrigation Company,* had long been central to the firm's control of water. Most recently, the *Herminghaus* decision had underscored the judicial support for this highly unpopular point. The MID based its argument on the 1928 constitutional amendment, which it claimed superseded these earlier decisions, and on notions of efficient use. By limiting all irrigators to a reasonable use of water, MID attorney Farmer argued, the 1928 amendment had truncated Miller & Lux's rights. The most reasonable use was that which produced the greatest value, so the vast quantities of water Miller & Lux used to flood its little-improved grasslands were, by definition, forfeit and available to appropriators, like the MID, that promised more efficient development. Woolley and Treadwell denied this point. Instead, they proposed Samuel Wiel's argument that the 1928 amendment recognized the riparian right to the full flow of the stream and insisted that any other reading violated the Fourteenth Amendment by taking property without paying compensation.[80]

Woolley and Treadwell also gave traditional water doctrine the creative twists needed to safeguard Miller & Lux's complex network of claims on the west side of the San Joaquin. They had to make the law conform to the pattern of economic development. And their efforts to establish the rights of the San Luis system and the claims to the surplus waters of the SJ&KRC&ICo, both of which irrigated large amounts of riparian land, produced tangled layers of argument. To protect the firm's riparian rights, Woolley and Treadwell postulated that the extensive modification (including the damming) of sloughs that Miller & Lux controlled did not change the riparian character of its land. The attorneys then argued that the various weirs and levies had created appropriative rights to the water delivered to this same riparian land because the structures had in fact altered the flow of the river. Such special constructions rested as much on impliction and inference as on any firm body of case law, with Miller & Lux's brief instead referring again and again to the treatise *California Jurisprudence.*[81]

Establishing Miller & Lux's claims to the power-released waters was the ultimate challenge to the forensic ingenuity of the firm's lawyers. While the state supreme court had ruled in *Herminghaus* that storage was a nonriparian use, it had issued no definitive statement on the status of the water returned to the river. The passionate rivalries over river development had engendered conflicting theories to explain the legal status of this water—pronouncing it variously natural water or foreign water or salvaged water—each theory purporting to be the logical outgrowth of existing legal categories, each theory reflecting the economic or ideological goals of its proponents.

The first theory examined was that adopted during the later negotiations with the San Joaquin storage district, holding that the liberated waters became part of the natural flow of the stream. Opening with a lengthy explication of this view excerpted from a brief MID attorney Farmer had written when representing Chowchilla Farms, Woolley and Treadwell presented a string of decisions from California, Colorado, and various eastern states dealing with seepage waters, irrigation runoff, and smaller reservoirs. Such a theory favored Miller & Lux because, as part of the natural flow, the power-released waters fed both Miller & Lux's riparian rights and its appropriations. Presenting the second theory, Woolley and Treadwell reprinted a recent ruling of the Division of Water Rights declaring power-released waters to be foreign waters available for appropriation. Based on the *Horst* decision,[82] this was the same argument that had been raised by the MID in 1921 and adopted by Harding in 1925. Woolley and Treadwell argued that since the MID had applied only to appropriate the waters of the San Joaquin, it had no claim to the power-released water if it was foreign water; Miller

& Lux, on the other hand, had filed to appropriate these specific waters in 1926. The third theory posited that the stored waters were salvaged waters, i.e., waters artificially developed that would otherwise have been lost. As such they were by law the property of the developer, in this case Southern California Edison, which had conveyed them to Miller & Lux.[83]

In a subsequent section, Woolley and Treadwell developed a more particular argument, holding that the stored waters had been jointly appropriated by Miller & Lux and the hydroelectric companies. Unlike most of the earlier explanations of its right to the released water, this argument reinforced the firm's most extreme contention: the stored water was its exclusive property and need not be shared with other riparian owners or with the canal company. Southern California Edison's rights as an appropriator had been recognized in *Herminghaus*. But even some within Miller & Lux worried about proving its claim to be a joint appropriator, since Miller & Lux had not made the original filing to appropriate and the power company's filing had not mentioned irrigation as a potential use. Here Woolley and Treadwell forged a chain of reasoning that linked the two companies through contract law: having been separated from the stream, the water stored in the reservoirs was the personal property of the power company, and it had been transferred to Miller & Lux by contract as compensation for a valuable right; thus, when released into the river, the water was not abandoned, but was being delivered (using the river as a legitimate conduit) to its lawful owner.[84]

In January 1932 Haines began his deliberations, punctuating them with occasional requests for clarifications from both Miller & Lux and the MID. In March he issued his opinion, a tome of some four hundred pages; the procedure of reading it aloud in court took over four days. By and large, it favored Miller & Lux in its interpretations of both facts and law. Haines granted Miller & Lux an injunction protecting its riparian and appropriative rights and limited the MID to the extraordinary flow of the river, which he defined as that above 20,000 cfs as measured at Friant. The SJ&KRC&ICo right was recognized at 1,360 cfs during its peak season, and a monthly flow schedule reflecting the canal company's actual use of the water was established and protected against the MID.

As in many of Miller & Lux's courtroom victories, a judicial commitment to property and the protection of vested rights was decisive. Early in the opinion, Haines explicitly rejected the view, offered by Harding and the state engineer's office, that stored water was foreign water to which no riparian

rights attached. Instead, he ruled that such waters were part of the natural flow of the stream. The question was one of "first impression," where
precedent provided no compelling answer, and Haines's decision reflected
his ideological and political regard for vested owners. To rule otherwise,
Haines explained, would harm "an old community" to favor "some upstart
community."[85] Of course, such a favoring of the newcomers was precisely
what the MID had hoped for when it raised arguments based on the need for
economic development. At the same time, Haines treated generously Miller
& Lux's irrigation facilities and its expansive use of riparian rights. Looking at the firm's established improvements and the complex of claims that
had caused such difficulty in creating the setup for the San Joaquin storage
district, Haines declared that Miller & Lux's damming of sloughs had not
changed the riparian character and rights of the land they crossed. At the
same time, he agreed that such artificial works had also created appropriative rights to the water.[86] Such material improvements, capital investments
in landed property, were to be protected.

Haines rejected the idea that the law and his court should fuel and guide
economic development. The doctrines of reasonable and beneficial use gave
judges broad powers for doing so, and reformers had long advocated that the
courts use them to narrow the hold of riparian owners and to increase access
water. Haines, however, refused to apply restrictive notions of beneficial use
and held that the cultivation of any crop, even grass, was inherently valuable, regardless of how much water was used or of any long-term damage to
the soil. Even the 1928 amendment, with its explicit extension of reasonable
use to riparians, placed no new burden on Miller & Lux. Haines accepted
the argument offered by Samuel Wiel that this amendment simply appended
to the constitution the findings in *Herminghaus* that the natural flooding of
riparian lands was both beneficial and reasonable.[87] In so doing, Haines assumed a division between private and public that separated the marketplace
from the courtroom. Although all water rights decisions, including his own,
affected economic development, Haines rejected the explicitly policy-based
arguments of reformers by implying the neutrality of judicial action. The
laws of economic competition, of private decisions and individual profits
and losses, not those of the courts, should regulate the crops raised and the
water used.[88]

Only on the issue of the deeds reserving riparian rights did Haines rule
against a major Miller & Lux argument. In this instance, Miller & Lux

had argued against long-standing interpretations of riparian doctrine for the purpose of preserving its control of vendable water. Haines noted that riparian water had always been inseparably linked to land and thus found that a completed sale eliminated the firm's riparian claims in favor of the new owner. However, he also noted that neither mere contracts reserving water rights nor deeds to land served by mutual companies could extinguish such rights. Given these qualifications, and because little of the firm's land had been deeded to new owners, this ruling had a limited impact.[89]

In late 1932, as the findings and judgment were being completed, the MID considered appealing the decision. Farmer recommended at least a limited appeal, primarily to challenge Haines's ruling that the damming of sloughs did not affect the riparian character of land. This ruling, he felt, violated *Lux* v. *Haggin* and could impose considerable expense on the MID when it condemned Miller & Lux's rights. Downey and Barnes were more skeptical of the efficacy of continued litigation. Since Miller & Lux could raise additional issues, Barnes feared that an appeal might undermine the few gains the district had achieved through the specification of the firm's riparian and appropriative rights. Believing that the district would get water rights by negotiating a purchase from Miller & Lux, he was unconcerned about the impact of the decision on a condemnation suit. Rather, he worried that further litigation would destroy the district, which lacked the money to take the case to the supreme court. More important, there was strong sentiment within the district, fanned in part by agents of Miller & Lux, against further litigation; if the directors filed an appeal, forces advocating the dissolution of the district might succeed.[90]

In the end, the MID chose to let the Haines judgment stand, only to regret its choice when the state supreme court handed down its ruling in *Gin Chow* v. *Santa Barbara*.[91] In *Gin Chow* the supreme court seemed to apply the 1928 amendment to the ordinary flow of a stream. While both Woolley and Farmer believed that this was only dicta, in Treadwell's view the decision sustained the 1928 amendment as a restriction on riparian rights. In any case, it clearly indicated that the views of the state supreme court were "entirely at variance" with those of Judge Haines. In fact, Farmer felt that had *Gin Chow* preceded the MID case, Haines would have denied an injunction protecting Miller & Lux's riparian rights. Miller & Lux would have been granted only reasonable methods and amounts, not the total volume of water coming to it in a natural state.[92] Although the developed state of Miller & Lux's property distinguished its controversy with the MID from that in *Gin Chow,* Farmer may well have been right. Justice John W. Shenk, who had dissented in the *Herminghaus* decision, authored *Gin Chow;* two years later, in *Peabody* v. *City of Vallejo,* he even more strongly asserted the notion that the 1928 amendment limited riparian rights. Riparian owners, Shenk argued, were allowed only a reasonable use of water, and it was the duty of the courts to determine whether this standard was met.[93] However, because the MID had chosen not to appeal the Haines decision, this reasoning was never applied or tested in the conflict between the MID and Miller & Lux.

While the Haines decision stabilized and protected Miller & Lux's property claims to water, the firm's financial situation was deteriorating. The refinancing scheme of 1925 had been predicated on a growing demand for land and a rising market for crops such as cotton. It had also anticipated the lucrative sale of water rights to the San Joaquin storage district, a transfer that not only would have raised cash but seemingly would have increased both the desirability and price of land in the region. None of this happened. Instead, land values fell, forcing Miller & Lux to readjust its pricing schemes, and the market for water rights withered. While most landowners demanded water storage, improved irrigation facilities, and an increased voice in their administration, they were unwilling to bear the costs of such developments even if they had been able to. Even the committed promoters of the Madera district retreated when they found it impossible to borrow the needed funds in financial markets after the crash of 1929. By 1931 Miller & Lux had sold $20 million of its debt. With land sales at a virtual standstill, it requested a revision of its trust indenture. The original note required that Miller & Lux apply 75 percent of the value of each unit sold (according to the 1916 appraisal) to discharge its debt. But forced to lower prices, to finance sales, and to pay commissions to its land agents, the firm frequently did not net enough cash at the time of purchase to meet this condition. By October 1932 Miller & Lux was in default, unable to pay the interest due its creditors after meeting operating expenses and taxes. It would not begin paying interest until late in 1934, and then only sporadically.[94]

Though formally in default, Miller & Lux continued to operate its ranches and to sell its lands as it had before. Praising the firm's management and blaming its problems on general economic conditions, Miller & Lux's creditors chose not to foreclose and attempt to run the company themselves, but instead formed oversight committees that were represented on the existing board of directors. In this period, Miller & Lux embarked on a new sales campaign that later led to accusations of fraud: it began accepting its own securities at par for the purchase of land. By picking up these securities on the open market, a buyer could obtain a substantial discount. In 1933 the prices of the firm's bonds and notes had dropped to all-time lows of 25 and 14½, respectively.[95] By accepting the notes, Miller & Lux could retire part of its debt, eliminating payments of both interest and principal that were rapidly coming due. The firm also began adjusting its sales contracts with the aid of federal farm mortgage money, realizing much-needed cash when the federal government refinanced those who had purchased its lands. Such refinancing, however, was one of the few New Deal programs the firm endorsed. Fickett charged that other farm legislation, especially the AAA's crop reduction plans, hindered its recovery by inhibiting both the sale of land and the profitable exploitation of the low-cost water and fertile tracts Miller & Lux still controlled.[96]

During the Depression, state and federal action subsumed private efforts at regional water development. While Miller & Lux and other landowners confronted the hostility of the state engineer's office and fumbled their efforts to set up a storage district, the California legislature was exploring ambitious plans to deliver water to the San Joaquin Valley. In 1933 the legislature passed the California Central Valley Project Act, a bill that reflected both the legislature's commitment to irrigation as an economic panacea and its equation of progress with the technological exploitation of resources. As part of a larger program, the state planned to construct a dam at the Friant site and divert the flow of the San Joaquin River to Tulare and Kern counties; the waters of the San Joaquin would be replaced by others from the Sacramento basin. In 1935, when California was unable to pay for the scheme, the federal government took over. The Bureau of Reclamation would construct the Central Valley Project and administer the promise of economic development.[97]

At that point, Miller & Lux, long desirous of selling some of its water rights, lacked the resources and the will for an extensive fight against the government project and the loss of private control it implied. While the firm continued its unfinished actions against upstream users,[98] financial problems limited its ability to operate through the courts. In 1936 twenty-two riparian landowners in Stanislaus County demanded that Miller & Lux, Southern California Edison, and other upstream users compensate them for injuries caused by reservoirs. Miller & Lux feared that an adverse judgment might force it into foreclosure, and it would have been unable to provide the bond required if an appeal were needed. As a result, Southern California Edison, contractually obliged to defend the reservoirs for Miller & Lux, agreed to pay both any judgment and the cost of an appeal to keep the company actively involved in the defense.[99] When confronted with the federal initiative, Miller & Lux filed pro forma protests and assertions of its rights and promptly entered into negotiations.

In 1939 Miller & Lux signed a contract to sell the excess waters flooding its "uncontrolled" grasslands to the federal government. Accepting the Haines decree as defining Miller & Lux's property rights to water, the Bureau of Reclamation paid $2.45 million for the water. This figure was based on the difference in value between the firm's unirrigated, often marginal riparian lands with their rights and access to water and those same lands considered as drylands; it represented damages of $9.00 per acre affected. At the same time, a flow schedule regulating storage at the new Friant reservoir guaranteed irrigation of Miller & Lux's croplands and its "controlled" grasslands (those checked and served by developed sloughs or canals). Miller & Lux and the SJ&KRC&ICo also signed contracts agreeing to accept the replacement waters from the Sacramento basin that would ultimately be delivered at Mendota. The contracts formed the models for subsequent contracts with riparian landowners and ultimately fixed the level of compensation.[100]

In the 1950s the Central Valley Project began delivering water to farmers in the San Joaquin basin. With a massive infusion of taxpayers' money to purchase capitalized water rights and to subsidize construction and operating costs, the project succeeded in expanding storage and irrigation facilities where the privately funded efforts of the storage district and the MID had failed. With regard to water development, state capitalism replaced private enterprise capitalism. Miller & Lux's dominance of water, made possible by its size, wealth, and litigation, was replaced by the control of a government bureaucracy. As the history of the Central Valley Project shows, however, the shift from private to public control produced only limited change. Some who had been excluded gained access to water, but power stayed in the hands of the largest landowners, and under the new system, as under the old, water was expected to be a source of profit for private exploiters of the land.

Miller & Lux's story, set in the West, illuminates broad questions about the relationship between law, economic development, and the distribution of wealth and power. In California and the rest of the arid West, scarcity made water an object of economic competition, a source of rents and profits for those who could command, exploit, and market it. It also became the focus of political and legal conflict. The control of water required not only the technical and financial competence to achieve physical mastery, but also the appropriate legal categories to recognize and legitimize such control. Command was achieved not by physical force or expertise but by gaining the state's recognition and definition of water as property. For Miller & Lux and its rivals, the struggle to frame the laws governing water became a central part of a struggle for wealth, and their efforts illuminate the complex, dialectical interplay between legal and economic power. In this context, legal and economic were simultaneously the same and different, each essential to success, alternately ascending and descending in importance, defying simplistic notions of either the influence of class and wealth over law or of law as an autonomous force in history.

When Miller & Lux began to develop its land, the laws governing water reflected the contingencies of time and culture, not the necessities of place. Riparianism had been adopted casually, even accidentally, when early legislators accepted the "common law" with which they were familiar. No effort was made to consider its application to the environment at hand; adoption was a matter of habit and custom, not forethought or planning. In turn, entrepreneurs invested energy and capital with little concern for legal formalities. The pattern was that of "drift and default," in which a general presumption favored existing notions of contract and the private exploitation of property.[1] Thus miners staked claims to land they did not own and moved water as a matter of need, developing conventions that were later adopted as law. Farmers and cattlemen did the same, digging ditches as suited their particular, immediate requirements. Henry Miller presumed that he owned water because he owned the land through which it flowed, and he proceeded to redirect its course, damming some sloughs and deepening others, draining swamps and irrigating dry pastures, negotiating deals with rivals to develop canals and reservoirs—all to generate profits from the land.

Population growth, economic development, and drought intensified the demand for water, and legal action and legal reform became crucial tools for denying competitors access, for securing and monopolizing the benefits of nature. Different doctrines favored different groups. Riparian rights attached water to the land of those, like Miller & Lux, whose holdings bordered rivers; prior appropriation allowed water to be moved to any location and permitted the irrigation of any land that the technology of ditches could reach; doctrines like reasonable use, beneficial use, and economical use allowed courts and politicians to judge the relative worth of various efforts to limit or expand claims; and any redefinition of property in water could transfer wealth from one individual to another, from some groups in society to others. Competition for scarce resources repeatedly exposed the contradictions in casually adopted legal doctrines, and the material developments that followed the resolution of each legal conflict exposed new cracks in the edifice.

Within this context, the legal system operated with immediate, apparent independence. Despite its wealth, its regional economic power, and its physical control of water, Miller & Lux could not dictate results. Popular agencies—juries, the legislature, or regulatory bureaus—were often hostile to the firm and its legal claims. Juries were a "vexatious" problem because they followed popular notions of justice rather than the letter of the law, and in the eminent domain cases, antimonopoly sentiments repeatedly led to judgments against the company far in excess of the economic worth involved. The legislature responded to popular sentiments by rewriting laws governing water to increase access for new groups seeking to exploit the resource. Administrative agencies like the water commission also seemed friendly to Miller & Lux's opponents. Operating under legislative mandate, the water commission moved the locus of control from the private arena of litigation to a public, political sphere where notions of expertise and efficiency restricted the firm's prerogatives and limited its independence. While Miller & Lux implemented some of the technical improvements suggested by reformers, it was unwilling to have such changes imposed from the outside, especially when someone else would benefit from the savings. Miller & Lux manipulated politicians when it could and worked hard to befriend those in elected positions, sending them Christmas and Thanksgiving turkeys, conducting hunting parties on its ranches, and loaning money to assessors and judges alike, but this activity provided no guarantee that laws would not be modified or enforced independently of the firm's wishes.

Miller & Lux preferred to take its disputes before judges, but even judges were unpredictable and unreliable. Miller & Lux viewed judges as the legal realists did, as figures who based decisions as much on their own views and psychology as on rules dictated by law. Some were infected with the boosterism of the local electorate; some were unfit and "imbecile"; some held antiriparian legal principles that reflected personal experience with irrigation; some were unimaginative, interpreting the law literally although the result was nonsensical. Miller & Lux used its vast size to bring suits in a variety of local, state, and federal courts, always seeking "a fearless court" where the judge was not only free from bias but "able mentally to cope with the ramified problems" of water rights litigation.[2] But even the best of judges, those holding "sound" views of the law, might rule in unexpected ways. Like other branches of the law, water law was laden with contradictions, and the firm's litigation often raised questions about new uses of resources for which precedent and history provided no easy certainty. Opportunities abounded for differing evaluations and answers, and there was no direct, determinant link between power and the outcome of any particular conflict.

Yet while decision making functioned independently of direct influence, the autonomy of the legal system was relative and constrained. With courts taking the main role in formulating California water doctrine, the actions of litigants and their lawyers bound legal evolution to the needs of powerful, private interests. The claims they pursued, the arguments they raised, the courts they selected, as well as the issues they chose to ignore, helped direct the resolution of specific economic conflicts and channeled the flow of doctrinal change. Thus while in some parts of California riparian rights were lost through simple neglect, Miller & Lux's persistent litigation bound the development of the San Joaquin Valley to its riparian claims; and while popular consensus dismissed riparianism as pernicious, Miller & Lux's repeated assertions fixed the doctrine at the core of California water law, expanding the narrow decision in *Lux* v. *Haggin* into a firm precedent that applied even to floodwaters. Similarly, in rate cases, the firm's determination and skillful argument helped transform the mere right to use water granted by riparian doctrine into a water right that was income-earning capital.

Miller & Lux was quite conscious of the role of law in its success and of its ability to direct the evolution of favorable doctrines. In a sense, it viewed the courts and the law as instruments of its economic power. California water law required that the firm be vigilant if it was to control water: legal victories validated its enterprise; defeats forced additional capital expenditures. As a result, it read judges' decisions carefully and appealed cases, however small the material consequences, because of the potential impact of adverse rulings. Working to establish precedents that served its interests and to prevent the development of trends that might harm it, Miller & Lux searched for the most sympathetic venue in which to bring its claims, and it avoided jurists like Erskine Ross who had opposing principles. Similarly, though often quick to bring suits against upstream appropriators, the firm delayed consideration of issues where the outcome or tactical benefits were uncertain. As the status of stored water was debated, Miller & Lux avoided the courts while using the prospect of litigation to extract legal concessions from rival claimants. It waited as long as possible, until its property claims were vested and highly developed, before raising this question of "first impression."

As much as these commonsense legal tactics enhanced Miller & Lux's power over water, legal power depended on economic success, on the ability to compete profitably in the international marketplace. Litigation was costly, and it was the firm's financial success that allowed it to bring the repeated suits that often exhausted its opponents; the extent of its landholdings provided its access to different courts. Similarly, wealth had allowed the firm to prevent the loss of water when reformers rewrote the law. It sponsored the referendum movement that delayed legal change, and was able to invest in additional irrigation systems to meet the requirements of the new statutes. But when the postwar agricultural depression slashed its income, Miller & Lux could not afford such responses. Despite its unchanged physical control of rivers, falling revenues and mounting debt impelled the firm to compromise and form a water storage district rather than pursue the court actions that earlier had given force to its riparian claims. As Miller & Lux faced financial problems, the protection and expansion of its irrigation systems, as well as the move from raising cattle to selling and renting land, required that it give up some of its command over water. In this situation, opponents manipulated Miller & Lux's financial distress, just as Miller & Lux used the threat of litigation, to win access to water. The conflicts over water reflected intraclass competition for a scarce resource universally seen as a source of profit, and while no person or interest group controlled the courts, economic power was an important factor in legal success. Both were prerequisites for the command of water.

Lawyers played a crucial role, for it was their job to mold and win acceptance for legal doctrines that reflected the pattern of material and economic development; frequently the exploitation of water had preceded legal definition of the rights involved. Miller & Lux relied on the basic notion of a contract as a meeting of the minds to develop its canal systems and its use of reservoirs; more than once it contracted to suspend riparian claims in exchange for capital improvements. Such arrangements with the SJ&KRC&ICo, with James Haggin and William Carr, and with Southern California Edison presumed that riparian rights were a legitimate item of exchange, though there was little in the law that addressed the issue. As these presumptions were challenged, the responsibility for bridging the chasm between established doctrine and Miller & Lux's use of water fell to attorneys such as Edward Treadwell and Frank Short. In the conflicts with customers and with other riparians, in the efforts to form a storage district and then to protect the reservoired water, Short and Treadwell presented new concepts of water rights. Starting from general premises of contract and property, they brought together railroad and land law, hydrology and public policy, the recent decisions of western courts and those of antebellum eastern jurists to contrive plausible and persuasive arguments. Pragmatic, yet broadly concerned with the legal and political issues of the period, they saw their work as serving not only the interests of Miller & Lux but also the good of the nation.

While the lawyer's prism refracted the material conflicts over water into legal categories, the lens of ideology refocused them. Ideology linked the private demands of Miller & Lux and the issues of western water law to broader changes in the capitalist economy and mediated the relationship between legal doctrine and material development. From the 1880s through the 1930s, a time when workers, farmers, and small proprietors challenged the growing concentration of industrial and financial capital, the nation's highest courts were dominated by a concern to protect property. Doctrines of liberty of contract and substantive economic due process helped protect big business against popular assaults as classes battled for power and position within the restructured political economy of corporate capitalism. Formalist reasoning, with its constant recitation of prior decisions, rationalized such rulings by fostering an image of courts bound by the dictates of an autonomous law. While Miller & Lux's opponents appealed to alternative strands of U.S. legal ideology—that the law should fuel economic development, that it should encourage the most efficient use of resources, that it should protect a just market to prevent monopoly and promote individual economic opportunity—Miller & Lux's interests were tied to the ascendant notions of protecting property. Repeatedly, it linked the criticism of riparianism to more general assaults on the rights of ownership and to the threat of social upheaval posed by Grangers and Populists, by trade unions and Socialists. Miller & Lux's ability to place its claims within the framework of the dominant ideology was at the heart of its success as a litigator and its impact on California water doctrine.

The role of property-centered ideology is illustrated by the actions of the California Supreme Court. While the courts in many other states modified riparianism and limited its impact, the California court was the mainstay of this doctrine and the protector of Miller & Lux's most extravagant notions. From its 1886 decision in *Lux* v. *Haggin* through the *Herminghaus* decision of 1926, the California Supreme Court endorsed the riparian right as a property right to the full flow of a stream. To the original McKinstry majority, the protection of property, including property in water, was the key to economic development. In contrast, prior appropriation offered no panacea for overcoming primitive conditions and in the circumstances was a call for confiscation that could not be endorsed. Later judges like Lucien Shaw and M. C. Sloss, who expanded the concept of police power to accept some Progressive reforms, continued to adhere to the property-centered view of water.[3] As Shaw explained, riparian rights became vested with the adoption of the common law in 1850; at that point, the "important public policy of protecting the rights of private property became paramount and controlling." This policy was responsible for "the remarkable progress and development" of the nation.[4] While Shaw's sense of history was flawed, his ideological paradigm conveyed authority.

The California court was not unwilling to innovate, and at times it conceded to the public demand for expanded access to water, but it generally did so only when such concessions did not contravene property rights. The same judiciary that accepted riparian rights, for example, radically rewrote the doctrines governing underground waters.[5] In litigation involving private canal companies like the one in Madera County, it noted that whenever possible courts should favor public utilities; and in both *Fresno Flume* and *Gallatin* v. *Corning*, the court limited riparian assertions by presuming in favor of innovators and against waste. In fact, reformers seized upon these two decisions to support their call for police-power restrictions on riparians. Yet until the 1930s their influence was limited; the crucial factor was the existence of real property claims. As Miller & Lux's attorneys had noted at the time of the rulings, in *Fresno Flume* and *Gallatin*, the courts had found no property damage.[6] But in most of the instances where antiriparians, irrigators, and boosters tried to apply such arguments to Miller & Lux, the damages to Miller & Lux's irrigated pastures were clear and palpable. The result was a string of decisions that further established riparianism as a rule of law.

In turn, the consistency and coherence required by the idea of rule of law constrained the short-term goals of powerful interests. Twice Miller & Lux attempted to protect the SJ&KRC&ICo against upstream riparian irrigators by calling on the supreme court to recognize the priority of an established public use over the private claims of riparians. The court rejected the plea. Despite popular support for such a ruling, the court refused to revise existing tenets that gave all riparians a property interest in the current and future use of water. The repeated recognition of riparianism as a coherent body of rights prevailed over the demands of both public and private interests. Miller & Lux was aware of the complications posed by the argument for public use and had raised it more to quiet the complaints of the SJ&KRC&ICo's rebellious customers than with an expectation, or even a desire, of victory. Ironically, while opponents insisted that riparianism promoted monopoly, the consistent application of the law encouraged access to water.

While an ideological and legal commitment to property rights protected riparian claims, riparianism itself clashed with dominant views of the role of property in a market economy. Riparianism protected the concurrent and coequal entitlement of all along a river to enjoy and use water; while this had been expanded in California to include the right to irrigate, traditionally the riparian owner could not transfer or rent water as a commodity separate from land. Yet throughout the nation the economic meaning of property was being expanded from a right to use some physical asset to a right to command earning power, and notions of liberty served to elevate the individual freedom to buy, sell, and contract over the kind of shared entitlements embodied in riparianism.[7] In the arid West, where scarcity created a market for water, riparianism complicated the transformation of water from use value into exchange value. The network of overlapping rights and interwoven benefits made it difficult to monetize water claims for easy transfer and complicated the private development of the large-scale, capitalized irrigation projects that many favored.

The contradictions embedded in considering riparian rights as property rights lay at the heart of many incongruities in Miller & Lux's legal efforts. The firm's various contracts with SJ&KRC&ICo, Southern California Edison, and others for the development of irrigation facilities had presumed that water rights were an independently vendable commodity, and in the rate case, Miller & Lux had won judicial recognition of water rights as income-earning capital. But at the same time, Miller & Lux frequently worked to prevent the monetary or physical measurement of its riparian property. Riparian claims were set up as negatives, valuable because of the water itself, but valued ultimately because they allowed owners to stop anyone from interfering with the flow of water. In case after case, the firm simply asserted that its rights were of immense value, fearing that to further define them would merely limit them, and before the 1928 amendment, its assertions were enough to enjoin rivals. However, when Miller & Lux agreed to sell some of its riparian rights to the proposed San Joaquin water storage district, the amorphous, shifting nature of water as property created problems, problems in which legal interpretations, engineering decisions, and financial concerns were intimately intertwined. The eminent domain suit against James Stevinson had sputtered along over the valuation of Stevinson's property in riparian waters, and the negotiations with the storage district floundered on the difficulties of measuring and justifying the price of such legal rights.

Underlying the legal debate over the value of riparian rights was a political struggle over who should bear the costs and risks of economic development. Ultimately, the federal government took over projects, like the storage district's Friant reservoir, that private capital had rejected as too risky and uncertain. Focusing on the role of the environment in history, Donald Worster has argued that the struggle to transform the West's natural condition in fact transformed its social landscape. Westerners, like the ancient Egyptians and others who tried to control water, created a "hydraulic society" in which the interests of individuals gave way to a hierarchical, centralized power that flowed from the command of water.[8] But command over resources emerged

from the broad interplay of economic and legal power; in the San Joaquin
Valley, the move to centralize control came not from those who had water,
but from those who lacked it. While the desire for reservoirs was a product of
the arid environment, the demand that the government build them reflected
the ever-present strand of American ideology that expected the state to guarantee economic growth and economic justice; the demand met with success
as power over the economy became centralized in the national government.

Under the terms of laissez-faire capitalism, the development of new industries involves speculation and a commitment to the future with no guarantee
of gain. Henry Miller had engaged in this type of gamble. Confident of the
benefits of irrigated pastures, he had invested in canals before they were
commonplace. The investment proved profitable as long as low wages subsidized ditching and until the influx of cattle raised on less capitalized land
forced down prices and revenues. Having launched his enterprise as an individual effort, Miller was suspicious of state interference and decried efforts
to regulate the use of water, seeing regulation as harmful to enterprise. Miller
& Lux and its lawyers rejected both populist political reforms and the statist
views of Progressives like Roosevelt in favor of the property-centered, judicial conservatism of Taft. By protecting property and abiding by the rule of
law, the courts seemed to provide a forum for resolving disputes that both
recognized and reflected the role of private initiative.

Many of Miller & Lux's opponents, especially the customers of the SJ&
KRC&ICo and the promoters of the Madera Irrigation District, advocated
another model of economic development and a different role for law. The
United States had a long tradition of state aid to enterprise. Canals and
railroads especially had benefited from the argument that economic development was one of the responsibilities of the state, that both the commonwealth
and the individual citizen would benefit if the state promoted and subsidized
costly but beneficial projects.[9] When Miller & Lux's opponents asserted the
public interest in appropriation, condemned the losses inherent in earthen
canals, and argued that efficient use be imposed, they were demanding that
the courts and the legislature aid their irrigation schemes, a demand seldom
far below the surface of their conflicts with Miller & Lux.

The constant rejection of eminent domain makes this struggle for subsidy clear. In California, irrigation companies and irrigation districts were
empowered to confiscate water. Eminent domain had been devolved on such
enterprises to encourage the development of water and to ease the transfer

of water from one group to another. Starting in the 1880s, the California Supreme Court had directed those proposing more profitable uses of the state's streams to exploit this option, but eminent domain was repeatedly ignored. Miller & Lux employed eminent domain in its struggle against the Stevinson injunction, but the hostility to private utilities that emerged in the Progressive era restricted its usefulness as a tool for easing economic development. Fear of debt and an unwillingness to take risks were an even more serious limit. Miller & Lux's challengers, from the Madera Canal Company to the MID and the numerous irrigation districts formed and dissolved on the west side of the valley, backed away from encumbering their land to purchase water rights. Their ambitious schemes to turn deserts into gardens required vast inputs of capital, and they wanted the courts to lessen their costs. If riparian rights had been rejected in favor of prior appropriation, if riparian rights had not been extended to floodwaters, these boosters could have taken water that Miller & Lux controlled without charge. Likewise, if the courts, the legislature, and the water commission had applied strict notions of reasonable or economical use, they would have reduced the need to compensate riparian owners. New reservoirs and canals would have received a subsidy at the expense of the owners of riparian property.

In the mid-nineteenth century such arguments were often successful. Courts frequently interpreted the rules of property, including those applying to water, to benefit transportation and manufacturing enterprises; even Chief Justice John Marshall, famed as the guardian of vested rights, condoned state actions that transferred property from one group to another when he refused to apply the Fifth Amendment to states.[10] By the turn of the century, such actions were less favored. The federal government aided overseas enterprises with its imperialist ventures, but at home the efforts of Grangers and others to regulate the recipients of public favor prompted businessmen and jurists to draw sharper lines between public and private property.[11] Social Darwinism and laissez-faire jurisprudence discouraged direct state aid, although the judicial attacks on striking workers and trade unions amounted to another kind of subsidy. Despite the political power of water reformers who marshaled antimonopoly rhetoric and appeals to the public interest behind their calls to change the law, the California court was not persuaded. Judicial interpretation did not become the avenue for promoting new, untested enterprises.

The subsidy that was granted came not through legal modification of rights, but in the form of cash. During the Great Depression, support swung back to the notion that government was responsible for the economic well-being of all citizens, and the responsibility moved from state and local governments to the national government. Agriculture came under federal supervision, as did labor relations, and in the San Joaquin Valley, the federal government assumed responsibility for the proposed state water plan, creating the Central Valley Project. The U.S. Bureau of Reclamation—in other words, the taxpayers—bought the rights to water that Miller & Lux had offered to the storage district and to the MID; the bureau built the reservoirs each had planned but could not finance. Under the Cental Valley Project, a reservoir at Friant provided water to the Madera Irrigation District, and the Kern-Friant Canal transported the bounty of the San Joaquin southward to Kern County, where Miller and Haggin had fought their early battle. Water from the Sacramento basin flowed from behind Shasta Dam through the Delta-Mendota Canal to supply the purchasers of Miller & Lux's land, the customers of the SJ&KRC&ICo, the irrigators of Stanislaus County, and the successors to the claims of Stevinson and James, among others, along the San Joaquin. While the first water arrived in the San Joaquin Valley only in 1951, by the 1970s the Central Valley Project supplied water to 2 million acres, a quarter of which had lain within the failed San Joaquin River Water Storage District. Irrigators who would have paid all the costs of a local project paid less than 20 percent of the cost of the federal system.[12]

Today, four decades after the opening of the Friant reservoir, westerners still complain about water shortages and waste. While some search for additional sources of water, many reformers condemn government control and call for changes in the law. Market mechanisms are the new panacea. Privatization and the sale of water to the highest bidder, they say, will enlarge the pie of available resources and provide incentives for cooperation and mutual solutions to shortage. And law should recognize the exchange value of water as a commodity to expedite its transfer.[13] In the sixty years covered by this study, the irrigation of the San Joaquin Valley advanced through private investment. Water law was an arena of economic competition as entrepreneurs strove to transform into property a resource made valuable by scarcity. The rules for distributing water evolved within a legal system that favored private initiative, private economic power, and private property. However, conflict, not cooperation, abounded, and many investors shunned the large projects taken for granted by current advocates of market mechanisms. Proposing more profitable uses of water, the newer agricultural capitalists of the period asked that the law and the state aid their enterprise by limiting private property rights. Today, the demand is different, but the goal is the same. The laws governing resources are inexorably linked to economic power. Privatization, like the earlier call for government action, is but a mechanism to transfer wealth, another call to subsidize one group of claimants at the expense of another.

NOTES

1. This call has been made most forcefully by James Willard Hurst, whose book *Law and Economic Growth: The Legal History of the Lumber Industry in Wisconsin, 1836–1915* (Cambridge: Harvard Univ. Press, 1964) laid the foundation for all studies of this sort. Proponents of Critical Legal Studies have rancorously attacked the work of Hurst, Lawrence M. Friedman, and others in the law and society movement, criticizing both the methodology and the interpretation of the role of law espoused by members of this group, but more recently even CLS has called for more "empirical" studies to provide answers to the theoretical questions. See Robert W. Gordon, "Critical Legal History," *Stanford Law Review* 36 (1984): 57–125, and David M. Trubek, "Where the Action Is: Critical Legal Studies and Empiricism," ibid.: 575–622.

2. Hurst's *Law and Economic Growth* (see n. 1) focused on Wisconsin, as did the work of many of his students; Morton Horwitz's *The Transformation of American Law 1780–1860* (Cambridge: Harvard Univ. Press, 1977) and the works of many other legal historians look primarily at Massachusetts.

3. Robert Glass Cleland and Osgood Hardy, *March of Industry* (Los Angeles: Powell Publishing, 1929), pp. 57–132; quotation from Frank Norris, *The Octopus* (1901; reprint, New York: Airmont Publishing, 1969), p. 337.

4. Edward F. Treadwell, *The Cattle King, A Dramatized Biography* (New York: Macmillan, 1931), pp. 28–61, quotation on p. 57. Treadwell was Miller's attorney; his account is uncritical, even laudatory, but provides a good picture of the scope of Miller's early enterprises.

5. Treadwell, *Cattle King*, p. 58; Paul W. Gates, "Adjudication of Spanish–Mexican Land Claims in California, *Huntington Library Quarterly* 21 (1958): 99–130; idem, "Pre–Henry George Land Warfare in California," ibid., 46 (1967): 121–48; Paul S. Taylor, "Foundations of California Rural Society," ibid., 24 (1945): 139–61; Leonard Pitt, *Decline of the Californios: A Social History of the Spanish-Speaking Californians* (Berkeley and Los Angeles: Univ. of California Press, 1966).

6. The Swamp Land Act was wantonly abused in California. Settlers were allowed to select swamplands on unsurveyed land, thus leaving the determination of what lands were actually overflowed to the claimants themselves. The law also set very liberal terms, charging only $1.00 per acre and allowing purchase on credit with only 20 percent down, the balance payable in five years. At the time that allegations of abuse were investigated, Miller & Lux had reportedly acquired more than 80,000 acres under this law. Paul W. Gates, *History of Public Land Law Development* (Washington,

D.C.: Government Printing Office, 1968), p. 327; idem, "Public Land Disposal in California," *Agricultural History* 49 (1975): 161–64.

7. Memoranda concerning lands filed on by F. A. Hyde for our a/c—Monterey County, Letterbook, carton 710, Miller & Lux Papers, Bancroft Library, University of California, Berkeley; Miller & Lux (Bolton) to D. Monroe, 15 May 1887, ibid.; Miller & Lux to H. G. Tanner, 25 August 1887, ibid.; Miller & Lux to F. A. Hyde, 5 September 1887, ibid.; Miller & Lux to M. T. Sickal, 26 August 1887, ibid.; John H. Bolton to Tanner, 10, 12, 14, 21 September 1887, 30 September 1887, ibid.; Miller & Lux (JLN) to D. Monroe, 7, 13, 29 February 1887, 20 March 1887, ibid.; Notice of Hearing, 13 November 1914, *United States* v. *Henry Miller* (U.S. Land Office, Vale, Ore., no. 01938-93), carton 488, Miller & Lux Papers; Decision of Register and Receiver, 22 July 1915, ibid.; Brief for Defendant, ibid.; Consual and Heltman to Edward F. Treadwell, 1 February 1916, ibid.; *United States* v. *Hyde*, 132 F. 545 (1904), 199 U.S. 62 (1905), 145 F. 393 (1906); San Francisco *Examiner*, 22, 29 August 1917; Treadwell, *Cattle King*, p. 60.

8. Autobiographical Statement of Henry Miller (dictated in 1891), Bancroft Library; Gates, "Public Land Disposal," pp. 171–73. For a list of the partnership's major landholdings in 1892, see *Jesse S. Potter* v. *Henry Miller, et al*, case no. 37,133 (34,056), Superior Court of San Francisco, Miller & Lux Papers.

9. Gates, "Public Land Disposal," pp. 159–78; Paul W. Gates, "Corporate Farming in California," in Ray Allen Billington, ed., *People of the Plains and Mountains* (Westport, Conn.: Greenwood Press, 1973), pp. 146–74.

10. Treadwell, *Cattle King*, pp. 280–81; Transcript of Record 3: 1066, 1084, 1158–59, *United States* v. *Nickel;* San Francisco *Call*, 11, 17, 19, 23 June 1908. The Miller & Lux Papers are filled with correspondence and invoices dealing with the firm's national sales of its products.

11. William A. Sullivan to R. F. Mogan, 28 May 1919, carton 464, Miller & Lux Papers; Miller & Lux to Holders of First Mortgage Bonds, 5 February 1918, box: General Correspondence 1918, January–March, 16f–58, Miller & Lux Papers; Alfred D. Chandler, *The Visible Hand: The Managerial Revolution in American Business* (Cambridge: Harvard Univ. Press, 1977), p. 512; Robert C. Fellmuth, *Politics of Land: Ralph Nader's Study Group Report on Land Use in California* (New York: Grossman Publishers, 1973), p. 10.

12. Donald Worster, *Rivers of Empire: Water, Aridity, and the Growth of the American West* (New York: Pantheon Books, 1985).

13. For an example of the court's early reasoning, see the decisions in *Conger* v. *Weaver*, 6 Cal 548 (1856) and *Crandall* v. *Woods*, 8 Cal 136 (1857). Samuel C. Wiel, "Public Policy in Western Water Decisions," *California Law Review* (1912–13): 11–26; idem, *Water Rights in Western States*, 3d ed., 2 vols. (San Francisco: Bancroft-Whitney, 1911) 1:97–101, 130–33; Charles W. McCurdy, "Stephen J. Field and Public Land Law Development in California, 1850–1866: A Case Study of Judicial Resource Allocation in Nineteenth-Century America," *Law and Society Review* 10 (1976): 253–63; Gordon Miller, "Shaping California Water Law, 1781 to 1928," *Southern California*

Quarterly 55 (1973): 9–42; Donald Pisani, *From Family Farm to Agribusiness: The Irrigation Crusade in California and the West, 1850–1931* (Berkeley and Los Angeles: Univ. of California Press, 1984); Robert G. Dunbar, *Forging New Rights in Western Waters* (Lincoln: Univ. of Nebraska Press, 1983).

14. See Frank W. Munger, Jr., "Commercial Litigation in West Virginia State and Federal Courts, 1870–1940," *American Journal of Legal History* 30 (1986): 344.

CHAPTER I

1. In the United States this doctrine changed throughout the nineteenth century to accommodate the needs of economic growth. Whereas water law had originally precluded any use of water that might lead to diminution of the flow, by midcentury usages such as damming for mills, drainage, and irrigation were allowed. The requirement that the flow be maintained was no longer a static concept to prevent the use of water but was applied to prevent monopoly; it allowed competitive development by permitting the use of water by all entitled to it. See Morton Horwitz, "The Transformation in the Conception of Property in American Law, 1780–1860," *University of Chicago Law Review* 40 (1972–73): 248–90. The development of American riparian doctrine and the possibilities of riparianism as a solution for modern water problems are explored in T. E. Lauer, "Reflections on Riparianism," *Missouri Law Review* 35 (1970): 1–25.

2. Robert L. Kelley, *Gold versus Grain: The Hydraulic Mining Controversy in California's Sacramento Valley* (Glendale, Calif.: A. A. Clarke, 1959).

3. Gates, *History of Public Land Law* (see intro., n. 6), p. 327; Transcript on Appeal 5: 64–97, *Lux* v. *Haggin*, 69 Cal 255 (1886); Argument of Hall McAllister, p. 11, *Lux* v. *Haggin*, ibid.

4. Wallace Morgan, *History of Kern County, California* (Los Angeles: Historic Record Co., 1914), p. 99; William Harland Boyd, *A California Middle Border: The Kern River Country, 1772–1880* (Richardson, Tex.: Havilah Press, 1972), p. 104; Treadwell, *Cattle King* (see intro., n. 4), pp. 78–80.

5. The members of the association included Cox and Clarke (with 14,520 acres of land), John H. Reddington (13,283 acres), George Cornwall (8,000 acres), L. H. Bonstell (1,920 acres), Horatio B. Livermore (22,541 acres), Horatio Stebbins (1,280 acres), and, of course, Miller & Lux (36,644 acres). They owned in total 98,188 acres of land in the Buena Vista Swamp and Kern River area. By 1888, many of the original landowners had sold out to Miller & Lux. Reporter's Transcript, pp. 25–33, *Title Insurance Company* v. *Miller & Lux*, Superior Court of Kern County (December, 1913) (no. 7093), Miller & Lux Papers; Transcript on Appeal 1: 26–27, 2: 181–82, 259, 309, 453–54, *Lux* v. *Haggin*, 69 Cal 255 (1886).

6. *Kern County Californian*, 16 April 1881, 14 May 1881.

7. Isaac F. Marcosson, *Anaconda* (New York: Dodd, Mead, 1957), pp. 34–35; David Lavender, *The Great Persuader* (Garden City, N.Y.: Doubleday, 1970), pp. 188, 191–

92, 225, 311; Rodman Paul, *Mining Frontiers of the Far West* (New York: Holt, Rinehart, 1963), pp. 147, 180, 185.

8. The first tract acquired by Haggin was part of the Gates tract, first owned by Isaac E. Gates of New York and Senator William M. Stewart of Nevada. The Kern County *Gazette* reported in 1877 that Stewart had received the land as a fee from the railroad and then was forced to unload it when the Crédit Mobilier investigation began. Margaret A. Cooper, "Land, Water and Settlement in Kern County, California, 1850–1890," M.A. thesis, University of California, Berkeley, 1954, pp. 76–77; Norman Berg, *A History of Kern County Land Company*, 32d Annual Publication (Bakersfield, Calif.: Kern County Hist. Soc. 1971), p. 6.

9. Gates, "Public Land Disposal (see intro., n. 6), 173–74; Cooper, "Land, Water and Settlement," p. 145; *United States v. Haggin*, in *Digest of the Decisions of the Department of the Interior Relating to Public Lands* 12: 34–42; General Land Office, *Report of the Secretary of the Interior, 1881*, 47th Cong., 1st sess., in *House Executive Documents*, vol. 9, no. 1, pt. 4, v. 1, pp. 35–36. The registrar gave Haggin the books, allowing him to reserve the sections he wanted before sales were opened to the public.

10. "Report of the Works and Practice of Irrigation in Kern County," Appendix B to *Report of the State Engineer to the Legislature of California, 1880*, in *Appendix to the Journals of the Senate and Assembly*, 23d sess., vol. 5, pp. 71, 78–79, 113.

11. James Ben Ali Haggin, *The Desert Lands of Kern County* (San Francisco: C. H. Street, 1877); see also articles supporting the Desert Land Act and Haggin's plan in *Courier-Californian*, 1 March 1877, 3 May 1877; and Kern County *Californian*, 23 April 1881. For a discussion of western attitudes toward outside investment, see Gene M. Gressley, *West by East: The American West in the Gilded Age*, Charles Redd Monograph, no. 1 (Provo, Utah: Brigham Young Univ. Press, 1972).

12. Transcript on Appeal, passim, *Lux v. Haggin;* Treadwell, *Cattle King*, pp. 81–84, 88–89.

13. Oral Argument of Hall McAllister, pp. 11–14, *Lux v. Haggin*, 69 Cal 255 (1886).

14. Oral Argument of John Garber, pp. 3, 65, *Lux v. Haggin*, ibid.

15. Gates, "Adjudication of Spanish–Mexican Land Claims (see intro, n. 5), 213–36; Paul W. Gates, "California's Embattled Settlers," *California Historical Society Quarterly* 46 (1967): 121–48; Taylor, "Foundations of California Rural Society" (see intro., n. 5), 139–61; Pisani, *From Family Farm to Agribusiness* (see intro., n. 13), pp. 191–249; Walton Bean, *California, An Interpretive History* (New York: McGraw-Hill, 1973), pp. 176–98; Ira B. Cross, *History of the Labor Movement in California* (Berkeley: Univ. of California Press, 1935); George B. Miller, *Railroads and Granger Laws* (Madison: Univ. of Wisconsin Press, 1971); Harry N. Scheiber, "Race, Radicalism, and Reform: Historical Perspectives on the 1879 California Constitution," *Hastings Constitutional Law Quarterly* 17 (1989): 35–80.

16. *Courier-Californian*, 10 May 1877, 11 September 1879; Kern County *Gazette*, 19 July 1879; Haggin, *Desert Lands*, pp. 25–27. Brundage had been elected judge on a reform platform; see Cooper, "Land, Water and Settlement in Kern County," p. 166.

17. Findings and Conclusions, Transcript on Appeal 4: 181–82, 186, 191–92, *Lux* v. *Haggin*.

18. Ibid. 4: 192.

19. Oral Argument of Hall McAllister, p. 15, *Lux* v. *Haggin*.

20. Transcript on Appeal, I: 28–30, *Lux* v. *Haggin*.

21. *Lux* v. *Haggin*, 4 P. 919, 926 (1884).

22. *Lux* v. *Haggin*, 4 P. at 929; J. Edward Johnson, *History of the Supreme Court Justices of California*, 2 vols. (San Francisco: Bender-Moss, 1963), 1: 130.

23. The water statutes at issue were sections 1410 and 1422 of title 8 of part 4, division 2 of the Civil Code, as follows: Section 1410. "The right to the use of running water flowing in a river or stream, or down a canyon or ravine, may be acquired through appropriation." Sec. 1422. "The rights of riparian proprietors are not affected by the provisions of this title." Sections 1411 through 1421 detailed the manner in which an appropriation could be made. Reprinted in *Lux* v. *Haggin*, 69 Cal 255 368–70 (1886).

24. *Lux* v. *Haggin*, 4 P. at 930–31.

25. Treadwell, *Cattle King*, pp. 87–88.

26. Paul, *Mining Frontiers*, pp. 172–73.

27. Section 9 of this law pertained to water, as follows: "Whenever, by priority of possession, rights to the use of water for mining, agricultural, manufacturing or other purposes, have vested and accrued, and the same are recognized and acknowledged by the local customs, laws and decisions of courts, the possessors and owners of such vested rights shall be maintained and protected in the same; and the right of way for the construction of ditches and canals for the purposes herein specified is acknowledged and affirmed; but whenever any person, in the construction of any ditch or canal, injures or damages the possession of any settler on the public domain, the party committing such injury or damage shall be liable to the party injured for such injury or damage." Wiel, *Water Rights*, pp. 106–8.

28. Petition for Rehearing, Steward and Herrin, attorneys, pp. 8, 14–15, 71, *Lux* v. *Haggin*, 69 Cal 255 (1886).

29. *Lux* v. *Haggin*, 69 Cal 255, 261 (1886). See also Eric T. Freyfogle, "*Lux* v. *Haggin* and the Common Law Burdens of Modern Water Law," *University of Colorado Law Review* 57 (1986): 485–525.

30. *Lux* v. *Haggin*, 69 Cal at 312–13.

31. Ibid., at 379.

32. Ibid., at 372–75 (quotation at 375).

33. Ibid., at 379. In his argument McKinstry stressed the constitutional relationship between the federal and state governments. The states could not legislate in a manner that interfered with federal powers or rights, including property rights. The issue was treated very differently in states like Colorado, which rejected riparian rights in favor of prior appropriation. See discussion in chap. 4 and Wiel, *Water Rights* 1:185–94.

34. Although this was the law, it was often not carried out because riparian proprietors in many cases did not sue to protect their water rights. Miller, "Shaping California Water Law" (see intro., n. 13), p. 25.

35. Gates, "Public Land Disposal," pp. 162–66.

36. Transcript on Appeal 1: 28–30, *Lux* v. *Haggin;* Berg, *Kern County Land Company*, pp. 1–2; Morgan, *Kern County*, pp. 54, 57; Boyd, *Middle Border*, p. 92; Cooper, "Land, Water and Settlement," pp. 88–90; *People ex rel Love* v. *Center,* decision of superior court, 1878, Bancroft Library, University of California, Berkeley; "An Act to provide for determining the rights of certain parties in certain swamp and overflowed lands in Fresno and Kern Counties," approved March 20, 1878. According to Cooper, the suit, which clouded title to more than 40,000 acres of land, was instigated by Haggin, who hoped to acquire the land in question if it reverted back to the state.

37. *Lux* v. *Haggin,* 69 Cal at 431.

38. Ibid., at 439.

39. Ibid., at 312–13.

40. Contract and Agreement between Henry Miller and others of the first part and James B. Haggin and others of the second part, 28 July 1888, Bancroft Library; Henry Miller to W. B. Carr, 1 July 1887, Letterbook, carton 710, Miller & Lux Papers; Treadwell, *Cattle King*, p. 94.

41. Figures compiled from Kern County assessor's rolls by William D. Lawrence, "Henry Miller and the San Joaquin Valley," M.A. thesis, University of California, Berkeley, 1933, p. 60.

42. Sheridan Downey, *They Would Rule the Valley* (San Francisco: n.p., 1947), p. 91; Berg, *Kern County Land Company*, p. 20.

43. "Agriculture by Irrigation," in *Eleventh Census of the United States, 1890*, vol. 5, part 2; *Thirteenth Census of the United States, 1910*, Abstract of the Census with a Supplement for California.

44. Arthur Maass and Raymond L. Anderson, *. . . and the Desert Shall Rejoice: Conflict, Growth, and Justice in Arid Environments* (Cambridge: MIT Press, 1978), pp. 228–29; Wiel, "Public Policy" (see intro., n. 13), p. 25; Lucien Shaw, "The Development of the Law of Waters in the West," *California Law Review* 10 (1922): 455–56.

45. Nickel to Charles Frohman, Kern River & Los Angeles Electric Power Company, 29 July 1902, HEH 9086, box 95, H. E. Huntington Papers, Huntington Library, San Marino, California; H. W. O'Melveny to Henry E. Huntington, 16 June 1904, HEH 7841, box 112, ibid. For a history of the various names under which these companies appeared and filed claims, see Frederick Hall Fowler, "Hydraulic Power Systems of California and their Extension into Oregon and Nevada," U.S. Geological Survey, Water Supply Paper no. 493 (1923). For a brief account of Huntington's enterprise, see William B. Fredericks, "A Metropolitan Entrepreneur Par Excellence: Henry E. Huntington and the Growth of Southern California, 1898–1927," *Business History Review* 63 (1989): 329–55.

46. O'Melveny to Huntington, 16 June 1904, HEH 7841, box 112, Huntington Papers. O'Melveny would later describe J. Leroy Nickel, who conducted some of the negotiations for Miller & Lux, as "insufferable in his disdain and assurance and ridicule" of the power company's ever being able to divert the waters of the Kern. William W. Clary, *History of the Law Firm of O'Melveny and Myers, 1885–1965* (Los Angeles: n.p., 1966), 1:272–74. R. F. Houghton, the attorney working with the cattle companies, was described as treating O'Melveny with contempt as well.

47. R. E. Houghton to Nickel, 5 March 1907, carton 9, Miller & Lux Papers.

48. Ibid.

49. Houghton and Houghton to Frank Short, 5 October 1906, General Correspondence, 1906, May–Dec, G–So, Miller & Lux Papers; Short to Nickel, 21 August 1906, ibid.

50. One second-foot is the flow of water equal to 1 cubic foot per second (cfs). Under the custom employed in California, a continuous flow of 1 cfs over twelve hours equals 1 acre-foot of water, which in turn is the volume of water required to cover 1 acre of land 1 foot deep. That volume equals 43,560 cubic feet of water or, under the customary relationship, 43,200 cubic feet.

51. Frank H. Short to Charles W. Willard, 31 October 1906, General Correspondence 1906, May–December, G–So, Miller & Lux Papers.

52. Nickel to Short, 7 July 1906, carton 9, Miller & Lux Papers.

53. Nickel to Isaac Bird, 4 January 1908, carton 18, Miller & Lux Papers.

54. Nickel to Short, 12 October, 1906, General Correspondence, 1906, May–December, G–So, Miller & Lux Papers.

55. Nickel to Page, McCutcheon, & Knight, 21 June 1907, carton 10, Miller & Lux Papers.

56. Houghton & Houghton to Nickel, 2 November 1906, carton 3, Miller & Lux Papers.

57. Testimony of Frank Clare, Reporter's Transcript, p. 488, *Union Colonization Company* v. *Madera Canal and Irrigation Company*, 179 Cal 774 (1919) (cited hereafter as *Union C.* v. *Madera*); Testimony of Isaac Bird, Reporter's Transcript, p. 206, ibid.; Affidavit of J. Leroy Nickel (February 13, 1905), Transcript on Appeal, pp. 241–43, *Miller & Lux* v. *Madera Canal and Irrigation Company*, 155 Cal 59 (1909).

58. Brief for Respondent, Frank Short, attorney (1906), pp. 2–6, *Miller & Lux* v. *Madera Canal and Irrigation Company*, 155 Cal 59; *Miller & Lux* v. *Madera Canal and Irrigation Company*, 155 Cal 59, 67 (1909); for an account of the earliest trial, see *California Pastoral and Agricultural Company* v. *Madera Canal and Irrigation Company*, 167 Cal 78 (1914). (These decisions are cited hereafter as *Miller & Lux* v. *Madera* and as *CP&A* v. *Madera*.)

59. *Lux* v. *Haggin*, 69 Cal at 333.

60. Miller & Lux contended that the opening of the reservoirs had stopped the entire flow of water to its land. While 1,000 cfs was the usual flow of the river during the winter, Miller & Lux officials testified that on 5 February 1905, after the reservoir began impounding water, only 99 cfs flowed to its land and that after 8 February, no

water flowed to its lands for the duration of the winter. Nickel, Transcript on Appeal, p. 248, *Miller & Lux* v. *Madera; Miller & Lux* v. *Madera;* 155 Cal 59.

61. See Worster, *Rivers of Empire.*

62. Oral Argument of T. J. Savage (1908), p. 15, *Miller & Lux* v. *Madera,* 155 Cal 59.

63. Brief of Leonard and Surr (1908), amici curiae, pp. 42–43, *Miller & Lux* v. *Madera,* ibid.

64. This has led Scheiber and McCurdy to interpret the decision as an "instrumentalist" ruling in which the court tried to mold the law to serve public policy; see Harry N. Scheiber and Charles W. McCurdy, "Eminent Domain Law in Western Agriculture, 1848–1900," *Agricultural History* 49 (1975): 124–25.

65. Brief of Leonard and Surr, amici curiae, p. 16, *Miller & Lux* v. *Madera.* The same rational flexibility of the common law formed the core of Justice Ross's dissent in the original decision in *Lux* v. *Haggin,* 4 p. 919.

66. Oral Argument of T. J. Savage, p. 19, *Miller & Lux* v. *Madera.*

67. Ibid., p. 8.

68. Brief of Leonard and Surr, pp. 37–38, *Miller & Lux* v. *Madera.*

69. Ibid., pp. 18–19, 24–25; Oral Argument of T. J. Savage, pp. 18, 24–25, *Miller & Lux* v. *Madera.*

70. Brief for Respondent, Frank H. Short, pp. 38–39, *Miller & Lux* v. *Madera.*

71. Reply to the Petition for Rehearing, Frank H. Short (1907), pp. 3, 5–6, *Miller & Lux* v. *Madera,* 155 Cal 59.

72. Brief for Respondent, W. B. Treadwell (1908), p. 9, *Miller & Lux* v. *Madera,* 155 Cal 59.

73. Oral Argument of Frank H. Short, pp. 26–28, *Miller & Lux* v. *Madera.*

74. Scheiber and McCurdy, "Eminent Domain Law," p. 128; Harry N. Scheiber, "Property Law, Expropriation, and Resource Allocation by Government: the United States, 1789–1910," *Journal of Economic History* 33 (1973): p. 248; idem, "The Road to *Munn*: Eminent Domain and the Concept of Public Purpose in the United States Courts," *Perspectives in American History* 5 (1971): 329–402; Lawrence Friedman, *A History of American Law* (New York: Simon & Schuster, 1973); Stanley Kutler, *Privilege and Creative Destruction: The Charles River Bridge Case* (New York: J. P. Lippincott, 1971); Horwitz, "Transformation in Conception of Property," pp. 248–90.

75. *Miller & Lux* v. *Madera,* 155 Cal 59, 63 (1909). Unlike the situation in *Lux* v. *Haggin,* 69 Cal 225, there was only one dissenter to this ruling.

76. Ibid., at 64.

77. Ibid., at 65.

78. Frank H. Short to J. Leroy Nickel, 3 January 1908, Miller & Lux Papers.

79. Complaint, Transcript on Appeal, pp. 3–8, *San Joaquin & Kings River Canal & Irrigation Company* v. *Fresno Flume and Irrigation Company,* 158 Cal 626 (1910) (this case is referred to hereafter as *SJ&KRC&ICo v. Fresno Flume*); testimony of C. B. Shaver, ibid., pp. 665, 672–73, 993; testimony of H. W. Swift, ibid., pp. 642–45; Answer of Amended Complaint, ibid., pp. 14–15, 28–29, 39.

80. Brief for the Defendant, pp. 2–3, 10–11, 14, 24, *SJ&KRC&ICo* v. *Fresno Flume*, 158 Cal 626.

81. Points and Authorities, E. F. Treadwell, pp. 29–43 (quotation on p. 43), *SJ&KRC&ICo* v. *Fresno Flume*, 158 Cal 626; *Fresno Morning Republican* (cited hereafter as *FMR*), 18 June 1907.

82. Findings of Fact and Conclusions of Law (August 4, 1905), pp. 49–52, *SJ&KRC&ICo* v. *Fresno Flume*, 158 Cal 69; H. Z. Austin, Opinion of the Court (February 27, 1905) in Findings of Fact . . . , pp. 56f–56g, ibid.; *SJ&KRC&ICo.* v. *Fresno Flume*, 158 Cal 626 (1910).

83. *SJ&KRC&ICo* v. *Fresno Flume*, 158 Cal at 629.

84. Ibid.

85. For an attempt to reconcile the two decisions, see Wiel, *Water Rights*, pp. 884–90.

86. Appellant's Opening Brief, L. L. Cory (March 1919), *SJ&KRC&ICo* v. *Fresno Flume*, Miller & Lux Papers; *SJ&KRC&ICo* v. *Fresno Flume*, 169 Cal 174 (1915).

87. The Madera Canal Company at one point argued that Miller & Lux's predecessors had consented to the canal company's diversion, thus abandoning the water rights of the land Miller & Lux now owned and asserted to be riparian. Reporter's Transcript, pp. 778–80, *Union Colonization Company* v. *Madera;* Answer of Madera Canal and Irrigation Company, Transcript on Appeal, pp. 47–49, *Miller & Lux* v. *Madera; FMR*, 2 January 1915.

88. Robert L. Hargrove, Reporter's Transcript, pp. 13–14, *Union C.* v. *Madera;* Oral Argument of E. F. Treadwell, Reporter's Transcript, pp. 3787–88, ibid.

89. Wiel, *Water Rights*, pp. 632–34, 498–501, 917.

90. *FMR*, 24 February 1915. Judge Conley of Madera County appointed an outside judge to hear the 1915 trial for the same reason Seawell had been appointed: he reasoned that the decision would be too easily overturned if a local judge sat in the case.

91. In 1900, when the suit was first filed, there were very few pumps in operation. By 1916, there were 112 pumping plants, irrigating 7,454 acres within the area nominally served by the canal company, a fact that, according to the Madera Canal Company, showed the benefits of its diversion of water. "In the matter of the Application of Madera Canal and Irrigation Company," *Decisions of the California Railroad Commission* 13:538.

92. Frank H. Short to Isaac Frohman, 9 March 1907, carton 9, Miller & Lux Papers; *California Pastoral & Agricultural Company* v. *Madera*, 167 Cal 78, 80–83 (1914).

93. Frank H. Short to J. Leroy Nickel, 28 November 1906, Miller & Lux Papers; Edward F. Treadwell to Isaac Frohman, 19 July 1909, ibid.

94. Short to Frohman, 16 January 1907, carton 9, Miller & Lux Papers.

95. Short to Nickel, 28 November 1906; W. B. Treadwell to Nickel, 4 March 1907; Nickel to W. B. Treadwell, 8 March 1907; Nickel to Short, 26 March 1907; Short to

Nickel, 29 March 1907; Short to W. B. Treadwell, 22 April 1907; Short to Nickel, 20 March 1908, Miller & Lux Papers. Oral Argument of Frank H. Short, Reporter's Transcript, pp. 4071–72, *Union C. v. Madera.*

96. *CP&A* v. *Madera*, 167 Cal at 84–90.

97. Robert L. Hargrove to Hiram W. Johnson, 23, 26 December 1914, Hiram W. Johnson Papers, Bancroft Library; Hargrove to State Water Commission, 12 December 1914 (copy attached to letter of 23 December 1914), Hiram Johnson Papers.

98. Amended Answer (February 1915), Reporter's Transcript, p. 76, *Union C. v. Madera;* Reporter's Transcript, p. 24, *Union C. v. Madera.*

99. Intervenor's Answer, Reporter's Transcript, vol. 2: Plaintiff's Exhibits, pp. 352L–352Q, *Union C. v. Madera; FMR*, 18 January 1913.

100. Hargrove to Hiram Johnson, 23 December 1914, Johnson Papers. Frank Adams, "Progress Report of Co-operative Irrigation Investigations in California, 1912–1914," California Department of Engineering, *Bulletin* no. 1 (Sacramento, 1915); Adams et al., "Investigations of the Economical Duty of Water for Alfalfa in Sacramento Valley, California, 1910–1915," ibid. no. 3 (Sacramento, 1917).

101. Affidavit of J. Leroy Nickel, Transcript on Appeal, pp. 227–29, *Miller & Lux* v. *Madera; FMR*, 2 January 1915; Reporter's Transcript, passim, *Union C. v. Madera.*

102. Answer of Madera Canal and Irrigation Company, Transcript on Appeal, p. 52, *Miller & Lux* v. *Madera.*

103. "Statistics of Irrigation," *Thirteenth Census of the United States, 1910*, abstract, with a supplement for California, p. 669.

104. Testimony of A. M. Acton, Steven Levin, Harry Barnes et al., Reporter's Transcript, pp. 362, 925, 2633–35, *Union C. v. Madera.* Levin, an employee of the Madera Canal Company, put the area irrigated at only 8,800 acres and acknowledged that this figure might overestimate the area irrigated by as much as 1,000 acres.

105. *G. W. Mordecai* v. *Madera Canal and Irrigation Company, Decisions of the California Railroad Commission* 3: 990.

106. Ibid., pp. 985–99; *FMR*, 20 April 1913.

107. Miller & Lux's attorneys tried to force water customers to make these statements during cross examination; see Reporter's Transcript, pp. 2044–2112, *Union C. v. Madera.*

108. *Union C. v. Madera.* 179 Cal 774 (1919).

109. Wiel, *Water Rights*, p. 507.

110. *Union C. v. Madera*, 179 Cal at 778; *CP&A* v. *Madera*, 167 Cal at 87; Oral Argument of E. C. Farnsworth, Reporter's Transcript, p. 3995, *Union C. v. Madera.*

111. The precise amounts that Miller & Lux spent on any given conflict cannot be determined. As an example, however, from 1900 to 1906 it spent more than $45,000 on various suits involving the San Joaquin River. From 1912 to 1916, its legal expenses in Oregon and California exceeded $137,000, a figure that excludes the amount spent by the San Joaquin Canal & Irrigation Company and all the costs of running its own legal department. Some of the cost of the litigation with Madera was

born by allies like the California Pastoral and Agricultural Company. The Madera Canal and Irrigation Company spent more than $45,000 between 1899 and 1915 in defending its rights against Miller & Lux. Klink, Bean and Co., accountants, "Estate of Henry Miller, Examination of the Accounts of Miller & Lux, Inc. and Affiliated Companies," 1916, Miller & Lux Papers; "Miller & Lux Incorporated in Account with California Pastoral & Agricultural Co. and its Successors," box: Canal and Water Companies, 1929–1950, Miller & Lux Papers; F. L. Humphrey to Judge Woolley, 9 April 1930, ibid.; "In the Matter of the Application of Madera Canal and Irrigation Company for an order authorizing increases in rates charged for water sold for irrigation," *Decisions of the California Railroad Commission* 13: 535.

112. Synopsis of Contracts, Barnes 169, Harry Barnes Papers, Water Resources Center Archives, University of California, Berkeley; Nickel to R. E. Houghton, 23 June 1910, carton 48, Miller & Lux Papers.

CHAPTER 2

1. Miller & Lux also owned the Chowchilla Canal, the Panoche Canal Company, the Gravelley Ford Canal Company, the San Luis Canal Company, and the Kern Valley Reclamation Company, among others. Kling, Bean and Company, accountants, "Estate of Henry Miller—Examination of Miller & Lux, Inc. and Affiliates," 1916, Miller & Lux Papers.

2. Wiel, *Water Rights* (see intro., n. 13), p. 1209.

3. San Joaquin and Kings River Canal and Irrigation Company (SJ&KRC&ICo), *Prospectus*, pp. 1, 5, Bancroft Library, University of California, Berkeley; SJ&KRC&I Co, *Report to the Stockholders, 1873*, pp. 11, 13–14, Bancroft Library; "List of Original Stockholders in SJ&KRC&ICo," Miller & Lux Papers.

4. SJ&KRC&ICo, *Prospectus*, p. 5.

5. Treadwell, *Cattle King* (see intro., n. 4), pp. 67–68.

6. SJ&KRC&ICo, *Report to the Stockholders 1873*, pp. 14–15; Transcript on Appeal, pp. 1074–81, *SJ&KRC&ICo* v. *Stanislaus*, 233 U.S. 454 (1914). The second of the contracts set up a timetable according to which the subsidy would be paid and water would be made available.

7. SJ&KRC&ICo, *Report to the Stockholders 1873*, p. 15.

8. Robert Brereton, *Reminiscences of an Old English Civil Engineer, 1858–1908* (Portland, Ore.: Irwin Hudson Co., 1908), pp. 29–30; *Fresno Morning Republican (FMR)*, March 27, 1910; Thomas E. Malone, "The California Irrigation Crisis of 1886; Origins of the Wright Act," Ph.D. diss., Stanford University, 1964, p. 56.

9. David Lavender, *Nothing Seemed Impossible: William Ralston and San Francisco* (Palo Alto, Calif.: American West Publishing, 1975), p. 354.

10. Brereton, *Reminiscences*, p. 25. A commission set up to study the area noted the potential for the development of irrigated agriculture in the area. See B.S. Alexander, George Davidson, and G.H. Mendel, *Report of the Board of Commissioners on*

the Irrigation of the San Joaquin, Tulare and Sacramento Valleys of the State of California (Washington, D.C., 1874; reprinted from House Executive Document 290, 43d Congress, 1st sess., 1874).

11. Transcript on Appeal, pp. 1082–83, *SJ&KRC&ICo* v. *Stanislaus;* Brief for Appellant (1903), pp. 123–25, *Stanislaus* v. *SJ&KRC&ICo,* 192 U.S. 201 (1903).

12. Brief for Appellant (1903), pp. 123–25, *Stanislaus* v. *SJ&KRC&ICo;* Transcript on Appeal, pp. 112–13, *SJ&KRC&ICo* v. *Stanislaus.*

13. Excerpt from the minutes of the Board of Directors of SJ&KRC&ICo, Brief for Appellant (1903), pp. 138–39, *Stanislaus* v. *SJ&KRC&ICo.*

14. John Outcalt, *History of Merced County* (Los Angeles: Historic Record Co., 1925), p. 221.

15. Brereton, *Reminiscences,* p. 25; Lavender, *Nothing Seemed Impossible,* p. 354; Maass and Anderson, *Desert Shall Rejoice* (see chap. 1, n. 44), pp. 210–12.

16. Transcript on Appeal, pp. 1082–83, *SJ&KRC&ICo* v. *Stanislaus;* Brief for Appellant (1903), pp. 123–25, 138–39, *Stanislaus* v. *SJ&KRC&ICo.*

17. Treadwell, *Cattle King,* p. 73; Testimony of C. Z. Merritt, Transcript on Appeal, pp. 345–46, *SJ&KRC&ICo* v. *Stanislaus;* "List of Original Stockholders in SJ&KRC&ICo," Miller & Lux Papers. Miller & Lux controlled stock held in the names of J. Leroy Nickel, E. T. Allen, D. Hensaw, and Thomas Bishop, as well as that owned by Miller's landholding company, the Las Animas and San Joaquin Land Company. Appellant's Opening Brief, pp. 212–15, *SJ&KRC&ICo* v. *Stevinson,* 26 Cal App 274 (1915) (no. 1250).

18. SJ&KRC&ICo, *Prospectus,* p. 11; Testimony of C. Z. Merritt, Transcript on Appeal, p. 236, *SJ&KRC&ICo* v. *Stevinson,* 63 Cal App 767 (1923) (no. 2345); Transcript on Appeal, pp. 445–47, *SJ&KRC&ICo* v. *Stanislaus.*

19. Testimony of C. Z. Merritt, Transcript on Appeal, pp. 360–63, *SJ&KRC&ICo* v. *Stanislaus;* Brief for Respondent (1903), p. 122, *Stanislaus* v. *SJ&KRC&ICo;* Testimony of C. Z. Merritt, Transcript on Appeal, pp. 209–12, *SJ&KRC&ICo* v. *Stevinson* (no. 2345). W. C. Hammatt, for example, was the hydraulic and civil engineer for both companies, receiving half his salary from each. Brief for Respondent, pp. 6–9, 77, *SJ&KRC&ICo* v. *Stevinson,* 26 Cal App 274 (1915) (no. 1250).

20. J. F. Clyne to C. Z. Merritt, 23 September 1909, Miller & Lux Papers; Merritt to Clyne, 1 November 1909, ibid.

21. C. Z. Merritt to D. M. Rouse, 3 December 1891, letterbook, vol. 178, Miller & Lux Papers.

22. SJ&KRC&ICo, *Report to the Stockholders,* pp. 13–14; Brief for Appellant (1903), p. 122, *Stanislaus* v. *SJ&KRC&ICo;* Appellant's Opening Brief, pp. 40, 328–31, *SJ&KRC&ICo* v. *Stevinson* (no. 1250); "Irrigation Season of 1907/08," Miller & Lux Papers.

23. Richard E. Copley, "A Historical Geography of the Dairy Industry of Stanislaus, California," M.A. thesis, University of California, Berkeley, 1961, pp. 41–49, 61–63; John T. Bramhall, *The Story of Stanislaus* (Modesto: Modesto Herald, 1914), pp. 14–15, 17; George H. Tinkham, *History of Stanislaus County, California* (Los

Angeles: Historic Record Co., 1921), pp. 211–12; John C. Graham, "The Settlement of Merced County, California," M.A. thesis, University of California, Los Angeles, 1957, pp. 120–25; *FMR*, 18 October 1907, 20 September 1908; *Merced County Sun*, 23 July 1909.

24. Graham, "Settlement of Merced County," pp. 72–74.

25. Miller to E. C. Morgan, 6 November 1890, 30 May 1891, 21 October 1891, letterbook, vol. 178, Miller & Lux Papers; Merritt to D. M. Rouse, 23 December 1895, carton 179, ibid.

26. Shannon to Nickel, 4, 17 July 1902, 15 August 1902, carton 714, Miller & Lux Papers; J. F. Clyne to Nickel, 25 August 1906, carton 2, ibid.; 13 August 1908, carton 22, ibid.

27. Merritt to Eastin and Griffin, 2, 4 February 1893, Letterbook, vol. 178, Miller & Lux Papers.

28. "Petition to the County of Stanislaus to Regulate the rates of SJ&KRC&ICo," Transcript on Appeal, p. 1211, *SJ&KRC&ICo* v. *Stanislaus;* Brief for Appellant (1903), pp. 40–41, *Stanislaus* v. *SJ&KRC&ICo; SJ&KRC&ICo* v. *Stanislaus,* 91 F. 517 (1898–99).

29. Transcript on Appeal, pp. 1084–85, *SJ&KRC&ICo* v. *Stanislaus;* Brief for Appellant (1903), p. 126, *Stanislaus* v. *SJ&KRC&ICo.*

30. Treadwell, *Cattle King,* p. 74; Brief for Appellant (1903), pp. 130–32, *Stanislaus* v. *SJ&KRC&ICo.* In one incident, a landowner attempted to irrigate with some of the wastewater as it passed through his land. When he refused to sign a contract with the canal company to pay for the water, Miller & Lux decided to prosecute him for stealing its water. Wangenheim, who was the leader of the Water Users' Association, advised the landowner neither to sign the contract nor pay for the water. J. F. Clyne to Miller & Lux, Inc., 26 August 1910, Miller & Lux Papers.

31. Transcript on Appeal, pp. 348, 1086–87, *SJ&KRC&ICo* v. *Stanislaus;* Minutes of the Board of Directors of SJ&KRC&ICo, 7 May 1899, Master's Report, p. 116, Transcript on Appeal, *SJ&KRC&ICo* v. *Stanislaus.*

32. Merritt to H. M. Briggs, 10 October 1892, letterbook, vol. 178, Miller & Lux Papers.

33. See Pisani, *From Family Farm to Agribusiness* (see intro., n. 13), chaps. 5, 6; Frank Adams, "Irrigation Districts in California, 1887–1915," California Department of Engineering, *Bulletin* 2 (1917): 118–121. The two most successful irrigation districts in the early twentieth century were the Modesto District and the Turlock District, both located in eastern Stanislaus County. The Modesto District, organized in 1887, was inactive from 1895 until 1902 but by 1914 it irrigated over 50,000 acres. The Turlock District, also founded in 1887, covered more than 175,000 acres.

34. Merritt to Rouse, 5, 9 May 1896, letterbook, vol. 179, Miller & Lux Papers.

35. *SJ&KRC&ICo* v. *Stanislaus,* 90 F. 516 (1898–99); *SJ&KRC&ICo* v. *Stanislaus,* 113 F. 931, 935–36 (1902).

36. *SJ&KRC&ICo* v. *Stanislaus.* 91 F. 519, 113 F. at 934.

37. Brief for Appellant (1903), p. 143, *Stanislaus* v. *SJ&KRC&ICo.*

38. Ibid., p. 146.

39. *SJ&KRC&ICo* v. *Stanislaus,* 113 F. at 939–43.

40. *Stanislaus* v. *SJ&KRC&ICo,* 192 U.S. 201 (1903).

41. Ibid., at 213–216. The Court's attitude can be seen in the later decisions in *Willcox* v. *Consolidated Gas Company,* 212 U.S. 1 (1909), and *Knoxville* v. *Knoxville Water Company,* 212 U.S. 19 (1909). In these decisions, the Court cited the rate cases to reemphasize its concern that customers not pay for the consequences of bad management and overcapitalization. On the role of Peckham in the debate over corporations, see Martin J. Sklar, *The Corporate Reconstruction of American Capitalism, 1890–1916: The Market, the Law, and Politics* (Cambridge: Cambridge Univ. Press, 1988), pp. 139–40.

42. *FMR,* 4 April 1907, 11, 17 May 1907; Wiel, *Water Rights,* p. 1194.

43. Frank H. Short to H. Z. Austin, 15 June 1906, Miller & Lux Papers.

44. See model in Jack Hirshleifer et al., "The Allocation of Water Supplies," in Edwin Mansfield, ed., *Micro-economics: Selected Readings* (New York: Norton, 1971), pp. 383–95; "Memorandum in Regard to Canal Company's Rates," 3 December 1914, Miller & Lux Papers; "Complainant's Computation of the Value of its Canals and the Minimum Rates Based on Said Values," Miller & Lux Papers.

45. Answer of Stanislaus County, Transcript on Appeal, pp. 32–45, *SJ&KRC&ICo* v. *Stanislaus.*

46. Short to Nickel, 18 November 1907, Miller & Lux Papers. One of Miller & Lux's superintendents also met with the district attorney of Merced County to persuade him of this position. The DA, he reported, had initially agreed to follow the lead of Stanislaus because he was inexperienced. D. W. Wallis to Nickel, 22, 25 November 1907, carton 634, Miller & Lux Papers; *FMR,* 12 October 1907.

47. In this year, rates were raised to $1.35, $2.75, and $3.25 per cfs when a drop in demand after an abundance of rain threatened to depress revenues. Miller urged J. F. Clyne, superintendent of the SJ&KRC&ICo, to pursue a conciliatory policy until the rate litigation was settled. Miller to Clyne, 19, 21 September 1909, Miller & Lux Papers; Clyne to San Francisco office, SJ&KRC&ICo, 14 August 1909, ibid.; Clyne to Nickel, 3 September 1910, ibid; *FMR,* 12 October 1907.

48. For a description of this phenomenon, see Miller, *Railroad and Granger Laws* (see chap. 1, n. 15).

49. *SJ&KRC&ICo* v. *Stanislaus,* 155 Cal 21 (1908).

50. Short to W. B. Treadwell, 16, 20 February 1907, Miller & Lux Papers; W. B. Treadwell to Short, 18 February 1907, ibid.; Short to J. Leroy Nickel, 14 February 1907, ibid.; *FMR,* 4 April 1907, 11 May 1907; In the matter of fixing the maximum rates which the SJ&KRC&ICo, a corporation, shall charge for water for irrigation purposes in Stanislaus County, Transcript of Hearing before the Board of Supervisors of Stanislaus County, 14 May 1907, 25 June 1907, Miller & Lux Papers.

51. See discussion in *Miller & Lux* v. *East Side Canal Company,* 211 U.S. 293 (1908).

52. Short to W. B. Treadwell, 10 August 1907, Miller & Lux Papers; Nickel to Short, 15 June 1907, ibid.

53. Henry Miller to J. F. Clyne, 16 September 1909, Miller & Lux Papers.

54. *San Diego Land & Town Co.* v. *City of National City*, 74 F. 79 (C.C.S.D., 1896).

55. C. Z. Merritt to D. M. Rouse, 7 March 1893, letterbook, vol. 178, Miller & Lux Papers.

56. C. Z. Merritt to Harry Schafer, 7 November 1896, letterbook, vol. 179, Miller & Lux Papers.

57. See chap. 1.

58. See *Turner* v. *East Side Canal Company*, 169 Cal 652 (1915). The East Side Canal, owned by James Stevinson, was to be used to irrigate his cattle lands and a proposed subdivision of his lands. For a discussion of this canal and of the litigation between Miller & Lux and Stevinson, see chap. 3.

59. Miller to S. J. Shannon, 2 May 1907, carton 398, Miller & Lux Papers.

60. Short to W. B. Treadwell, 10 August 1907, Miller & Lux Papers; Short to Nickel, 19 November 1908, carton 25, ibid.; Short to Edward F. Treadwell, February 16 1909, *ibid.*

61. *SJ&KRC&ICo* v. *Stanislaus*, 191 F. 875, 897 (C.C.N.D. Cal., 1911).

62. Complaint, *SJ&KRC&ICo* v. *E.D. Roberts*, no. 47222 (1912) and no. 40598 (1911), Miller & Lux Papers; Letter of complaint to state comptroller and state treasurer from SJ&KRC&ICo, 19 August 1911, Miller & Lux Papers. In an undated letter to the state Board of Equalization, the canal company cited the rate cases in order to get the valuation of its franchise lowered from $190,000. The letter argued that the franchise was "only valuable insofar as the said company is permitted to collect such water rates." Miller & Lux and the SJ&KRC&ICo ultimately won these suits, and the payments were refunded.

63. *SJ&KRC&ICo* v. *Stanislaus*, 163 Cal 567 (1908).

64. On Heacock and Morrow in other cases, see Lucy Salyer, "Captives of Law: Judicial Enforcement of Chinese Exclusion Laws, 1891–1905," *Journal of American History* 76 (1989): 91–117.

65. Master's Report, Transcript on Appeal, *SJ&KRC&ICo* v. *Stanislaus;* Objections and Exceptions to the Master's Report, Transcript on Appeal, *SJ&KRC&ICo* v. *Stanislaus; SJ&KRC&ICo* v. *Stanislaus*, 191 F. at 879–81.

66. Value of the Water Right (handwritten note), Miller & Lux Papers; *SJ&KRC&ICo* v. *Stanislaus*, 191 F. at 895–96.

67. *SJ&KRC&ICo* v. *Stanislaus*, ibid., at 889–91.

68. Master's Report, *SJ&KRC&ICo* v. *Stanislaus*, p. 113; "Complainant's Objections to the Master's Report," Miller & Lux Papers.

69. Master's Report, *SJ&KRC&ICo* v. *Stanislaus*, p. 136.

70. Points and Authorities of Company to Have Value of Franchise and Water Right Considered, *SJ&KRC&ICo* v. *Stanislaus*, no. 14554, Legal Department Correspondence, 1911–1915, Miller & Lux Papers.

71. Ibid.

72. Short to Edward F. Treadwell, 11 October 1911, Miller & Lux Papers.

73. See chap. 3.

74. Water use was calculated in terms of the number of second-feet delivered over twenty-four hours. SJ&KRC&ICo, *Rules and Regulations, Instructions to Zanjeros . . .* (1909), Bancroft Library.

75. *FMR*, 4 April 1907, 17 August 1908; Deposition of Abram E. Clary, *SJ&KRC&ICo* v. *Stanislaus*, 8 November 1907, Miller & Lux Papers; Answer of Defendants, *SJ&KRC&ICo* v. *Stanislaus*, Miller & Lux Papers; Nickel to Short, 24 June 1908, Miller & Lux Papers.

76. Clyne to Nickel, 17, 31 August 1908, carton 22, Miller & Lux Papers; Merritt to Clyne, 25 November 1908, ibid.

77. N. S. Ellis, R. M. Osborn, D. M. Steyer, R. H. Zackerias, and Wm. E. Bunker to Henry Miller, 10 December 1910, carton 413, Miller & Lux Papers; *FMR*, 22 January 1911, 2 March 1911. Clyne later attributed this plan to "Mr. Steyer and his Socialist friends." Clyne to Treadwell, 3 February 1911, carton 463, Miller & Lux Papers.

78. Shannon to Nickel, 17 July 1902, carton 714, Miller & Lux Papers; E. F. Treadwell to Short, 9 March 1911, 13, 19, 29 April 1911, ibid.; E. F. Treadwell to Nickel, 18 March 1911, ibid.; Wangenheim to Treadwell, 11, 15 March 1911, carton 463, ibid.; Wangenheim to Treadwell, 10 April 1911, ibid.; Nickel to Clyne, 18, 21 April 1911, carton 63, ibid.; Clyne to Nickel, 19 April 1911, carton 63, ibid.; Treadwell to Nickel, 4 October 1911, General Correspondence, 1911, Oct–Dec 101–135, ibid. In his letter to Nickel of 18 March 1911, Treadwell mentions a discussion of giving money to the Water Users' Association and of making a gesture to indicate that Miller & Lux and the canal company were "acting fairly." During this period, the Water Users' Association acted to aid the canal company in its suits against James and Stevinson, both of whom were riparian owners diverting water from the San Joaquin River. See chap. 3.

79. *FMR*, 6, 8, 20 July 1911; complaint, *SJ&KRC&ICo* v. *Stanislaus, Merced and Fresno*, Miller & Lux Papers.

80. Clyne would later argue that this tactic had curbed waste while measurement had not. Clyne to SJ&KRC&ICo, 25 February 1914, General Correspondence, 1914, Miller & Lux Papers.

81. Wangenheim to Frank Anderson, 20 July 1911, carton 463, Miller & Lux Papers; Wangenheim to Nickel, 20 July 1911, ibid.; Clyne to Nickel, 19, 21, 25 July 1911, carton 67, ibid.; Clyne to Treadwell, 29 July 1911, carton 463, ibid.; Nickel to Clyne, 17, 24 July 1911, carton 67, ibid.; Nickel to Treadwell, 1 August 1911, carton 463, ibid.

82. Treadwell to Short, 25 September 1911, carton 57, Miller & Lux Papers.

83. *SJ&KRC&ICo* v. *Stanislaus*, 191 F. at 891–92.

84. Short to Treadwell, 27, 30 October 1911, carton 463, Miller & Lux Papers.

85. Treadwell to Nickel, 4 October 1911, carton 463, Miller & Lux Papers; Lawrence Kennedy to Treadwell, 6 October 1911, ibid.; Nickel to Treadwell, 7 October 1911, ibid.; Nickel to Clyne, 29 January 1912, carton 69, ibid., Nickel to Clyne, 3 February 1912, carton 463, ibid.; Clyne to Nickel, 11 February 1912, carton 69, ibid.

86. Treadwell to Nickel, 11 March 1914, carton 110, Miller & Lux Papers.

87. *SJ&KRC&ICo* v. *Stanislaus*, 233 U.S. 454 (1914).

88. E.F. Treadwell, transcript of Railroad Commission Hearing, December 1914, Miller & Lux Papers. In an earlier letter to Nickel, Treadwell had stated that in his view the supervisors' rates gave a fair return of 6 percent on a water right of $962,500. He based this return on the company's profits that year of $111,750. His only question concerning the company's goal of a higher $2.25 rate for Stanislaus County was whether or not it could be achieved. In his opinion, "It would be better to let it go than to take the entire matter before the Railroad Commission." E.F. Treadwell to Nickel, 16 June 1914, Miller & Lux Papers.

89. Petition to the Railroad Commission, 1914, Miller & Lux Papers; Transcript of Railroad Commission Hearing, December 1914, Miller & Lux Papers; Letter from SJ&KRC&ICo to "The Irrigators of the SJ&KRC&ICo, Inc.," 31 December 1914, Miller & Lux Papers; E.S. Wangenheim to E.F. Treadwell, 1 October 1914, Miller & Lux Papers; *FMR*, 28 June 1914.

90. The man who organized this protest, a Mr. Fink, owned 63.5 acres of land. In 1915 Clyne wrote that he expected little more trouble from "Mr. Fink or his imaginary objectors [to the $2.25 rate] at Crows Landing until he wants more water." Clyne to E.F. Treadwell, 22 June 1915, Miller & Lux Papers; "List of those objecting to the $2.25 Stanislaus rate," Miller & Lux Papers; Treadwell to Board of Directors, SJ&KRC&ICo, 2 February 1915, carton 123, Miller & Lux Papers.

91. California Railroad Commission, Decision no. 2656, Supplemental Order, 3 August 1915, Miller & Lux Papers.

92. *Leavitt* v. *Lassen Irrigation Company*, 157 Cal 82 (1910).

93. *Limoneira* v. *Railroad Commission of the State of California*, 174 Cal 232 (1917).

94. "Canal Company Irrigation Account," Miller & Lux Papers; Miller & Lux, Inc., schedule 6, Appraisement no. 7, Miller & Lux Papers.

95. Miller & Lux, Inc., "Balance Sheet for 1915," Miller & Lux Papers.

96. *FMR*, 11 August 1911.

97. S. Kempsky, "SJ&KRC&ICo, Valuation for Rate Fixing" (1929), pp. 25–27, Miller & Lux Papers.

98. Hirschleifer, "The Allocation of Water Supplies."

CHAPTER 3

1. Pisani, *From Family Farm to Agribusiness*: (see intro., n. 13), p. 290; Transcript on Appeal, p. 472, *SJ&KRC&ICo* v. *Fresno Flume*, 158 Cal 626 (1910); Outcalt, *History of Merced County* (see chap. 2, n. 14), pp. 353–54, 394; Elwood Mead, *Irrigation in California*, Department of Agriculture, *Bulletin* no. 100 (Washington, D.C., 1901), pp. 223–26.

2. Amended Complaint (March 10, 1900), Transcript on Appeal, pp. 2–11, *Stevin-*

son v. *SJ&KRC&ICo*, 162 Cal 141 (1912); Oral Argument of Frank H. Short, pp. 2–3, *Stevinson* v. *SJ&KRC&ICo*, ibid.

3. Answer to the Amended Complaint, Transcript on Appeal, pp. 11–25, *Stevinson* v. *SJ&KRC&ICo; Stevinson* v. *SJ&KRC&ICo*, 162 Cal 141, 142–43 (1912); M. L. Short, "Decision and Decree," Transcript on Appeal, pp. 20–106, *Stevinson* v. *SJ&KRC&ICo.*

4. In 1915, for example, the canals carried 1,600 cfs. Edward F. Treadwell, argued that irrigators who protested canal company policies threatened their own supply of water by forcing the exposure of the true amounts diverted. Fink v. SJ&KRC&ICo, Case no. 834, California Railroad Commission Hearing, 19 November 1915, pp. 13–15, Records of the Public Utilities Commission, California State Archives, Sacramento.

5. Clyne to Nickel, 28, 29, 30 June 1906, 11 July 1906, carton 2, Miller & Lux Papers; Nickel to McCain, 20 August 1907, 2 October 1907, carton 15, ibid.; Nickel to Hammatt, 20 August 1907, carton 13, ibid.; Miller to Superintendent, 26 July 1906, ibid.

6. Federal judges, of course, were not always sympathetic to the firm's arguments, as was clear in the rate case. That case, however, had not yet been decided, and the politics and connections of local judges were well known.

7. Short to Nickel, 27 September 1907, carton 15, Miller & Lux Papers.

8. Nickel to Short, 22 September 1906, General Correspondence, 1906, May–December, G–So, Miller & Lux Papers.

9. Treadwell, *Cattle King*, pp. 81–82, 153–74; Nickel to Short, 18 June 1906, General Correspondence, 1906, May–December, G–So, Miller & Lux Papers; Short to Nickel, 2 July 1906, ibid.; Nickel to Short, 10 September 1909, carton 15, ibid.

10. Nickel to Miller, 9 July 1907, Miller & Lux Papers; Nickel to McCray, 21 August 1907, 3 September 1907, ibid.; Nickel to Short, 10 September 1907, carton 15, ibid.

11. Nickel to McCray, 23 November 1907, 20 December 1907, carton 15, Miller & Lux Papers. Stevinson had rented a house in which he installed his witnesses, who were rounded up by H. A. V. Torchiana, a former SJ&KRC&ICo superintendent who later wrote a novel that criticized Miller & Lux in fictional form.

12. In the period 1916–22, Miller & Lux paid Treadwell $92,000 and spent $43,000 on its legal offices; it spent $90,000 on outside legal services, almost half of this on the inheritance tax protest. Treadwell, who had been in practice for ten years prior to taking the position with Miller & Lux, initially earned $350 a month; at the time of his resignation, his annual salary had reached $20,000. In 1924 he won a suit against Nickel for $300,000 in compensation for saving the family more than $10 million in inheritance taxes. Nickel's refusal to pay Treadwell this fee prompted his resignation in 1922. *Treadwell* v. *Nickel*, 194 Cal 243 (1924); Appellant's Opening Brief, pp. 33–34, 138, *Treadwell* v. *Nickel*, ibid., carton 563, Miller & Lux Papers; *Bench and Bar of California*, 1937–38, pp. 10–11; Treadwell, *How it Began* (pamphlet),

Bancroft Library, pp. 4–5; *San Francisco Chronicle*, 1 August 1924; *San Francisco Examiner*, 18 February 1923; Nickel to Treadwell, 13 May 1922, carton 517, Miller & Lux Papers; Treadwell to Nickel, 8, 13 May 1922, carton 517, ibid.; Miller & Lux, Inc., "Expenses of Outside Legal Services, October 1, 1916 to July 1, 1922," carton 517, ibid.

13. Gordon Morris Bakken, "Industrialization and the Nineteenth Century California Bar," in Gerard W. Gewart, ed., *The New High Priest: Lawyers in Post–Civil War America* (Westport, Conn.: Greenwood, 1984); Friedman, *History of American Law* (see chap. 1, n. 74), pp. 641–42; Clary, *History of O'Melveny and Myers* (see chap. 1, n. 46), pp. 270–73, 280.

14. *Miller & Lux v. East Side Canal Co.*, 211 U.S. 293 (1908). In contrast, Miller & Lux had been able to bring its rate case against Stanislaus County in the federal courts because the suit questioned the constitutional protections of property under the Fourteenth Amendment. See chap. 2 following n. 33.

15. Rector had ruled in Miller & Lux's favor in a number of other water cases but was also considered to be friendly with Stevinson. Nickel to Short, 18 June 1906, General Correspondence, 1906, May–December, G–So, Miller & Lux Papers.

16. *Turner v. East Side Canal Company*, 168 Cal 103, 142 P. 69 (1914); *Turner v. East Side Canal Company*, 169 Cal 652, 147 P. 579 (1915).

17. The second trial did not take place until the 1920s. At that trial, Judge Finch of Merced County recognized the East Side's right to divert 281 cfs from the San Joaquin but found that 35 cfs of this water was attached to land owned by Miller & Lux. The decision was appealed by both parties and had not been settled by the end of the decade. Treadwell to Nickel, 15 November 1923, carton 232, Miller & Lux Papers; Nickel to Treadwell, 20 November 1923, ibid.; "Memorandum of litigation affecting water rights of Miller & Lux and the SJ&KRC&ICo," April 1927, carton 544, ibid.

18. Nickel to Treadwell, 25 August 1912, carton 463, Miller & Lux Papers; *FMR*, 2 August 1913.

19. Oral Argument of Frank H. Short (May 2, 1911), pp. 15–16, *Stevinson v. SJ&KRC&ICo* 162 Cal 141; Petition for Rehearing, p. 4, ibid.

20. *Stevinson v. SJ&KRC&ICo*, 162 Cal 141, 144–46 (1912).

21. Quotation from Oral Argument of Short, p. 6, *Stevinson v. SJ&KRC&ICo;* Notice of Appeal, pp. 36–37, ibid.; Petition for Rehearing, pp. 1–3, 8, 21, ibid.

22. Oral Argument of Short, pp. 18–20, *Stevinson v. SJ&KRC&ICo.*

23. Ibid., pp. 24–25.

24. Petition for Rehearing on Behalf of the Water Users' Association as a Friend of the Court, J.P. Langhorne, attorney (1911), pp. 2–3, *Stevinson v. SJ&KRC&ICo*, 162 Cal 141.

25. Appellant's Opening Brief, p. 8, *SJ&KRC&ICo v. Stevinson*, 26 Cal App 274 (1915) (no. 1250); *SJ&KRC&ICo v. Stevinson*, 63 Cal App 767 (1923).

26. Frank H. Short to Edward F. Treadwell, 25 March 1909, Miller & Lux Papers.

27. *Stevinson* v. *SJ&KRC&ICo,* 162 Cal at 143–46.

28. Short to Treadwell, 10 July 1909, Miller & Lux Papers. Earlier they had successfully fought Peck's request for a jury trial in the East Side case, "dispos[ing] of that very undesirable and vexatious problem." Short to Nickel, 11 September 1907, carton 15, Miller & Lux Papers.

29. Short to Nickel, 9 September 1909, Miller & Lux Papers. In part, Short worried that a new judge would have to be "educated" on the issues and even at that could not be counted on to be friendly to the company. Short to Nickel, 3 September 1911, carton 463, Miller & Lux Papers.

30. Short to Treadwell, 21 October 1911, carton 463, Miller & Lux Papers.

31. Short to Treadwell, 21, 25 November 1912, carton 463, Miller & Lux Papers. *SJ&KRC&ICo* v. *Stevinson,* 164 Cal 221 (1912).

32. Nickel to Clyne, 29 November 1912, Miller & Lux Papers; Clyne to Nickel, 10 December 1912, carton 85, ibid.

33. Appellant's Opening Brief, pp. 37–38, 328–31, *SJ&KRC&ICo* v. *Stevinson* (no. 1250); Transcript on Appeal, pp. 216–17, 275–80, *SJ&KRC&ICo* v. *Stevinson,* 63 Cal App 767 (1923) (no. 2345).

34. Testimony of Burton Smith, Transcript on Appeal, pp. 439–44, *SJ&KRC&ICo* v. *Stevinson* (no. 2345); Testimony of Samuel McCullough, ibid., pp. 374–75; Testimony of D.M. Rouse, ibid., pp. 365–67; Testimony of H.A.V. Torchiana, ibid., pp. 314–17.

35. Transcript on Appeal, pp. 70–75, *SJ&KRC&ICo* v. *Stevinson.* (no. 2345).

36. Ibid., p. 6.

37. Brief for Respondent, pp. 41, 47, *SJ&KRC&ICo* v. *Stevinson.* (no. 1250).

38. Appellant's Opening Brief, pp. 11–12, 52–53, 75, *SJ&KRC&ICo* v. *Stevinson.* (no. 1250).

39. Transcript on Appeal, pp. 282–84, *SJ&KRC&ICo* v. *Stevinson* (no. 2345).

40. Older earthen canals typically lost 50 percent of the water diverted through seepage; new canals usually lost 60 percent. Wiel, *Water Rights,* p. 498.

41. Appellant's Opening Brief, pp. 31–33, *SJ&KRC&ICo* v. *Stevinson* (no. 1250).

42. Appellant's Opening Brief, *SJ&KRC&ICo* v. *Stevinson* (no. 1250); Respondent's Petition for Rehearing, p. 9, ibid.

43. Appellant's Opening Brief, pp. 83–85, 93–99, *SJ&KRC&ICo* v. *Stevinson* (no. 1250).

44. Short to Treadwell, 11 September 1907, carton 15, Miller & Lux Papers.

45. Respondent's Reply Brief, p. 79, *SJ&KRC&ICo* v. *Stevinson* (no. 1250); Wes S. Malone, "The Formative Era of Contributory Negligence," *Illinois Law Review* 41 (1946): 155–58; Henry Miller to Isaac Bird, 18 December 1907, carton 13, Miller & Lux Papers; Daugherty & Lacy to Miller & Lux, 6 December 1909, carton 41, ibid.; D. W. Wallis to Nickel, 10 November 1914, carton 116, ibid.; Nickel to Clyne, 13 November 1914, carton 116, ibid.; Treadwell to Nickel 28 December 1914, carton 116, ibid.

46. *Crow* v. *SJ&KRC&ICo,* 130 Cal 309 (1900).

47. Instructions quoted in Appellant's Opening Brief, pp. 163–65, *SJ&KRC&ICo* v. *Stevinson* (no. 1250).

48. *FMR*, 19 July 1913, 2 September 1915; *SJ&KRC&ICo* v. *Stevinson*, 26 Cal App 274, 276 (1915).

49. Appellant's Opening Brief, pp. 3–6, 54–57, 61, 129–30, *SJ&KRC&ICo* v. *Stevinson* (no. 1250).

50. Ibid., pp. 80–82; quotation on p. 82.

51. For a discussion of the Charles River Bridge case, see Kutler, *Privilege and Creative Destruction*.

52. *Hough* v. *Porter*, 51 Ore 318, 95 p. 732, 98 Pac 1083 (1909).

53. *Little Walla Irrigation Union* v. *Finis Irrigation Co.*, 62 Ore 348, 124 Pac Rep 666 (1912). For further discussion of this trend, see Samuel Wiel, "What Is Beneficial Use of Water?" *California Law Review* 3 (1914–15): 460–75.

54. Frank Adams, "The Economical Use of Water as Affecting the Extent of Rights under the Doctrine of Prior Appropriation," *California Law Review* 2 (1913–14): 367–76.

55. Quotation from Treadwell to Short, 22 October 1914, carton 117, Miller & Lux Papers; *SJ&KRC&ICo* v. *Stevinson*, 26 Cal App at 276–79.

56. Ibid., at 281.

57. Ibid., at 282.

58. Ibid., at 283 (emphasis added).

59. Appellant's Petition to the Supreme Court, pp. 2–10, 47, *SJ&KRC&ICo* v. *Stevinson* (no. 1250).

60. *CP&A* v. *Madera*, 168 Cal at 87.

61. *SJ&KRC&ICo* v. *Stevinson*, 26 Cal App at 284–85.

62. *FMR*, 19 November 1915, 15, 24 December 1915, 4 February 1916; *SJ& KRC&ICo* v. *Stevinson*, 30 Cal App 405, 407–8 (1916).

63. *SJ&KRC&ICo* v. *Stevinson* 179 Cal 533, 593 (1919).

64. Treadwell to Berkeley B. Blake, 8 November 1919, Miller & Lux Papers.

65. *FMR*, 17 September 1919.

66. Forest A. Cobb to Berkeley [Blake], 1 October 1919, carton 464, Miller & Lux Papers; John A. Wall to Treadwell, 28 October 1919, carton 464, ibid.; J. J. Griffen to Treadwell, 3, 5 November 1919, carton 464, ibid.; *SJ&KRC&ICo* v. *Stevinson*, 63 Cal App 767 (1923); *Decisions of the California Railroad Commission*, 1929, case no. 2658, pp. 422–25, 650.

67. This case provides a concrete qualification to the view of eminent domain in Scheiber and McCurdy, "Eminent-Domain Law" (see chap. 1, n. 64), pp. 112–30. In this article, Scheiber and McCurdy cite a number of nineteenth-century decisions in which the court's interpretation of eminent domain law seems "to perpetuate significant cost-reducing, subsidy effects." Such interpretations were not applied in this case. The importance of localism in eminent domain proceedings is also stressed in Tony Freyer's article, "Reassessing the Impact of Eminent Domain in Early American Economic Development," *Wisconsin Law Review* (1981): 1263–86.

68. When James died in 1910, the *Fresno Morning Republican* (29 March 1910) estimated that his estate was worth between $1.5 million and $2 million.

69. *Miller & Lux* v. *Enterprise Canal and Irrigation Company*, 142 Cal 208 (1904); *Miller & Lux* v. *Enterprise*, 145 Cal 652 (1905).

70. Mead, *Irrigation in California*, pp. 223–26. Curiously, some years later a Fresno court ruled that Fresno Slough was not a natural watercourse linking the Kings and San Joaquin rivers and thus the Kings was not tributary to the San Joaquin. That ruling was overturned by the state supreme court in *Chowchilla Farms* v. *Martin*, 219 Cal 1, 25 P(2d) 435 (1933) and *Miller & Lux* v. *Tulare Lake Basin Water Storage District*, 219 Cal 41, 25 P(2d) 451 (1933).

71. *Turner* v. *James*, 155 Cal 82 (1909).

72. *Miller & Lux* v. *Enterprise*, 169 Cal 415 (1915).

73. *SJ&KRC&ICo* v. *Fresno Flume*, 158 Cal 626 (1910).

74. *Miller & Lux* v. *Enterprise*, 169 Cal 415, quotation at 444.

75. Nickel to Short, 2, 31 July 1906, General Correspondence, 1906, May–December, G–So, Miller & Lux Papers; Short to Nickel, 14 August 1906, ibid; Houghton and Houghton to Nickel, 7 February 1908, box 19, ibid; Treadwell to Nickel, 8 April 1912, carton 70, ibid.

76. In this case Miller & Lux owned a half-interest in the Antelope Valley Land and Cattle Company, which took control of the land formerly owned by Thomas Rickey. Owning land in California, Rickey had asserted riparian rights against the appropriative claims that Miller & Lux had in Nevada. Treadwell, memo to Nickel, 26 October 1915, carton 125, Miller & Lux Papers; *Miller & Lux* v. *Rickey*, 123 F. 604 (C.C. Nev, 1903), 127 F. 573 (C.C. Nev., 1904), 146 F. 574 (C.C. Nev., 1906); *Rickey Land and Cattle Co.* v. *Miller & Lux*, 152 F. 10 (9th Cir., 1907), 218 U.S. 258 (1910); *Pacific Live Stock Co.* v. *Rickey*, 8 F. Supp. 772 (D.C. Nev., 1934).

77. FMR, 18 April 1912, 26 July 1912. The *Republican* reported that Miller & Lux was willing to mortgage its Fresno County properties to finance this purchase.

78. Appellant's Points and Authorities (July 1912), p. 62, *Miller & Lux* v. *Enterprise*, 169 Cal 415.

79. Memorandum of Appellant Canal Company in Reply to Respondent's Brief on Rehearing, p. 6, *Miller & Lux* v. *Enterprise*, 169 Cal 415.

80. Short to Treadwell, 3 April 1912, Miller & Lux Papers.

81. Appellant's Points and Authorities, p. 77, *Miller & Lux* v. *Enterprise*. James denied that the SJ&KRC&ICo was an agent of the public, insisting that the various contracts granting Miller & Lux special privileges made it merely the private agent of the cattle company. While James cited numerous cases requiring that public service corporations provide their customers with equal access to water, he had no success because the court had earlier ruled in *Crow* v. *SJ&KRC&ICo* (130 Cal 309) that the canal company was a public utility. Brief of Defendants on Rehearing (July, 1914), pp. 34–41, *Miller & Lux* v. *Enterprise*, 169 Cal 415.

82. Short to Treadwell, 23 April 1912, 3, 5, 8 June 1912, Miller & Lux Papers;

Petition for Rehearing by Appellant, the SJ&KRC&ICo (1914), pp. 3–26, *Miller & Lux* v. *Enterprise*, 169 Cal 415; Appellant's Reply Brief (1913), pp. 4–17, ibid.

83. *Miller & Lux* v. *Enterprise*, 47 Cal Dec 1; Short to Treadwell, 24 December 1913, Miller & Lux Papers.

84. Brief of J. P. Langhorne, amicus curiae (January 1914), p. 9, *Miller & Lux* v. *Enterprise*, 169 Cal 415.

85. Treadwell to Short, 18, 22 July 1914, carton 113, Miller & Lux Papers.

86. Statement quoted in Appellant's Reply Brief (1917), p. 21, *Miller & Lux* v. *J. G. James*, 180 Cal 39 (1919). This appeal was the response to a later decision in Merced County granting the canal company the rights to more than 1,300 cfs of water.

87. *Miller & Lux* v. *Enterprise*, 169 Cal at 431–34. This decision was rejected by James, who petitioned for another rehearing of the case. He argued that the earlier decision was final because the court, when it opened the case for rehearing, had limited arguments to the question of the public use but had then reversed itself on another issue. Miller & Lux had submitted a memorandum to the court at the time of the rehearing to argue (successfully) that the court did not have to decide the case in rehearing only on the issue of the public use. The controversy continued, and in 1919 in *Miller & Lux* v. *James* (180 Cal 39), the court offered a detailed justification of the 1915 reversal of the decision on rehearing. Petition for Second Rehearing by Respondent J.G. James Co. (March 1915), *Miller & Lux* v. *Enterprise*, 169 Cal 415; Appellant's Reply Brief (1917), p. 21, *Miller & Lux* v. *James*, 180 Cal 39 (1919).

88. After James's death in 1910, his land was sold to B.F. Graham for $3 million. In 1919, the James land was subdivided and put on the market at $175 an acre. At that time it was advertised as receiving water from thirty-five artesian wells. Forty thousand acres were sold in the first six months the land was on the market. *FMR*, 18 April 1912, 26 July 1912, 14 September 1919, 10 April 1920; *SJ&KRC&ICo* v. *J. G. James*, 180 Cal 38 (1919).

89. Decision of E.N. Rector, *SJ&KRC&ICo* v. *Worswick*, filed December 15, 1919; *FMR*, 4 March 1912, 24 May 1913.

90. In 1912 Miller & Lux spent $445,000 for feed and rent; in 1913 it spent $311,000. On the other hand, in 1915, after the drought had ended, it spent only $103,000 for rent and feed, and in 1916 only $60,000. It also expended more on freight in 1912 and 1913 than in the later two years, as a result of the greater movement of cattle. Nickel to H. Miller, 8 March 1913, Miller & Lux Papers; Nickel to Clyne, 19 March 1913, 18 April 1913, carton 413, ibid; *FMR*, 24 May 1913; Klink, Bean and Co., accountants, Estate of Henry Miller: Examination of the Accounts of Miller & Lux, Inc. and Affiliated Companies, 1916, Miller & Lux Papers.

91. Treadwell to Board of Directors, SJ&KRC&ICo, 12 February 1914, General Correspondence 1914, January–March, 18a–27, Miller & Lux Papers; *SJ&KRC&ICo* v. *Worswick*, 187 Cal 674, 677-79 (1922); Appellant's Opening Brief, pp. 75–95, *SJ&KRC&ICo* v. *Worswick*, 187 Cal 674.

92. Appellant's Opening Brief, pp. 26–27, 73–74, *SJ&KRC&ICo* v. *Worswick*;

SJ&KRC&ICo v. *Worswick,* 187 Cal 674. In 1909 the Oregon court had adopted this reasoning in *Hough* v. *Porter,* which limited the role of riparian rights in that state. See chap. 4, n. 11.

93. Treadwell to Board of Directors, SJ&KRC&ICo, 25 January 1917, carton 150, Miller & Lux Papers; Treadwell to Board of Directors, SJ&KRC&ICo, 1 February 1918, box: General Correspondence, 1918, Jan–April, 16f–58, ibid.

94. *SJ&KRC&ICo* v. *Worswick,* 187 Cal 674.

95. Shaw, "Development of Law of Waters," p. 455.

96. Miller & Lux appealed to the U.S. Supreme Court on grounds that two federal laws were at issue (the Swamp Land Act and the Desert Land Act) and that these laws had been the subjects of contrasting interpretations in various state courts. Special Brief on Motion for Reconsideration of Decision Denying Application for Writ of Certiori, Will R. King (1922), *SJ&KRC&ICo* v. *Worswick, Miller & Lux* v. *Worswick.*

97. *Herminghaus* v. *Southern California Edison,* 200 Cal 81 (1926).

98. Oral Argument of Edward F. Treadwell, pp. 49–70, 121–23, *Herminghaus* v. *Southern California Edison,* 200 Cal 81.

99. Brief on Behalf of the State of California, amicus curiae, *Herminghaus* v. *Southern California Edison,* 200 Cal 81.

100. J. E. Woolley, Memorandum Re: *Herminghaus* v. *Southern California Edison,* 7 August 1925, carton 257, Miller & Lux Papers; Milton J. Farmer to Miller & Lux Inc., 4 August 1925, carton 257, ibid.; Woolley to Nickel, 19 September, 29 October 1925, carton 262, ibid. Roy V. Reppy assured Woolley in a brief letter that Southern California Edison would honor its contractual relationship with the cattle company. Reppy to Woolley, 22 August 1925, carton 540, Miller & Lux Papers. For a full account of this case, see M. Catherine Miller, "Water Rights and the Bankruptcy of Judicial Action: The Case of *Herminghaus* v. *Southern California Edison,*" *Pacific Historical Review* 58 (1989): 83–107.

101. *Herminghaus* v. *Southern California Edison,* 200 Cal at 105.

102. Southern California Edison eventually settled its dispute with Herminghaus by purchasing the land involved. It later negotiated a water rights adjustment contract with the federal government to allow the development of the Central Valley Project. Leland O. Graham, "The Central Valley Project: Resource Development of a Natural Basin," *California Law Review* 38 (1950): 598.

CHAPTER 4

1. Thomas Edward Malone, "The California Irrigation Crisis of 1886: Origins of the Wright Act," Ph.D. diss., Stanford University, 1964, pp. 180–88, 213; Pisani, *From Family Farm to Agribusiness,* pp. 250–56.

2. *In re Bonds of Madera Irrigation District,* 28 P. 272 (1891).

3. For example, John Norton Pomeroy, chief teacher at the Hastings Law School

riparians charged that Miller & Lux paid for the publication of this piece. George C. Gorham, Jr., to J. DeBarth Shorb, 17 April 1886, box 48, Shorb Papers, Huntington Library, San Marino, Calif.

4. Alaska, Arizona, Colorado, Idaho, New Mexico, Nevada, Utah, and Wyoming adopted the so-called Colorado doctrine. Nebraska, Texas, and Oregon (after 1909) adopted the Colorado doctrine in part. Wiel, *Water Rights* 1:141.

5. Ibid., 1: 185–94; Dunbar, *Forging New Rights* (see intro., n. 13), pp. 78–85.

6. Dunbar, *Forging New Rights*, pp. 99–132; Wiel, *Water Rights* 1: 435–41.

7. Donald J. Pisani, "Water Law Reform in California, 1900–1913," *Agricultural History* 54 (1980): 295–317.

8. Dunbar, *Forging New Rights*, pp. 116–17; John Bird, "A History of Water Rights in Nevada, Part 2," *Nevada Historical Society Quarterly* 20 (1976):28–29; *Ormsby County v. Kearney*, 37 Nev 314, 142 P. 803 (1914); Donald J. Pisani, "Federal Reclamation and Water Rights in Nevada," *Agricultural History* 51 (1977): 547–48.

9. Curiously, in its most complex Nevada litigation, Miller & Lux was involved in a suit asserting the rights of Nevada appropriators against the claims of a riparian owner in California on the issue of how to administer interstate streams. The Nevada state engineer worked closely with Miller & Lux to resolve the conflicts among the Nevada claimants in this litigation. See *Miller & Lux v. Rickey*, 123 F. 604 (C.C. Nev., 1903), 127 F. 573 (C.C. Nev. 1904), 146 F. 574 (C.C. Nev., 1906); *Rickey Land and Cattle Co.* v. *Miller & Lux*, 152 R. 10 (9th Cir., 1907), 218 U.S. 258 (1910); *Pacific Live Stock Co.* v. *Rickey*, 8 F. Supp. 772 (D.C. Nev., 1934); *Pacific Live Stock Co.* v. *Malone*, 294 P. 538 (1931).

10. Dunbar, *Forging New Rights*, 122–25; Earl Pomeroy, *The Pacific Slope* (Seattle: Univ. of Washington Press, 1965), 196–99; Wiel, *Water Rights* 1: 149–56.

11. *Lux v. Haggin*, 69 Cal at 339–340; Wiel, *Water Rights* 1: 157–60; Dunbar, *Forging New Rights*, pp. 46–47, 77; Gates, *History of Public Land Law*, p. 538; *Hough* v. *Porter*, 51 Ore 318, 95 P. 732, 98 P. 1083 (1909).

12. Signed into law in 1894, the Carey Act assigned each of the eleven western states up to 1 million acres of arid land to be reclaimed and sold in 160-acre tracts. Settlers had to irrigate one-eighth of their parcel before a patent would be issued. The states generally contracted with development corporations to reclaim the land and required that settlers purchase water rights as well as land. This act had the support of many of the major railroad companies in the West but led to little development. After eight years, only 11,321 acres had been patented under its provisions; some sixty years later, slightly more than 1 million acres had been patented, out of almost 4 million acres that had been set aside. Dunbar, *Forging New Rights*, pp. 39–40; Gates, *History of Public Land Law*, pp. 650–51; Wiel, *Water Rights* 2: 1265–74.

13. Isaac Frohman to Miller & Lux, 2 July 1906, 4 October 1906, carton 3, Miller & Lux Papers; Frohman to State Land Board, 19 July 1906, carton 3, ibid.

14. John L. Rand to Treadwell, 29 March 1912, 28 October 1912, 14, 22 November 1912, carton 463, Miller & Lux Papers; Treadwell to Nickel, 16 July 1912, carton

15. Rand to Treadwell, 22 November 1912, carton 463, Miller & Lux Papers; *Pacific Live Stock Company* v. *Cochran,* 144 Pac 668 (1914); *In re Silvies River,* 199 F. 495 (D.C. Oregon, 1912); *Pacific Live Stock Company* v. *Lewis,* 217 F. 95 (D.C. Oregon, 1914), 241 U.S. 440 (1916).

16. Wiel to Treadwell, 26 November 1915, carton 489, Miller & Lux Papers; Treadwell, Oral Argument, 16 March 1916, *PLSCo* v. *Lewis,* 241 U.S. 440, carton 489, ibid.

17. George T. Cochran, Brief, *PLSCo* v. *Lewis,* 217 F. 95, carton 489, Miller & Lux Papers; Argument Submitted by Oliver P. Morton, District Counsel, U.S. Reclamation Service, appearing as amicus curiae, *PLSCo* v. *Lewis,* ibid.

18. In 1917 Cochran recommended that the water board recognize virtually all of Miller & Lux's claims, awarding it 4 acre-feet per acre. Treadwell to Nickel, 18 November 1917, box 41, Miller & Lux Papers.

19. *PLSCo* v. *Lewis,* 241 U.S. 440; *In re Willow Creek,* 144 P. 505 (1914).

20. Franklin Hichborn, *The Story of the California Legislature of 1913* (San Francisco: James H. Barry Co., 1913), p. 137.

21. *Report of the Conservation Commission of the State of California,* Sacramento, 1912.

22. Ibid., pp. 6–7.

23. Hichborn, *Story of California Legislature,* p. 137; Elmo Richardson, *The Politics of Conservation, Crusades and Controversies, 1897–1913,* University of California Publications in History, vol. 70 (Berkeley and Los Angeles: Univ. of California Press, 1962), p. 43; *Report of the Conservation Commission,* p. 9.

24. *Report of the Conservation Commission,* p. 7.

25. Ibid., p. 8.

26. Ibid., p. 28.

27. Ibid.

28. *SJ&KRC&ICo.* v. *Fresno Flume,* 158 Cal 626, 112 P. 182 (1910).

29. *Gallatin* v. *Corning Irrigation Co.,* 163 Cal 405, 126 P. 864 (1912).

30. *Report of the Conservation Commission,* pp. 29–30.

31. Ibid., pp. 30–31.

32. Ibid., pp. 21–26.

33. *Miller & Lux* v. *Madera Canal and Irrigation Company,* 155 Cal 59 (1909).

34. 1913 Cal. Stats. 586.

35. Frank Adams to W. F. McClure, 11 February 1913, Adams Papers, Water Resources Center Archives, University of California, Berkeley; Frank Adams, University of California, on irrigation, reclamation, and water administration, 1959, interview by Willa Klug Baum, Regional Cultural History Project, University of California, Berkeley, p. 214; Samuel Wiel, "Determination of Water Titles and the Water Commission Bill," *California Law Review* 2 (1913–14): 449; Commonwealth Club of California, *Transactions* 7 (June 1912): 292.

36. E. S. Wangenheim, for example, was upset that when Pardee was governor, he had refused "to sign a bill to curb the Miller & Lux interests." Although it is not

clear what legislation this was, Short in turn had praised Pardee for obstructing the Curtin bill, an action Short claimed served all irrigation interests. E. S. Wangenheim to George Pardee, 31 July 1911, George Pardee Papers, Bancroft Library, University of California, Berkeley; Short to Pardee, 8, 30 March 1903, Pardee Papers.

37. One of the members of the executive board was F. G. Munzer, secretary of the various canal companies controlled by the Kern County Land Company. Letterhead of the San Joaquin Valley Water Problems Association, John Fairweather to Hiram Johnson, 13 December 1913, Hiram Johnson Papers, Bancroft Library, University of California, Berkeley; *FMR*, 5 January 1913; *Report of the State Water Commission of California*, 1 January 1917, in *Appendix to the Journals of the Senate and Assembly of California*, 42d sess., 1917, vol. 4, pp. 287–304 passim; *FMR* 12 November 1912, 4, 5 January 1913.

38. *FMR*, 20 July 1912, 12 November 1912, 4, 5 January 1913; John Fairweather to George Pardee, 4 December 1904, 16 April 1911, George Pardee Papers; *Herminghaus* v. *Southern California Edison*, 200 Cal 81, 86 (1926); Tinkham, *History of Stanislaus County*, p. 523.

39. *FMR*, 22, 23 February 1913.

40. Short to Treadwell, 6 March 1911, 16 December 1911, carton 463, Miller & Lux Papers; Short to Milton R. U'ren, 10 December 1910, ibid.

41. Miller & Lux was an unwavering opponent of the eight-hour workday. In 1911 it locked out unionized engineers who refused to work twelve-hour days, earning it a place on the building trades council's unfair list. Similarly, it insisted on running its abbatoirs from 7:00 a.m. to 5:00 p.m.; meat inspectors worked only from 7:00 to 4:00, but Miller & Lux got a court order commanding them to be on hand from 4:00 to 5:00 (*San Francisco Call*, 19 January 1911, 16 March 1911). Miller & Lux also belonged to and helped fund various anti–single tax groups. The single tax is generally identified with Henry George, who in 1871 proposed that railroad land grants and other speculative holdings could be retrieved for the public by means of a tax equal to the rental value of the land. The idea continued to find support in the Progressive era, and proposals for such a tax were occasionally raised in the legislature. The cattle company, with its thousands of acres of land, opposed all efforts to increase property taxes, especially those that promised confiscation.

42. Short to Treadwell, 20 December 1912, carton 463, Miller & Lux Papers.

43. Treadwell to Short, 14 December 1912, carton 86, Miller & Lux Papers.

44. Pisani, "Water Law Reform," pp. 303–8.

45. *FMR*, 5 January 1913.

46. Ibid.

47. Hichborn, *Story of California Legislature*, pp. 152–53; George E. Mowry, *The California Progressives* (Chicago: Quadrangle Books, 1963), p. 152.

48. Edward F. Treadwell to Frank Short, 27 February 1913, Miller & Lux Papers.

49. L. J. Kennedy to J. Leroy Nickel, 7 March 1913, Miller & Lux Papers; Treadwell to Short, 12 March 1913, carton 98, ibid.; Kennedy to Short, 29 August 1913,

ibid. Pledges of $100 to $500 were received from companies such as Pacific Gas and Electric, Oro Electric, Northern California Power, and Northern California Water and Power Company. However, most of the $7,000 in expenses due to Perry, was paid by land and water companies in the San Joaquin Valley. Miller & Lux and the San Joaquin & Kings River Canal & Irrigation Company together paid $2,500; the Fresno Canal and Irrigation Company, the Kern County Land Company, and the Stevinson interests each paid $1,120.

50. George O. Perry, Northern California Water Association, *Confiscation Not Conservation: A Protest against the Enactment of the Glavis–Pardee Water Commission Act*, pp. 1–2, Miller & Lux Papers.

51. Mowry, *California Progressives*, p. 152.

52. *FMR*, 5 July 1910. In a July 4 speech in Los Banos, Short called the initiative, referendum, recall, and the direct primary part of the "fallacies of Populism." He argued that the reformers who "in their eagerness would change the fundamental character of the government were the chief obstacles to reform."

53. L. J. Kennedy to Treadwell, 1, 2 July 1913, Miller & Lux Papers; Treadwell to Nickel, 3 July 1913, ibid.; Pat R. Parker to Treadwell, 30 June 1913, ibid. Pledges were again received from such companies as Pacific Gas and Electric, Oro Electric, and Northern California Power; as in the earlier campaign, however, the largest pledges came from large land and irrigation companies, such as the Crocket–Huffman Land and Water Company, the Kern County Land Company, and Miller & Lux, not from the power companies. List of Original Subscribers to Water Commission Fund, Miller & Lux Papers.

54. "Some Objections to the 'Water Commission Act' and Reasons Why It Should Be Submitted to a Referendum" (printed flyer), Miller & Lux Papers.

55. Mowry, *California Progressives*, p. 197; *Farmers News*, September 1914, October 1914; Farmers Protective League to George O. Perry, 2 December 1914, Miller & Lux Papers.

56. Treadwell to Nickel, Memorandum, 7 July 1914, carton 112, Miller & Lux Papers; Treadwell to Nickel, 28 December 1914, carton 116, ibid.; Miller & Lux to "Dear Sir," 18 October 1912, carton 85 (files of Clyne), ibid.

57. C. Z. Merritt to Clyne, 22 September 1914, carton 116, Miller & Lux Papers; *FMR*, 15 July 1913, 7 January, 12 March, 27 September, 11 October 1914.

58. *FMR*, 20 September 1914.

59. Ibid., 18 October 1914, 1 November 1914.

60. Ibid., 27 September 1914, 18 October 1914.

61. The cost of hiring solicitors and checking signatures was placed at $4,300 by the Northern California Water Association, which handled the bulk of this work. "Account and Report of Perry and Daley with Northern California Water Association," Miller & Lux Papers.

62. J. W. Hawkes to Treadwell, 8 July 1913, Miller & Lux Papers; Bruce Geil to Treadwell, 18 July 1913, ibid.; J. F. Clyne to Treadwell, 14 August 1913, ibid.

63. *FMR*, 7 May 1915.

64. Ibid., 30 April 1915.

65. *FMR*, 27 January 1915, 30 April 1915, 7 May 1915; California Legislature, *Final Calendar of Legislative Business, 1915*, 41st sess.

66. California Legislature, *Final Calendar, 1915*, 41st sess.

67. Mowry, pp. 195–242.

68. Treadwell to Nickel, 26 October 1915, carton 127, Miller & Lux Papers; Treadwell, "Modernizing the Water Law," *California Law Review* 17 (1928): 14; Treadwell, Oral Argument, 16 March 1916, *PLSCo* v. *Lewis*, 241 U.S. 440, carton 489, Miller & Lux Papers.

69. Among the sixteen members of the conference were the heads of the legislative committees on irrigation and drainage, and the chairmen of the water commission, the reclamation board, and the conservation commission. State Water Problems Conference, *Report*, 25 November 1916, in *Appendix to the Journals of the Senate and Assembly of California*, 42d sess., 1917, vol. 6, p. 7.

70. *California Blue Book or State Roster, 1913–1915*, pp. 473–513 passim.

71. State Water Problems Conference, *Report*, pp. 5–7, 12.

72. Ibid., pp. 54–55; Treadwell to Nickel, 4 January 1917, carton 150, Miller & Lux Papers.

73. State Water Problems Conference, *Report*, p. 99.

74. Adams, "Economical Use of Water," pp. 372–73.

75. Ibid., pp. 373–74.

76. Ibid., pp. 375–76; Frank Adams, "Progress Report of Cooperative Irrigation Investigations in California, 1912–1914," California Department of Engineering, *Bulletin* 1 (1915): 56.

77. A. E. Chandler, "Water Rights in California—in which the Principal Matter Discussed is that of Riparian Rights," in *Report of the State Water Commission of California*, 1917, p. 57.

78. *Hough* v. *Porter*, 51 Or. 318, 98 P. 1083 (1909); *Little Walla Irrigation Union* v. *Finis Irrigation Company*, 62 Ore 348, 124 P. 666 (1912).

79. Wiel, "What Is Beneficial Use?" (see chap. 3, n. 55), p. 475.

80. Henry Miller to Clyne, 19 September 1913, Miller & Lux Papers; Nickel to Clyne, 26 March 1913, carton 413, ibid.

81. Treadwell to Nickel, 8 August 1913, carton 95, Miller & Lux Papers.

82. Nickel to Clyne, 20 August 1913, carton 413, Miller & Lux Papers.

83. Nickel to Clyne, 26 March 1913, 7 April 1913, 20 August 1913, carton 413, Miller & Lux Papers; Nickel to D. W. Wallis, 20 June 1913, ibid.

84. Nickel to Treadwell, 2 October 1913, Miller & Lux Papers; Treadwell to Nickel, 3 October 1913, ibid.

85. Nickel to Clyne, 19 December 1914, carton 116, Miller & Lux Papers; see also Nickel to Clyne, 12, 17, 18 December 1914, carton 116, ibid.

86. Nickel to Clyne, 17 September 1918, carton 382, Miller & Lux Papers.

87. Barclay McCowan to State Water Commission, 21 September 1915, box 161, Miller & Lux Papers; J. A. Patten to Tulare Water Company, 22 September 1915, ibid.; A. E. Chandler to Tulare Water Company, 14 August 1919, ibid.; Treadwell to State Water Commission, 18 August 1919, ibid.; *Tulare Water Co.* v. *State Water Commission,* 187 Cal 533, 202 P. 874 (1921).

88. Wiel, "Determination of Water Titles," p. 449.

89. *Herminghaus* v. *Southern California Edison,* 200 Cal 81 (1926); *Fall River Valley Irrigation District* v. *Mt. Shasta Power Corporation,* 202 Cal 56 (1927); *Scott* v. *Fruit Growers Supply Company,* 202 Cal 47 (1927); *Tulare Irrigation District* v. *Lindsay-Strathmore Irrigation District,* 45 Pac (2d) 972 (1935). Even though the court found in the Fall River case that the riparian owners had used all the water beneficially and thus that section 11 did not apply, it made a point of stating that section 11 was not valid. Justice Shenk dissented from the decision, arguing that the majority opinion would further entrench riparian owners in making unreasonable demands.

90. *Herminghaus* v. *Southern California Edison,* 200 Cal 81 (1926).

91. 1927 Cal. Stats. 2373.

92. Samuel Wiel, "The Pending Water Amendment to the California Constitution, and Possible Legislation," *California Law Review,* 16 (1928): 170–75. Wiel himself felt that the amendment would strengthen the aspects of *Herminghaus* that prevented the confiscation of riparian rights. Many members of the panel of lawyers commissioned to discuss the legal aspects of a state water project also shared this point of view. Henry E. Monroe et al., "Report of Legal Committee to Joint Legislative Committee Appointed to Investigate the Water Problems of the State and Recommend Some State-wide Policy for the Conservation and Use of Water," 27 October 1928, Bancroft Library. See also Miller, "Water Rights" (see chap. 3, n. 100), pp. 103–5.

93. Frank Adams, University of California, on irrigation, reclamation, and water administration, 1959, interview by Willa Klug Baum, Regional Cultural History Project, University of California, Berkeley, p. 219.

94. J. E. Woolley to Nickel, 1 November 1928, carton 282, Miller & Lux Papers.

CHAPTER 5

1. For example, see Nickel to John Gilcrest, 26 November 1914, carton 116, Miller & Lux Papers; on Miller's style of management, see Treadwell, *Cattle King* (see intro., n. 4). See also Ralph Milliken's interviews with Louie Arbura, 31 March 1930, F1:229, Milliken Collection, California State University, Stanislaus; and with Archie Smith, n.d., F1:241, Milliken Collection.

2. Jimmy M. Skaggs, *Prime Cut: Livestock Raising and Meatpacking in the United States, 1607–1983* (College Station: Texas A & M University, 1986) p. 135; Miller & Lux to E. Sebbelov, 14 November 1913, carton 100, Miller & Lux Papers; Nickel to F. H. Raffo, 17 November 1913, ibid.; Nickel to George W. Nickel, 18 November

1913, ibid.; R. L. Adams to Miller & Lux, 13 November 1913, ibid.; Leon K. David to Nickel, 4 December 1913, ibid.

3. Nickel to Clyne, 10, 12, 14, 30 December 1914, carton 116, Miller & Lux Papers; Nickel to Miller & Lux, 29 December 1914, ibid.

4. The federal government initially demanded $4 million in inheritance taxes; penalties for nonpayment later pushed the total demanded above $6 million; California, Oregon, and Nevada together demanded some $4 million more income, estate, & inheritance taxes. Nickel's protests included a challenge to the application of the federal tax law, which had been adopted three years after the inter vivos trust had been formed, and a rejection of the government's valuation of the estate. Although the heirs won the tax protest, the floating of bonds to pay the government's early demands cost the firm close to $2.5 million in interest and legal costs. When the battle was won, Nickel refused to pay the fee Treadwell asked for his efforts, which included appearing as amicus curiae in related cases in other states and cooperating with other estates in challenging the law. Treadwell resigned and sued Nickel for the fee. He won the case in 1924. *Treadwell* v. *Nickel*, 194 Cal 243 (1924). Appellant's Reply Brief, pp. 17–25, *Treadwell* v. *Nickel*, ibid.; *San Francisco Chronicle*, 7 September 1921. The lawsuits that challenged the various state and federal laws included *In re Miller's Estate*, 184 Cal 674, 195 P. 413 (1921); *Nickel* v. *State of California*, 175 P. 641 (1918); *Nickel* v. *State of Nevada*, 185 P. 565 (1919); *Cole* v. *Nickel*, 177 P. 409 (1919); *Nickel* v. *Cole*, 256 U.S. 222 (1921); *Shwab* v. *Doyle*, 269 F. 321 (C.C.A., 6th, 1920), 258 U.S. 529 (1922); *Union Trust* v. *Wardell*, 273 F. 733 (D.C. Cal, 1921), 258 U.S. 537 (1922); *Levy* v. *Wardell*, 258 U.S. 542 (1922).

5. J. W. Matthews, Memorandum Book and Diary, 6 April 1899 to 11 August 1900, Bancroft Library. Matthews worked as a laborer on Miller & Lux's San Joaquin ranches during this period.

6. Clyne to Nickel, 1 April 1918, cartons 164, 382, Miller & Lux Papers; Nickel to Clyne, 3 April 1918, ibid.; Nickel to Miller & Lux, 13 August 1917, carton 152, ibid.; Miller & Lux to Nickel, 10 August 1917, ibid.; wage schedule attached to Clyne to Nickel, 8 November 1918, carton 382, ibid.

7. Nickel to Clyne, 12 March 1921, 11 August 1921, carton 384, Miller & Lux Papers.

8. Treadwell to Nickel, 24 December 1914, carton 116, Miller & Lux Papers; Alexander C. Shaw to Oswald West, 22 December 1914, carton 116, ibid.; *In re Silvies River*, 199 Fed 495 (D. C. Ore., 1912); *Pacific Live Stock Co.* v. *Cochran*, 144 P. 668 (1914); *Pacific Live Stock Co.* v. *Lewis*, 217 Fed 95 (D.C. Ore., 1914), 241 U.S. 440 (1916); A. R. Olsen to Nickel, 6 December 1919, carton 682, Miller & Lux Papers; *State* v. *Pacific Live Stock Company*, 93 Or. 196, 182 P. 828 (1919).

9. Treadwell to Nickel, 12 July 1910, carton 42, Miller & Lux Papers; *Pacific Live-Stock Co.* v. *Hanley et al.*, 98 F. 327 (C.C.D. Ore., 1899); *Pacific Live Stock Co.* v. *Hanley et al*, 200 F. 468 (9th Cir., 1912).

10. Wood to Treadwell, 6 January 1919, carton 464, Miller & Lux Papers.

11. Treadwell to Ben Newman, 18 November 1916, carton 143, Miller & Lux Papers; Treadwell to PLSCo, 24 August 1917, carton 152, ibid.; Nickel to Wm. Hanley, 1 September 1917, carton 465, ibid.; Treadwell to Nickel, 28 June 1918, carton 178, ibid.; Nickel to PLSCo, 7 April 1919, carton 207, ibid.; Olsen to Nickel, 17 April 1919, carton 207, ibid.; Olsen to Nickel, 5 June 1919, carton 178, ibid.; Treadwell to Olsen, 18 June 1919, carton 178, ibid.; *William Hanley Co.* v. *Harney Valley Irrigation District No. 1*, 180 P. 724 (1919), 182 P. 559 (1919).

12. Olsen to Treadwell, 1 July 1919, 6 December 1919, carton 464, Miller & Lux Papers; Olsen to Nickel, 6, 7 December 1919, carton 682, ibid.; Olsen to Nickel, 22 February 1920, carton 192, ibid.; Treadwell to Nickel, 8 April 1920, carton 192, ibid.; *Harney Valley Irrigation District* v. *Weittenhiller*, 101 Or. 1, 198 P. 1093 (1921); *Allen* v. *Levens*, 101 Or. 466, 198 P. 907 (1921), 199 P. 595 (1921); *Harney Valley Irrigation District* v. *Bolton*, 109 Or. 486, 221 P. 171 (1922).

13. Treadwell to PLSCo, 17 January 1920, carton 192, Miller & Lux Papers; William Hanley to Nickel, 29 March 1920, carton 466, ibid.; Treadwell, Memorandum as to Report on Harney Valley Irrigation District, 23 December 1920, carton 197, ibid.

14. Nickel to Olsen, 24 December 1919, carton 682, Miller & Lux Papers; Nickel to PLSCo, 15 March 1921, carton 200, ibid.

15. Treadwell, Memorandum as to Report on Harney Valley Irrigation District, 23 December 1920, carton 197, Miller & Lux Papers; Olsen to Treadwell, 9 November 1921, carton 208, ibid.; *Harney Valley Irrigation District* v. *Bolton*, 221 P. 171.

16. Treadwell to Nickel, 20 October 1916, carton 143, Miller & Lux Papers; Treadwell to Short, 7, 19, 25 October 1916, carton 144, ibid.; Treadwell to Nickel, 3 February 1917, carton 150, ibid.; Nickel to Treadwell, 8 September 1917, carton 510, ibid.; Nickel to Treadwell, 26 September 1917, carton 465, ibid. This district was not the same as the Madera Irrigation District that was initiated in the 1880s (see chap. 4, n. 2). This second MID was closely tied to the former manager of the Madera Canal & Irrigation Company, Robert Hargrove, who had been an activist in the San Joaquin Water Problems Association. For the official history of the second district, see Madera Irrigation District, Sixth Annual Report, 1981.

17. Clyne to Treadwell, 24 January 1918, carton 601, Miller & Lux Papers.

18. Clyne to Treadwell, 24 January 1918, 15, 28 May 1918, 1, 7 June 1918, 10 July 1918, carton 601, Miller & Lux Papers; Treadwell to Clyne, 4 June 1918, 11 July 1918, carton 382, ibid.

19. Delger Trowbridge to Berkeley B. Blake, 20 April 1919, carton 464, Miller & Lux Papers. For the history of Pope & Talbot, see Edwin T. Coman, Jr., and Helen M. Gibbs, *Time, Tide and Timber: A Century of Pope & Talbot* (Stanford, Calif.: Stanford Univ. Press 1949).

20. Trowbridge to Treadwell, 11 April 1919, carton 464, Miller & Lux Papers; Trowbridge to Blake, 20 April 1919, carton 464, ibid.; *San Francisco Bulletin*, 16 April 1919 (clipping), carton 495, ibid.

21. Elwood Mead to Farnham P. Griffiths, 1 April 1919, carton 495, Miller & Lux Papers; *San Francisco Bulletin*, 16 April 1919 (clipping), ibid.; W.F. McClure to Lee Gebhart, 15 April 1919, ibid.

22. Treadwell to Clyne, 20 May 1919, carton 178, Miller & Lux Papers.

23. Nickel to Clyne, 28 August 1919, cartons 383, 178, ibid.

24. Treadwell to Nickel, 4 November 1919, carton 181, ibid.

25. W. M. Conley to Treadwell, 24 February 1920, carton 466, Miller & Lux Papers; Cowell to Treadwell, 23 February 1920, carton 466, ibid.; Miller & Lux to Arthur Leavenrich et al., 25 February 1920, carton 192, ibid.

26. Samuel Fortier to Treadwell, 8 May 1920, carton 466, Miller & Lux Papers.

27. Agreement between State Water Commission and Madera Irrigation District, June 1920, Barnes 169, Harry Barnes Papers, Water Resources Center Archives, University of California, Berkeley; W. A. Johnstone to Treadwell, 18 May 1920, carton 510, Miller & Lux Papers; Treadwell to Johnstone, 19 May 1920, ibid.; Johnstone to Treadwell, 25 May 1920, ibid.; Treadwell to Johnstone, 1 June 1920, ibid.

28. Numerous examples appear in the Milliken interviews; see interviews with L. A. Sischo, 8 March 1945, F1:241; Archie Smith, n.d., F1:241; Hattie Safstrom, 20 March 1962, F1:206; Mrs. Icie Jameson, 30 October 1953, F1:235.

29. Clyne to Nickel, 22 August 1918, carton 601, Miller & Lux Papers; A. L. Cowell to Treadwell, 29 December 1919, carton 464, ibid.

30. *Mordecai v. Board of Supervisors*, 192 P. 40 (1920).

31. Nickel to Clyne, 21 July 1920, carton 194, Miller & Lux Papers.

32. Treadwell to Madera Irrigation District, 1 November 1920, carton 196, Miller & Lux Papers; see also Cowell to Treadwell, 1 March 1920, carton 466, Miller & Lux Papers.

33. "Litigation in re Madera Irrigation District," carton 517, Miller & Lux Papers; statement quoted in Address of Sherwood Green before the Rotary Club, Madera County, California, June 22, 1922, p. 11, Barnes 72, Barnes Papers.

34. Nickel to Clyne, 16 August 1920, carton 194, Miller & Lux Papers.

35. Treadwell to Berkeley B. Blake, 16 October 1920, carton 466, Miller & Lux Papers; Treadwell, Memorandum, 11 December 1920, carton 466, ibid.

36. K. Cameron to Nickel, 14 June 1924, carton 242, Miller & Lux Papers. This method proved to be an obstacle in 1924, when litigation with the Tranquillity Irrigation required just such a proof of water rights. It was also be a major problem in the later attempts to set up a water storage district, as discussed in chap. 6.

37. Nickel to Clyne, 28 July 1920, carton 194, Miller & Lux Papers.

38. SJ&KRC&ICo to Clyne, 3 February 1921, Miller & Lux Papers; Nickel to Clyne, 3 February 1921, carton 200, ibid.

39. Clyne to Nickel, 29 March 1919, 4 April 1919, carton 383, Miller & Lux Papers; Clyne to Nickel, 17, 24, 28 May 1919, 20 June 1919, carton 682, ibid.; Berkeley B. Blake to Treadwell, 26 May 1919, carton 464, ibid.; Nickel to Blake, 31 May 1919, carton 179, ibid.; Nickel to Clyne, 23 June 1919, carton 178, ibid. This effort

involved the establishment of a corporation to be funded by the landowners for the purpose of building the canal. Miller & Lux would provide legal and engineering aid, and when the canal was completed, the SJ&KRC&ICo would manage it.

40. Nickel to Clyne, 16 August 1920, carton 194, Miller & Lux Papers; Clyne to Treadwell, 10 September 1920, carton 466, ibid.

41. Treadwell, Memorandum as to Senate Bill 242, 21 June 1921, carton 203, Miller & Lux Papers.

42. A. L. Cowell to Treadwell, 16 September 1920, carton 466, Miller & Lux Papers; Nickel to Clyne, 11 September 1920, carton 197, ibid.

43. Cowell to Treadwell, 16 September 1920, carton 466, Miller & Lux Papers.

44. Treadwell, Memorandum for Adjustment of Irrigation District Matters, 24 September 1920, carton 466, Miller & Lux Papers.

45. Cowell to Treadwell, 17 December 1921, carton 384, Miller & Lux Papers; Nickel to Clyne, 19 December 1921, carton 384, ibid.

46. Nickel to Clyne, 11, 12 March 1921, 11 August 1921, carton 384, Miller & Lux Papers.

47. Clyne to Nickel, 14, 21 December 1921, carton 384, Miller & Lux Papers; Nickel to Clyne, 16 December 1921, carton 208, ibid.; Nickel to Clyne, 19 December 1921, carton 384, ibid.; W. F. Hume to Clyne, 6 March 1922, ibid.; Hume to Nickel, 6 March 1922, carton 386, ibid.

48. L. L. Dennett to Treadwell, 22 June 1921, carton 511, Miller & Lux Papers.

49. Nickel to Clyne, 6 February 1922, carton 386, Miller & Lux Papers.

50. Clyne to Nickel, 8, 15 February 1922, carton 222, Miller & Lux Papers.

51. J. Leroy Nickel, Jr., to Nickel, 30 January 1922, carton 222, Miller & Lux Papers; Cowell to Treadwell, 5 February 1922, carton 386, ibid.; Nickel to Clyne, 6 February 1922, carton 386, ibid.; S. T. Harding, Records of the Relation of the State Engineer's office to the San Joaquin River Water Storage District, July 1, 1928, pp. 1–2, Harding 37, S. T. Harding Papers, Water Resources Center Archives, University of California, Berkeley.

52. Clyne to Wangenheim, 23 February 1922, carton 386, Miller & Lux Papers; Wangenheim to Clyne, 27 February 1922, carton 386, ibid. Bottoms had asked for fifty cents for every acre in the irrigation district. When, under pressure from Miller & Lux, the district refused to pay Bottoms, he sued for his fee. Transcript of Reporter on Appeal, pp. 143–63, 375–421, 1224–35, *Herminghaus v. Southern California Edison*, 200 Cal 81 (1926); *Madera Mercury*, 8 August 1922, 25 October 1925; Nickel to Treadwell, 30 March 1923, carton 225, Miller & Lux Papers; Clyne to J. Leroy Nickel, Jr., 16 March 1923, carton 224, ibid.; T. P. Wittschen to Nickel, 21, 27, 28 December 1922, carton 517, ibid.

53. Tri-Party Agreement—Miller & Lux, West Side Storage District, and Madera Irrigation District, 7 September 1922, Barnes 169, Barnes Papers.

54. Ibid.; Harding, Records of the Relations of the State Engineer's Office to the SJRWSD, p. 7–10, Harding 37.

55. Hammatt to Milton T. Farmer, 20 December 1922, carton 386, Miller & Lux Papers; McClure to Farmer, 15 December 1922, carton 221, ibid.; Sidney T. Harding, "A Life in Western Water Development," oral interview edited by Gerald J. Giefer (Statewide Water Resources Center, University of California, in cooperation with Regional Oral History Office, Bancroft Library, University of California, Berkeley, 1967), pp. 98–99.

56. McClure had appointed Harding as consulting engineer for water storage district matters, a position he held through 1928. Harding, "Life in Water Development," p. 73; idem, "Discussion of the Functions of the State Engineer in Relation to Water Storage Districts," December 1922, Harding 38-1; W. F. McClure to Board of Directors, Madera Irrigation District, 15 December 1922, ibid.; Gail C. Larkin to Nickel, 22 September 1922, carton 222, Miller & Lux Papers.

57. Nickel to Farmer, 29 December 1922, carton 221, Miller & Lux Papers.

58. Farmer to McClure, 16 December 1922, carton 221, Miller & Lux Papers.

59. *Tulare Water Co.* v. *State Water Commission*, 187 Cal 533, 202 P. 874 (1921).

60. Nickel to Clyne, 7, 8 June 1923, carton 230, Miller & Lux Papers.

61. McClure to Miller & Lux Inc., 6 June 1923, carton 230, Miller & Lux Papers.

62. Nickel to Clyne, 8, 13 June 1923, carton 230, Miller & Lux Papers; K. Cameron to Nickel, 6 June 1923, carton 227, ibid.

63. Clyne to Nickel, 21 April 1923, carton 224, Miller & Lux Papers; Clyne to Nickel, 9, 13 June 1923, carton 230, ibid.

64. Treadwell to Nickel, 3 May 1923, carton 230, Miller & Lux Papers; Nickel to Clyne, 21 April 1923, carton 224, ibid.

65. *Tarpey* v. *McClure* 190 Cal 593, 213 P. 983 (1923).

66. Kenneth C. Gillis to Nickel, Memo Re Water Storage District Act, 10 July 1923, carton 230, Miller & Lux Papers.

67. T. P. Wittschen to Nickel, 19 July 1923, carton 227, Miller & Lux Papers.

68. Clyne to Nickel, 12 July 1923, carton 230, Miller & Lux Papers; Nickel to Clyne, 10 July 1923, carton 230, ibid.

69. Harding, Records of the Relations of the State Engineer's Office to the San Joaquin River Water Storage District, p. 8, Harding 37.

70. The board of directors consisted of Nickel, J. F. Clyne, J. Leroy Nickel, Jr., and George Bowles, all representing Miller & Lux; D. B. Harris of the Madera Irrigation District; O. A. Robertson, manager of Chowchilla Farms, a large east side ranching company; E. S. Wangenheim, manager of Simon Newman Co. in Stanislaus County; and W. E. Bunker, a prominent irrigator from the SJ&KRC&ICo who was active in the formation of the West Joaquin District. The ninth member, selected by these eight, was W. A. Sutherland, a Fresno attorney who was the former partner of Frank Short. Farmer continued as the district's attorney and Barnes as its resident engineer. See Barnes to Nickel, 7 July 1925, carton 257, Miller & Lux Papers; Harding, Summary of the History of the San Joaquin Water Storage District to July 7, 1928, p. 3, Harding 37.

71. Barnes to Farmer, 5 January 1927, Barnes 115.

72. Nickel to Clyne, 19 March 1923, carton 224, Miller & Lux Papers; Clyne to Nickel, 23 March 1923, carton 224, ibid.

73. Clyne to Nickel, 23 December 1922, carton 386, Miller & Lux Papers.

74. K. Cameron to Nickel, 6 June 1923, carton 227, Miller & Lux Papers.

75. T. P. Wittschen to Nickel, 21 December 1922, carton 386, Miller & Lux Papers.

76. Hammatt to S. T. Harding, 11 July 1922, carton 510, Miller & Lux Papers.

77. Wittschen to Nickel, 23 March 1923, carton 225, Miller & Lux Papers; Wittschen to Nickel, 4 April 1923, carton 224, ibid.; Harding, Records of the Relation of the State Engineer's Office to the SJRWSD, p. 14, Harding 37.

78. Wittschen to Nickel, 11 April 1923, carton 224, Miller & Lux Papers.

79. Harding, Records of the Relation of the State Engineer's Office to the SJRWSD, p. 16, Harding 37.

80. James E. Fickett to Barnes, 16 November 1925, carton 747, Miller & Lux Papers. Farmer earlier dated the San Luis appropriation from December 1914; Farmer to W. C. Hammatt, 31 December 1925, Barnes 115.

81. Nickel to Wittschen, 28 November 1924, carton 247, Miller & Lux Papers; Wittschen to Nickel, 31 January 1925, carton 252, ibid.; Wittschen to Clyne, 31 January 1925, carton 252, ibid.; Nickel to Clyne, 23, 29 January 1925, 3 February 1925, carton 252, ibid.; Nickel to Clyne, 2 February 1925, carton 388, ibid.; Clyne to Nickel, 2 February 1925, carton 252, ibid.

82. Wittschen to Nickel, 9, 29 November 1924, carton 247, Miller & Lux Papers; Wittschen to Barnes, 8 April 1925, carton 252, ibid. Until this point, MID attorneys had insisted that neither Miller & Lux nor Southern California Edison had a property right to the stored water. See W. L. Huber to F. M. Carter, 7 December 1920, Huber 153, Walter Leroy Huber Collection, Water Resources Center Archives, University of California, Berkeley.

83. T. P. Wittschen to Nickel, 10 July 1924, carton 242, Miller & Lux Papers.

84. Barnes to Wangenheim, 16 September 1926, Barnes 115. The value per acre-foot was calculated from the total value of the grassland right, which was estimated to yield 373,000 acre-feet of water per year. Barnes was very skeptical of Tibbetts's figures, as he had come up with at least four sets of values that varied dramatically, the largest being four times that of the smallest. He averaged the four to arrive at the figure of almost $7 million.

85. Wangenheim and Barnes had independently hired a bank appraiser named Whistler to appraise the canal company's right-of-way. His appraisal was quite low, and Miller & Lux had worked hard to limit its influence on Kempkey. Tibbetts worried that the low valuation would affect land values throughout the area. Wangenheim, Whistler, and others later stated that the grasslands were worth at the most $10 an acre. Clyne placed their value at $40–50 an acre. Nickel to Clyne, 26, 29 September 1924, carton 387, Miller & Lux Papers; Clyne to Nickel, 27 September 1925, carton 387, ibid.; Nickel to Clyne, 2 January 1925, carton 252, ibid.; Clyne to Nickel, 3 January 1925, carton 388, ibid.

86. Barnes to Wangenheim, 16 September 1925, carton 115, Miller & Lux Papers; Harding, Records of the Relation of the State Engineer's Office to the SJRWSD, pp. 22–23, Harding 37.

87. Barnes to Board of Directors, 11 April 1925, Barnes 115; Hammatt to Barnes, 28 April 1925, carton 747, Miller & Lux Papers; Hammatt to Nickel, 17 March 1925, carton 747, ibid.; Nickel to Clyne, 22 January 1925, carton 252, ibid.; Harding, Record of the Relation of State Engineer's Office to the SJRWSD, pp. 21, 24–26, Harding 37.

88. McClure here was following Harding's lead. Harding had reviewed the plan in April and later wrote the formal evaluation of the plan. His report was not issued until September, but its main points were well known by early June. Harding, "Life in Water Development," pp. 102–3.

89. McClure stated that he meant no criticism of Kempkey as an engineer and recognized that he was just doing the job he had been assigned. His statement may, however, have been insincere. Harding later claimed that the accusation of bias could have been sustained because Kempkey's appraisal was inconsistent and favored Miller & Lux. Harding believed that Kempkey had let himself be misled when he failed to seek information from all quarters, in particular from Barnes. While Kempkey alleged that Barnes was prejudiced against Miller & Lux, Harding insisted that Barnes was not anti–Miller & Lux but rather pro-district. Harding, Records of the Relation of the State Engineer's Office to the San Joaquin River Water Storage District, 1 July 1928, pp. 30–31, Harding 37.

90. McClure to A. Kempkey, 24 June 1925, carton 388, Miller & Lux Papers; Harding, Report on the Proposed Plan of the SJRWSD as Submitted Informally to the State Engineer by Resolution No. 76 to the Board of Directors of the SJRWSD, 1 September 1925, pp. 27–28, Harding 37-A.

91. Nickel to Clyne, 2 June 1925, carton 256, Miller & Lux Papers; Clyne to Nickel, 24 June 1925, carton 256, ibid.

92. Harding, "Life in Water Development," p. 102–3; quotations from Harding, Record of the Relations of the State Engineer's Office to the SJRWSD, pp. 27–28, Harding 37.

CHAPTER 6

1. Harry N. Scheiber, Harold G. Vatter, and Harold Underwood Faulkner, *American Economic History*, 9th ed. (New York: Harper and Row, 1976), pp. 345–46; Mary Montgomery and Marion Clawson, *History of Legislative and Policy Formation of the Central Valley Project* (Bureau of Agricultural Economics, 1946), p. 22; Clyne to Nickel, 31 December 1925, carton 270, Miller & Lux Papers.

2. Donald P. Spears, "California Besieged: The Foot-and-Mouth Epidemic of 1924," *Agricultural History* 56 (1982): 528–41; Miller & Lux Inc. to Nickel, 25 March

1924, carton 239, Miller & Lux Papers; Nickel to Nickel, Jr., 4 June 1924, carton 242, ibid.

3. Copy of a petition, To the Honorable Railroad Commission, 29 July 1924, attached to H. G. Matthews to SJ&KRC&ICo, 30 July 1924, carton 387, Miller & Lux Papers.

4. Clyne to Wittschen, 25 October 1924, carton 387, Miller & Lux Papers.

5. SJ&KRC&ICo to S. J. Mason, 22 March 1924, carton 387, Miller & Lux Papers.

6. Miller & Lux to Southern California Edison Company, 19 May 1924, carton 387, Miller & Lux Papers.

7. SJ&KRC&ICo to Mason, 22 March 1924, carton 387, Miller & Lux Papers. The canal company could change the level of water by opening and closing the headgates of the canal. In fact it had long asserted that much of the water in the slough was its own water, impounded for the use of canal company customers.

8. Nickel to Wittschen, 2 May 1924, carton 237, Miller & Lux Papers; Wittschen to Nickel, 6 May 1924, carton 237, ibid.; Joseph Sharp to Nickel, 21 May 1924, carton 242, ibid.; Wittschen to Nickel, 19 December 1924, carton 247, ibid.; Milton T. Farmer to Hammatt, 23 June 1925, carton 388, ibid.; Nickel to Clyne, 2 July 1925, carton 388, ibid.; Hammatt to Nickel, 2 July 1925, carton 388, ibid.; Nickel, Memorandum regarding Proposed Settlement with the Tranquillity Irrigation District, [3 July 1925], carton 388, ibid.; Clyne to Nickel, 3 July 1925, carton 388, ibid.; Nickel to Clyne, 6, 7 July 1925, carton 388, ibid.; [J.] Woolley to Clyne, 9 July 1925, carton 256, ibid.; Nickel to Clyne, 24 July 1925, carton 388, ibid.; Woolley to Clyne, 18 November 1925, carton 262, ibid.

In 1930 a Madera County judge apportioned the San Joaquin to give Miller & Lux the right to 88 percent of the flow at the junction of Fresno Slough and the San Joaquin River; the James interests were granted rights to the remaining 12 percent of its flow. Both were subject to the prescriptive right of the SJ&KRC&ICo to 1,360 cfs. The decision presumed the conditions at this junction to be natural and considered the power-released waters to be part of the natural flow of the stream. A notice of appeal was filed, but action on it was not completed. Miller & Lux v. San Joaquin Valley Farm Lands Co., case no. 3094, the Superior Court of Madera County, 14 April 1930, carton 522, Miller & Lux Papers.

9. Nickel to Superintendents of Miller & Lux, 10 April 1924, carton 239, Miller & Lux Papers.

10. Nickel to Clyne, 8 October 1924, carton 242, Miller & Lux Papers.

11. Nickel to Clyne, 2 October 1924, carton 247, Miller & Lux Papers.

12. Nickel to Clyne, 3 November 1924, carton 387, Miller & Lux Papers; Clyne to Nickel, 17 November 1924, carton 387, ibid.

13. Deed of Trust, July 1, 1910, Miller & Lux Incorporated to Mercantile Trust Company of San Francisco; Deed of Trust, June 15, 1920, Miller & Lux Incorporated to Bank of California, National Association, Trustee, carton 594, Miller & Lux Papers.

14. In 1916–17 the federal government set the value of the firm's property at $46

million; Miller & Lux, in its efforts to lower taxes, asserted that this figure was too high. Miller & Lux to Holders of First Mortgage Bonds of Miller & Lux Incorporated, 5 February 1918 (unsigned copy), box: General Correspondence, 1918, January–March, 16f–58, Miller & Lux Papers; Treadwell to Britton and Gray, 23 October 1918, carton 166, ibid.; Skaggs, *Prime Cut* (see chap. 5, n. 2), pp. 133–34.

15. Ad for the Miller & Lux bond issue, Barnes 168, Barnes Papers.

16. Trust Indenture, October 1, 1925, Miller & Lux Incorporated to Bank of California, carton 594, Miller & Lux Papers; ad for the Miller & Lux bond issue, Barnes 168; Nickel to Board of Directors, Miller & Lux Inc., 16 November 1925, carton 262, Miller & Lux Papers. *San Francisco Chronicle*, 8 October 1925, 19 February 1930, 15 March 1930. The company that bought the firm's cattle also leased some 80,000 acres of west side land from Miller & Lux.

17. Nickel to Clyne, 2 June 1925, carton 256, Miller & Lux Papers.

18. Nickel to Wittschen, 6 June 1925, carton 257, Miller & Lux Papers.

19. Nickel to Wittschen, 9 June 1925, carton 257, Miller & Lux Papers.

20. Nickel to J. E. Woolley, 29 October 1925, carton 262, Miller & Lux Papers; Haehl, Etcheverry, Herrman to Board of Directors, 27 August 1925, carton 256, ibid.; Farmer to Haehl, Herrman, and Etcheverry, 10 September 1925, Barnes 115.

21. C. H. Mead to Fickett, 27 July 1926, 28 September 1926, 1, 15 November 1926, carton 271, Miller & Lux Papers; C. H. Mead, Memorandum for James E. Fickett, 28 September 1926, carton 271, ibid. For example, M. Silva owed the firm $15,290 on 45 acres of land, a debt of $342 per acre on land then appraised at $220 an acre. He had paid nothing since 1920. Miller & Lux planned to reduce Silva's debt by 25 percent under a new contract if he would make a substantial payment of $3,000 to $5,000. Another case is that of Emil Alberti, who owed the firm $14,400 on 96.58 acres of land; he had already reduced his original debt on this land by almost $20,000. Although Alberti was "hostile" and claimed that Miller & Lux had misrepresented the land, the firm felt it was safe with his debt—Alberti had invested so much that he would pay the rest.

22. Woolley to Nickel, 1 February 1926, carton 270, Miller & Lux Papers; Barnes to Valuation Committee, Board of Directors, 12 February 1926, Barnes 115; James E. Fickett to Board of Directors, 16 March 1926, carton 270, Miller & Lux Papers; Nickel to San Joaquin River Water Storage District, 23 March 1926, carton 747, ibid.

23. Hammatt also developed explanations based on a general appreciation in value over time. Hammatt to Nickel, 11 September 1926, carton 271, Miller & Lux Papers; Hammatt, Memorandum Regarding Increased Value of Water Right of SJ&KRC&ICo over its Value at the Time of its Appraisal in the Rate Case, [11 September 1926], carton 271, ibid.; Barnes to Wangenheim, 16 September 1926, Barnes 115.

24. James Peck represented the Stevinson interests in this suit. *San Francisco Chronicle*, 12 March 1926; J. E. Woolley, Memo, 12 March 1926, box 164, Miller & Lux Papers; Woolley to Malcolm C. Glenn, 8 May 1926, carton 271, ibid.; Woolley to Fickett, 13 April 1926, carton 270, ibid.

25. The irrigators were represented by the firm of Downey, Brand, Seymour, and Dunn of Sacramento; the California Farm Bureau Federation was represented in a verbal protest by attorney Edson Abel. *San Francisco Chronicle*, 3 June 1926.

26. McClure died in the middle of this process of replacement, which was completed by his successor, Paul Bailey. Harding, Records of the Relations of the State Engineer's Office to the San Joaquin River Water Storage District, p. 35, Harding 37, Harding Papers.

27. Barnes to Valuation Committee, 12 February 1926, Barnes 115, Barnes Papers.

28. Barnes to Valuation Committee, 9 March 1926, Barnes 115; Nickel to Clyne, 1 March 1926, carton 270, Miller & Lux Papers; Clyne to Nickel, 3 March 1926, carton 270, ibid.

29. Hammatt to Barnes, 9 April 1926, Barnes 115; Barnes to Farmer, 14 April 1926, ibid.

30. As evidence of the problem with "agreement," Barnes stated that, based on the data and records given him, he could justify a right of 215,800 acre-feet, versus Hammatt's 205,223 acre-feet. Barnes to Farmer, 14, 23 April 1926, Barnes 115.

31. Barnes to Valuation Committee, 6 May 1926, Barnes 115.

32. Harding, Materials Relating to the Herminghaus Case Prepared for the U.S. by State Attorney U.S. Webb, Harding 40; Harding, Report on the Effect Which Would Result from the Establishment of the Right to Store as a Part of the Rights of Riparian Owners on the Feasibility of Proposed Irrigation Projects, Particularly on the San Joaquin and Kings Rivers, 1 October 1925, pp. 28–30, ibid.; Harding to McClure, 30 September 1925, 13, 24 October 1925, 7 November 1925, ibid.

33. Farmer to Barnes, 17 April 1926, Barnes 115; Woolley to Barnes, 3 June 1926, cartons 271, 747, Miller & Lux Papers; Barnes to T. C. Mott, 19 April 1927, carton 747, ibid.

34. See *Pabst* v. *Finmand*, 211 P. 11 (1922).

35. Wittschen to Nickel, 12 December 1925, carton 262, Miller & Lux Papers; Farmer to Hammatt, 31 December 1925, Barnes 115.

36. Farmer to Barnes, 17 April 1925, Barnes 115; Woolley to Nickel, 26 April 1926, carton 270, Miller & Lux Papers. Miller & Lux attorney Woolley stated that he never had any doubt about the validity of such a dual right.

37. Fickett to Barnes, 16 November 1926, cartons 271, 747, Miller & Lux Papers.

38. Fickett to Barnes, 17 January 1927, carton 747, Miller & Lux Papers.

39. Barnes to Board of Directors, SJRWSD, 19 July 1927, Barnes 115.

40. Mildred H. Bentley to Madera Irrigation District, 12 October 1925, Barnes 115.

41. Barnes to Farmer, 28 May 1925, Barnes 115; Farmer to Barnes, 30 December 1925, ibid. The contract between Miller & Lux and the storage district drafted in 1925 treated the power-stored and -released water as a separately owned entity. However, in 1920 attorneys for the MID had insisted that neither Miller & Lux nor Southern California Edison had a property right in this water; the contracts might bind them to each other but the contracts divided something neither company owned. See W. L. Huber to F. M. Carter, 7 December 1920, Huber 153, Huber Collection.

42. *Horst* v. *New Blue Point Mining Co.*, 171 Pac 417.

43. Harding, "Report on the Proposed Plan of the San Joaquin River Water Storage District as Submitted Informally to the State Engineer," pp. 35–53 (quotation from p. 43), Harding 37a; Plaintiff's Authorities, Madera Irrigation District v. Miller & Lux and Southern California Edison, no. 2455, carton 510, Miller & Lux Papers.

44. Hammatt to Barnes, 8 May 1926, carton 747, Miller & Lux Papers; Hammatt to Farmer, 24 June 1926, carton 747, ibid.

45. Woolley to Barnes, 7 July 1926, cartons 747, 271, Miller & Lux Papers.

46. Farmer to Barnes, 19 April 1926, Barnes 115.

47. Farmer to Hammatt, 23 June 1926, Barnes 115; Barnes to Farmer, 6 July 1926, carton 747, Miller & Lux Papers; Farmer to Barnes, 3 August 1926, Barnes 115.

48. The Barnes report of August 25, 1926 is discussed in Hammatt to Nickel, 11 September 1926, and Hammatt, Memorandum in Regard to Power Released Water, [11 September 1926], carton 271, Miller & Lux Papers.

49. Barnes to Wangenheim, 25 September 1926, Barnes 115.

50. Ibid.

51. Quotation from Barnes, Memorandum of Conference with Mr. Fickett and Mr. Mott on November 8, 1926, carton 747, Miller & Lux Papers. Hammatt, "Memorandum in Regard to Power Released Water," [11 September 1926], carton 271, ibid.; Farmer to Barnes, 22 November 1926, Barnes 115; Fickett to Farmer, 10 December 1926, carton 747, Miller & Lux Papers; Barnes to Fickett, 18 December 1926, carton 747, ibid.

52. Woolley to Harold Conkling, 1 January 1927, carton 282, Miller & Lux Papers; Woolley to Mott, 3 January 1927, carton 282, ibid.; Barnes to Woolley, 20 January 1927, carton 747, ibid.; Barnes to Farmer, 20 January 1927, carton 711, ibid.

53. Woolley was the judge who had originally heard the *Herminghaus* case. He replaced T. P. Wittschen in mid-1925, when Wittschen resigned to become the attorney of the East Bay Municipal Utility District, a group hoping to establish a mountain water supply for Oakland similar to the Hetch Hetchy supply to San Francisco. Nickel had berated Wittschen on receiving his resignation, insisting that had could not approve of his departure until the storage district work was completed. However, he would not let any attorney employed by Miller & Lux represent another corporation on even a part-time basis, thus forcing Wittschen to choose between them. Wittschen to Nickel, 6, 10 June 1925, carton 257, Miller & Lux Papers; Nickel to Wittschen, 9 June 1925, carton 264, ibid.

54. Barnes to Farmer, 31 December 1926, carton 711, Miller & Lux Papers.

55. Barnes to Farmer, 20 January 1927, carton 711, Miller & Lux Papers; Barnes to Board of Directors, 5 April 1927, carton 711, Miller & Lux Papers, and Barnes 115; Barnes to Fickett, 13 April 1927, cartons 600, 747, Miller & Lux Papers.

56. Woolley to Barnes, 20 April 1927, carton 747, Miller & Lux Papers; Farmer to Board of Directors, 23 July 1927, Barnes 115.

57. The storage district had also asked Miller & Lux to pay its interest charges until the Friant dam was operational, a request that was quickly refused. Barnes to

W. A. Sutherland, 16 January 1928, Barnes 115; Fickett to Barnes, 19 March 1928, 23 March 1928, carton 282, Miller & Lux Papers; Barnes to Board of Directors, 26 March 1928, 3, 23 April 1928, Barnes 115; Fickett to Wangenheim, 19 April 1928, carton 282, Miller & Lux Papers; Resolution No. 200, Barnes 115; Barnes, Memorandum of Meeting Held on April 19, 1928, at 10 a.m. in office of J. Leroy Nickel in Merchants Exchange Building, San Francisco, ibid.; Barnes, Memorandum of Informal Meeting of the Directors Held at the Office of E. S. Wangenheim, 110 Market Street, San Francisco, on the afternoon of April 24, 1928, ibid.; Woolley to Edward Hyatt, Jr., 19 June 1928, carton 282, Miller & Lux Papers.

58. Nickel, Jr., to Nickel, 20 June 1928, carton 282, Miller & Lux Papers; Woolley to Fickett, 29 June 1928, carton 711, ibid.; Woolley to Nickel, 5 July 1928, carton 282, ibid.; Woolley to T. C. Mott, 9 July 1928, carton 282, ibid.; Woolley to Nickel, 12 September 1928, carton 282, ibid.; Woolley to Mott, 12 December 1928, carton 282, ibid.; Fred B. Wood to B. Grant Taylor, 4 February 1928, box 164, ibid.

59. Harding, Summary of History of San Joaquin River Water Storage District to July 1, 1928, Harding 37.

60. Sutherland to Walter C. Ficklin, 4 February 1929, Barnes 115; Barnes to Board of Directors, 4 September 1928, carton 711, Miller & Lux Papers, and Barnes 115.

61. It had begun this process in September 1926. Woolley to Bank of California, N.A., trustee, 2 September 1926, carton 271, Miller & Lux Papers; Woolley, Memorandum, 1 September 1926, carton 271, ibid.

62. Woolley to Edward Hyatt, Jr., 19 June 1928, 11 July 1928, 22 December 1928, carton 282, Miller & Lux Papers; Fickett to W. A. Sutherland, 15 August 1928, carton 711, ibid.; Nickel, Jr., to Mott, 18 September 1928, carton 282, ibid.; Barnes to Board of Directors, 27 November 1928, Barnes 115; Woolley to County Treasurer, Merced County, 27 February 1929, carton 287, Miller & Lux Papers; Woolley to Clare Berg, 2 March 1929, carton 287, ibid.

63. MID to Miller & Lux, 15 January 1929, in Compilation of Data Relative to the Proposed Purchase by the Madera Irrigation District of Certain Water Rights of Miller & Lux, carton 441, Miller & Lux Papers; Fickett to George Mordecai, 16 January 1929, ibid.

64. Harry Barnes, Statement Relative to the Position of the District, August 1929, Barnes 168; Woolley to George Mordecai, 15 August 1929, carton 287, Miller & Lux Papers; Woolley to Fickett, 29 July 1929, carton 289, ibid.; Stephen W. Downey to SJ&KRC&ICo, 12 September 1929, carton 438, ibid.; Mott to Fickett, 4 March 1930, in Compilation of Data . . . , carton 441, ibid.; A. R. Olsen to Fickett, 16 September 1929, carton 438, ibid.; Woolley to Olsen, 17 September 1929, 5 November 1929, carton 438, ibid.; Woolley to Mott, 13 August 1929, carton 282, ibid. In 1928, Fickett had also begun proceedings to raise the water rates charged by the canal company.

65. Barnes, Memorandum Relative to the Proposed Plan of Madera Irrigation District, 7 February 1930, in Compilation of Data . . . , carton 441, Miller & Lux Papers. On district costs, see Barnes to Board of Directors, SJRWSD, 3, 23 April 1928, Barnes 115.

66. Barnes, Memorandum Relative to Proposed Plan, in Compilation of Data . . . , carton 441, Miller & Lux Papers.

67. Ibid.

68. Olsen to Fickett, 5 March 1930, carton 510, Miller & Lux Papers.

69. Engineering Department, K. C[ameron], Memorandum—Harry Barnes' Proposed Plan of the Madera Irrigation District, February 7, 1930, 6 March 1930, carton 510, Miller & Lux Papers. In 1924 Cameron had also lamented that the employment of legal and engineering talent was not solving the problems inherent in forming the storage district; Cameron to Nickel, 22 August 1924, carton 242, Miller & Lux Papers.

70. Mott to Fickett, 3 March 1930, carton 510, Miller & Lux Papers.

71. Woolley, report on Conference held in forenoon of March 19, 1930, with W. B. Harris representing the Madera Irrigation District, and James E. Fickett, T. C. Mott, and J. E. Woolley, carton 510, Miller & Lux Papers.

72. The MID had acceded to some of the earliest demands; M. B. Harris to Woolley, 30 April 1930, 19 May 1930, carton 510, Miller & Lux Papers; Woolley to Harris, 13, 20 May 1930, carton 510, ibid.; Mordecai to Woolley, 6 June 1930, carton 510, ibid.; Woolley to Board of Directors, MID, 13 June 1930, carton 510, ibid.

73. Miller & Lux had, in fact, agreed to stipulate the amount of compensation if MID recognized the firm's cropland rights and condemned only the grassland rights. However, the district did not have the money to pay the judgment within the time period Miller & Lux demanded. Woolley to Mordecai, 11, 21 July 1930, 22 September 1930, carton 510, Miller & Lux Papers; Mordecai to Woolley, 18 July 1930, 13 August 1930, 19 September 1930, carton 510, ibid.; Fickett to Mordecai, 19 August 1930, carton 510, ibid.; Mordecai to Fickett, 20 August 1930, carton 510, ibid.; Woolley to Mott, 21 October 1930, carton 511, ibid.

74. There were technically three suits: *Miller & Lux* v. *Madera Irrigation District, et al*, no. 25729, Fresno Superior Court; *San Luis Canal Company* v. *Madera Irrigation Company, et al*, no. 25731, Fresno Superior Court; and *SJ&KRC&ICo* v. *Madera Irrigation District, et al*, no. 25730, Fresno Superior Court. However, those of Miller & Lux and the San Luis Canal Company were joined because they dealt with the same issues and facts. San Luis Canal, wholly owned by Miller & Lux, was in fact simply a holding company for its San Luis canal system.

75. An action to quiet title is defined in *Black's Law Dictionary* (5th ed.) as follows: "One in which plaintiff asserts his own estate and declares generally that defendant claims some estate in the land without defining it, and avers that the claim is without foundation, and calls on the defendant to set forth the nature of his claims, so that it may be determined by decree."

76. This group, designated the People's Protective Association in 1930, originated with the proponents of the West Joaquin District. It was represented by Cowell when the cross-complaint was filed in the 1920s, then by Stephen Downey, and in the trial itself by C. R. Perrier. A. Cowell to Woolley, 16 September 1930, carton 511, Miller & Lux Papers; C. R. Perrier to Woolley, 24 March 1931, carton 511, ibid.

77. Treadwell, in fact, had some concern that Haines would be biased, since he owned land within the Merced Irrigation District and his family owned bonds of that district. But most other names had been rejected for more serious reasons. Woolley to S. L. Strother, 14 November 1930, carton 511, Miller & Lux Papers; Treadwell to Woolley, 3 November 1930, carton 511, ibid.

78. Woolley to Mott, 10 November 1930, carton 511, Miller & Lux Papers; Memorandum as to Miller & Lux v. Madera Irrigation District, no. 25729, n.d., carton 711, ibid.

79. Woolley to Mott and Olsen, 26 January 1931, carton 511, Miller & Lux Papers.

80. Plaintiff's Opening Brief, part 2, Argument on the Law, pp. 1–30, *Miller & Lux* v. *MID* (no. 25729, 25731), carton 510, Miller & Lux Papers; Plaintiff's Reply Brief, pp. 13–20, ibid.

81. Plaintiff's Opening Brief, part 2, pp. 19–26, 30–42, ibid.

82. *Horst* v. *New Blue Point Mining Co.*, 171 P. 417 (1918). See text at notes 43, 44.

83. Plaintiff's Opening Brief, part 2, pp. 43–74, *Miller & Lux* v. *MID*, carton 510, Miller & Lux Papers.

84. Ibid., pp. 75–83. Part of the opening brief was devoted to the case law supporting Miller & Lux's argument that the river channel could be used as a conduit of privately owned water. Treadwell corresponded with attorneys of Southern California Edison on the development of some of these arguments. At one point, Southern California Edison tried to get the issue eliminated from the case, fearing that it would involve the priority of its filings in relation to those of the MID, an issue that it did not want settled in a case to which it was not a party. The San Joaquin Light & Power Company declined to testify for Miller & Lux, stating that it wanted to stay on good terms with customers favoring the MID. Treadwell to Roy V. Reppy, 3 October 1931, carton 511, Miller & Lux Papers; George E. Trowbridge to Treadwell, 26 February 1931, 13 October 1931, carton 511, ibid.; Treadwell to Trowbridge, 24 February 1931, carton 511, ibid.; Reppy to Farmer, 30 September 1931, Barnes 167; Farmer to MID, 1 October 1931, ibid.; Farmer to Southern California Edison, 1 October 1931, ibid.

85. Judge Haines, Opinion, Miller & Lux Inc. v. MID, San Luis Canal Company v. MID, SJ&KRC&ICo v. MID, p. 36, 51, Water Resources Center Archives.

86. Ibid., p. 155.

87. Ibid., pp. 368–76.

88. Ibid., pp. 162–63.

89. Ibid., pp. 235–41. In the case of deeded land, Haines did not determine whether the new owners had water rights, leaving that for another case.

90. In fact, Miller & Lux agents worked unsuccessfully to elect a board of directors that would vote to dissolve the district; Fickett to Max B. Arnold, 2 January 1935, carton 441, Miller & Lux Papers; Arnold to Fickett, 22 January 1935, carton 441, ibid.; T. Mott to Fickett, 14 February 1935, carton 441, ibid.; Farmer to Barnes, 14 October 1932, Barnes 168; Downey to Farmer, 13 October 1932, ibid.; Barnes, Notes Regarding Litigation, n.d., Barnes 167.

91. *Gin Chow* v. *Santa Barbara* 217 Cal 673 (1933).

92. Farmer to Barnes, 5 May 1933, Barnes 168.

93. *Peabody* v. *City of Vallejo* 2 Cal(2d) 351, 40 P(2d) 486 (1935). This decision was taken with considerable care after a rehearing with arguments from numerous friends of the court. In its first decision in *Peabody*, the court expressed a much more limited view of the impact of the 1928 amendment. Its views in 1933 were closer to those expressed by Judge Haines in his ruling in the suit between Miller & Lux and the MID. See *Peabody* v. *City of Vallejo*, 25 P(2d) 454 (1933).

94. Fickett to the Holders of Miller & Lux Inc. First Mortgage 6% Gold Bonds and Secured 7% Gold Notes, 8 July 1931, carton 594, Miller & Lux Papers; Miller & Lux Inc. Bondholder's Protective Committee to Holders of First Mortgage 6% Gold Bonds of Miller & Lux Inc., 1 November 1932, carton 594, ibid.; Bondholders Protective Committee and Noteholders Protective Committee to Holders of . . . , 11 February 1933, 11 August 1933, 26 February 1934, 7 September 1934, 30 November 1934, 15 March 1935, 6 March 1936, 24 October 1936, carton 594, ibid.

95. See n. 94; Nickel, Jr., to L. B. Peet, 15 July 1935, carton 441, Miller & Lux Papers; Memo, James E. Fickett, 12 September 1934, carton 441, ibid. Members of the board of directors were accused of buying much of the firm's land, including oil land, at well below true value by means of this scheme. *Miller & Lux* v. *J. Leroy Nickel, Jr.*, 141 F. Supp. 41 (1956), 149 F. Supp. 463 (1957); *Miller & Lux* v. *R. H. Anderson, Miller & Lux* v. *Allen Chickering*, 318 F. Supp. 831 (1963).

96. Miller & Lux declined to participate in these programs until penalties for noncompliance were enacted. In 1935, however, the firm found it difficult to meet the requirements of the cotton reduction program. Miller & Lux relied on tenants to raise cotton on approximately 7,500 acres a year, rotating the planting of cotton and its tenants over some 30,000 acres of land. This practice made it difficult to establish the land as cotton land, since federal definitions relied on a history of repeated planting. When the AAA declared the firm's renters to be "managing share tenants" and thus decided that the individual tract that each tilled, not the entire 30,000 acres, was a farm, little of this land qualified for benefit payments. However, Miller & Lux eventually found its way around the system, becoming a major recipient of such subsidies. In 1967 Miller & Lux interests collected close to $400,000 from USDA programs and in 1968, over $250,000. Olsen to William H. Alison, 13 September 1933, carton 441, Miller & Lux Papers; Olsen, Memorandum to Mr. Fickett: Relative to 1935 Cotton Planting, 23 February 1935, carton 441, ibid.; telegram, Olsen to Fickett, 28 February 1935, carton 441, ibid.; Henry I. Richards, *Cotton and the AAA* (Washington, D.C.: The Brookings Institute, 1936), pp. 49–53, 120, 141–43; *Congressional Record*, 90th Cong., 2d sess., 9 September 1968, pp. 26054-26056; *Congressional Record*, 91st Cong. 1st sess., 21 May 1969, pp. 13274-13275, 26 June 1969, p. 17554.

97. Montgomery and Clawson, *History of the Legislative and Policy Formation of the Central Valley Project*; Worster, *Rivers of Empire* (see intro., n. 12), pp. 239–43; William Karhl, *The California Water Atlas* (Sacramento: State of California, 1977), pp. 47–49.

98. The lengthiest of these was a suit to stop a proposed appropriation of water on

the Kings River. In this case, the Tulare Lake Basin Water Storage District asserted that the Kings River was not a tributary of the San Joaquin. This proposition was accepted by the local court despite the numerous earlier court decisions and government reports linking the Kings to the San Joaquin through Fresno Slough. On appeal, the state supreme court ruled that the Kings was indeed a tributary of the San Joaquin. With this ruling, the Tulare district was enjoined, but after the *Peabody* decision, it won the right to store some of the waters of the Kings on the grounds that they were not reasonably used by the downstream owners. *Chowchilla Farms* v. *Martin,* 219 Cal 1, 25 P(2d) 435 (1933); *Miller & Lux* v. *Tulane Lake Basin Water Storage District,* 219 Cal 41, 25 P(2d) 451 1933; *SJ&KRC&ICo* v. *Tulare Lake Water Storage District,* case no. 40474, Superior Court of Fresno County, Judgment, 18 March 1937, carton 525, Miller & Lux Papers.

99. Miller & Lux was to pay for any part of the judgment that resulted from its use of water after it left the reservoirs, an amount to be determined through arbitration. As it was, the jury found in favor of Miller & Lux and the power companies. In a retrial, the judge ruled against the riparian challengers to the reservoirs, citing the limitations placed on riparian claims by the 1928 constitutional amendment. A. R. Olsen to James E. Fickett, 13 May 1936, carton 442, Miller & Lux Papers; *Woolley et al* v. *Superior Court in and for Stanislaus County,* 66 P(2d)680 (1937); *L. A. Vandervort* v. *Southern California Edison,* case no. 14642, Superior Court of Stanislaus County, opinion of Judge Roy B. Maxey (carbon copy, n.d.), carton 532, Miller & Lux Papers.

100. Fickett to Edward Hyatt, 8 March 1935, carton 441, Miller & Lux Papers; Woolley to Bureau of Reclamation, 20 September 1935, carton 441, ibid.; *Central Valley Project Documents,* House Committee on Interior and Insular Office, 85th Cong., 1st sess., House doc. no. 246, Part 2, Operating Documents, pp. 554–89; *United States* v. *Gerlach Live Stock Co.,* 399 U.S. 725 (1949); *Gerlach Live Stock Co.* v. *United States,* 76 F. Supp. 87 (1948); *Rank* v. *Krug,* 90 F. Supp. 773 (1950).

CONCLUSION

1. James Willard Hurst, *Law and the Conditions of Freedom in the Nineteenth-Century United States* (Madison: Univ. of Wisconsin Press, 1956), p. 53.

2. J. E. Woolley to Dave Barnwell, 30 June 1927, carton 525, Miller & Lux Papers.

3. Frank H. Sloss, "M. C. Sloss and the California Supreme Court," *California Law Review* 46 (1958): 715–38; Comment, *California Law Review* 11 (1923): 109–10.

4. Shaw, "Development of Law of Waters" (see chap. 1, n. 44), p. 455.

5. *Katz* v. *Walkinson,* 141 Cal 114 (1903).

6. Short to Treadwell, 23, 26 August 1912, carton 463, Miller & Lux Papers.

7. Sklar, *Corporate Reconstruction* (see chap. 2, n. 41), pp. 49–50; John R. Commons, *Legal Foundations of Capitalism* (New York: Macmillan, 1939), pp. 11–28.

8. Worster, *Rivers of Empire.*

9. For a recent overview of this issue, see Harry N. Scheiber, "State Law and

'Industrial Policy' in American Development, 1790–1987," *California Law Review* 75 (1987): 415–44; earlier studies include Carter Goodrich, *Government Promotion of American Canals and Railroads, 1800–1890* (New York: Columbia Univ. Press, 1960); Goodrich, "American Development Policy: The Case of Internal Improvements," *Journal of Economic History* 16 (1956): 449–60; Goodrich, "Internal Improvements Reconsidered," *Journal of Economic History* 30 (1970): 289–311; Louis Hartz, *Economic Policy and Democratic Thought: Pennsylvania, 1776–1860* (Cambridge: Harvard Univ. Press, 1954); Oscar Handlin and Mary Flug Handlin, *Commonwealth: A Study in the Role of Government in the American Economy: Massachusetts, 1774–1861* (New York: New York Univ. Press, 1947); Harry N. Schieber, *Ohio Canal Era: A Case Study of Government and the Economy, 1820–1861* (Athens: Ohio Univ. Press, 1969).

10. *Barron* v. *Baltimore*, 7 Peters 243 (1833). Kutler, *Privilege and Creative Destruction* (see chap. 1, n. 74); William E. Nelson, *The Americanization of the Common Law: The Impact of Legal Change on Massachusetts Society, 1760–1830* (Cambridge: Harvard Univ. Press, 1975); Horwitz, *Transformation of American Law* (see intro., n. 2); Schieber, "Road to *Munn*" (see chap. 1, n. 74), pp. 329–402; Scheiber, "Property Law" (see chap. 1, n. 74); pp. 232–51.

11. Charles W. McCurdy, "Justice Field and the Jurisprudence of Government-Business Relations: Some Parameters of Laissez Faire Constitutionalism, 1863–1897," *Journal of American History* 61 (1975): 970–1005.

12. William L. Karhl, *California Water Atlas*, pp. 48–49, 56; Worster, *Rivers of Empire*, pp. 239–56.

13. Terry L. Anderson, *Water Crisis: Ending the Policy Drought* (Baltimore: Johns Hopkins Univ. Press, 1983).

The main sources for this study are court decisions and the collection of Miller & Lux Papers at the Bancroft Library, University of California, Berkeley. The Miller & Lux collection is massive, containing more than seven hundred cartons and boxes of files, as well as numerous bound volumes of court transcripts and lawyers' briefs. It includes legal department papers and correspondence from the firm's San Francisco headquarters and from the various branch offices in Oregon and California. The collection retains the original organization and includes information on business and agricultural practices well beyond my focus on law and the control of water. Unfortunately, the collection is minimally cataloged. In fact, the labeling of cartons was done only after I had started my research, so in many cases I have been unable to give carton numbers for cited letters. The guide to the collection lists file titles for each carton, but the titles are sometimes inaccurate, there is no identification of the office from which the files came, and the substantive content is not indicated. Researchers must determine on their own which are the characters (cattle bosses, local farming supervisors, business managers, etc.) relevant to their particular study.

There is only one published book on the firm, Miller & Lux attorney Edward F. Treadwell's worshipful biography of Henry Miller, *The Cattle King: A Dramatized Biography* (New York: Macmillan Company, 1931). This book is of little help in identifying the major units and figures in the firm. For example, it does not mention the role of J. Leroy Nickel, Miller's son-in-law, who managed the firm for many years.

Other major sources for this study are the S. T. Harding and Harry Barnes collections, housed at the Water Resources Center Archives at University of California, Berkeley. This archive is most frequently employed by researchers interested in the history of the flow of the region's rivers, but the Harding and Barnes collections include carbon copies of extensive correspondence on the formation of the San Joaquin River Water Storage District. Barnes, as engineer for the Madera Irrigation District and for the San Joaquin River Water Storage District, and Harding, a professor at Berkeley and adviser to the state engineer, were deeply involved in the storage district project. These collections furnish access to information on the actions of the state engineer that is not easily available from the State Archives. The Henry E. Huntington, H. H. Sinclair, and H. W. O'Melveny collections at the Huntington Library, San Marino, California, provide information on the early efforts to establish reservoirs to generate hydroelectric power. Recently the Huntington has also received material on Miller & Lux as part of another collection. The Millikin Museum in Los Banos, California, houses numerous artifacts, interviews, and copies of correspondence on the building of the SJ&KRC&ICo canals; some of these materials are also available at the library of the California State University, Stanislaus, in Turlock.

The work of J. Willard Hurst provides the foundation for examining law in its broad economic and social context. Hurst's *Law and Economic Growth: The Legal History of the Lumber Industry in Wisconsin, 1836–1915* (Cambridge: Harvard University Press, 1964) is a model for work done in this area. Harry Scheiber's articles are essential starting points in analyzing public policy questions. Especially important to my work are Scheiber's "The Road to *Munn*: Eminent Domain and the Concept of Public Purpose in the State Courts" (*Perspectives in American History* 5 [1971]: 329), "Property Law, Expropriation, and Resource Allocation by Government: The United States, 1789–1910" (*Journal of Economic History* 33 [1973]: 232), and "State Law and 'Industrial Policy' in American Development, 1790–1987," (*California Law Review* 75 [1987]: 415). Morton J. Horwitz's *The Transformation of American Law, 1780–1860* (Cambridge: Harvard University Press, 1977) is an important, though flawed, discussion of the winners and losers in battles over legal doctrine. The controversies provoked by his interpretations of specific areas of the law emphasize the need for detailed and focused investigations of the real impact of legal change. Robert W. Gordon, "Critical Legal History" (*Stanford Law Review* 36 [1984]: 57) and David M. Trubek, "Where the Action Is: Critical Legal Studies and Empiricism" (*Stanford Law Review* 36 [1984]: 575) illuminate more subtle interpretive paradigms associated with the Critical Legal Studies movement. Especially useful here are the discussion of the autonomy of the law. Martin J. Sklar's *The Corporate Reconstruction of American Capitalism, 1890–1916: The Market, the Law, and Politics* (Cambridge: Cambridge University Press, 1988) focuses on the national debate over antitrust regulations that occurred contemporaneously with Miller & Lux's battles over water. His insights into evolving notions of property and the role of the state help clarify the changes being proposed by the lawyers involved in water reform. So do Michael E. Tigar and Madeleine E. Levy, *Law and the Rise of Capitalism* (New York: Monthly Review Press, 1977) and Hugh Collins, *Marxism and Law* (Oxford: Oxford University Press, 1982).

The writings of Paul W. Gates are essential to understanding the context of land and agricultural policy in which firms like Miller & Lux operated. Gates was probably the first historian to look at the Miller & Lux papers, at a time when they were stacked in a stadium storeroom. His writings on California agriculture, especially "Public Land Disposal in California" (*Agricultural History* 49 [1975]: 158), and his *History of Public Land Law Development* (Washington, D.C.: Government Printing Office, 1968) are essential references. On the agricultural crisis of the post–World War I period and the specific dynamics of the cattle industry, see James H. Shideler *Farm Crisis, 1919–1923* (Berkeley and Los Angeles: University of California Press, 1957) and Jimmy M. Skaggs, *Prime Cut: Livestock Raising and Meatpacking in the United States, 1607–1983* (College Station, Tex.: Texas A & M Press, 1986).

A number of recent studies of California water conflicts are especially important. William L. Kahrl's *The California Water Atlas* (Sacramento: State of California, 1979) is a excellent introduction to the history and geography of water development in the state. Gordon R. Miller's "Shaping California Water Law, 1781–1928" (*Southern California Quarterly* 55 [1973]: 9) provides a brief, accessible chronology of the early developments in California water law. Harry N. Scheiber and Charles McCurdy's "Eminent-Domain Law and Western Agriculture" (*Agricultural History* 49 [1975]: 112) and Eric T. Freyfogle's "*Lux* v. *Haggin* and the Common Law Burdens of Modern Water Law" (*University of Colorado Law Review* 57 [1986]: 485) place California's adoption of riparianism in the context of broader issues of legal ideology in the Gilded Age. Thomas Edward Malone's unpublished dissertation, "The California Irrigation Crisis of 1886: Origins of the Wright Act" (Ph.D. dissertation, Stanford University, 1964), is essential to understanding this early effort at water reform. Donald J. Pisani's *From Family Farm to Agribusiness: The Irrigation Crusade in California and the West, 1850–1931* (Berkeley and Los Angeles: University of California Press, 1984) is an important account of water reform and agricultural development, but is somewhat uneven and not as comprehensive as its length and subtitle would indicate.

The writings of Samuel C. Wiel furnish some of the most useful accounts of western water law issues in the late nineteenth and early twentieth century. His treatise *Water Rights in the Western States*, 3d ed., 2 vols., (San Francisco:

Bancroft–Whitney Company, 1911) is the best guide through the specific legal developments of the period. Wiel was also a participant in the debates, advocating a modified riparianism, and his publications in the *California Law Review* and the *Harvard Law Review* are important as historical documents as well. Robert G. Dunbar's *Forging New Rights in Western Water* (Lincoln: University of Nebraska Press, 1983) is a good, recent overview of western water history despite a pronounced appropriationist perspective. Donald Worster's *Rivers of Empire: Water, Aridity and the Growth of the American West* (New York: Pantheon Books, 1985) is a flawed but provocative account of concentration of power and environmental arrogance on the part of the advocates of irrigation. T. E. Lauer's "Reflections on Riparianism" (*Missouri Law Review* 35 [1970]: 60) and Arthur Maass and Raymond L. Anderson's . . . *and the Desert Shall Rejoice: Conflict, Growth and Justice in Arid Environments* (Cambridge: MIT Press, 1978) sound important counterpoints to the notion that either riparian rights or irrigation itself is inherently undemocratic and authoritarian. More recent reformers have advocated market-based treatment of water issues. This perspective can be seen in Terry L. Anderson, *Water Crisis: Ending the Policy Drought* (Baltimore: Johns Hopkins University Press, 1983).

Although water reform was an important political issue for California Progressives, the accounts of Progressivism in the state give water law little attention. George E. Mowry's *The California Progressives* (Chicago: Quadrangle Books, 1963) and Olin C. Spencer, Jr.'s, *California's Prodigal Sons: Hiram Johnson and Progressives, 1911–1917* (Berkeley and Los Angeles: University of California Press, 1968) explore California Progressivism but virtually ignore water law reform. Franklin Hichborn's contemporary discussion, *Story of the Session of the California Legislature of 1913* (San Francisco: Press of the James H. Barry Company, 1913), is similarly limited. An account of early reform efforts is found in Pisani's "Water Law Reform in California, 1900–1913" (*Agricultural History* 54 [1980]: 295) and his earlier mentioned book. Samuel P. Hays does not discuss California water issues in *Conservation and the Gospel of Efficiency: The Progressive Conservation Movement, 1890–1920* (Cambridge: Harvard University Press, 1959; New York: Atheneum, 1969), but his examination of engineers and ideology illuminates the dilemmas and controversies surrounding water law reform in the state. Most information on Progressivism and water, however, must be gleaned from the public documents of the water reformers themselves. Important here are the reports of the California Conservation Commission and the State Water Commission, the publications of the Commonwealth Club of California, and the writings of the engineer Frank Adams, who conducted numerous studies for these agencies.

Similarly, the local context must be pieced together. In the early twentieth century, the Los Angeles–based Historic Record Company published histories of many California counties and communities. Unfortunately, these histories tend to be dominated by biographical lists of self-styled local dignitaries. Geared to the promotion of the local community, they discuss little of real controversy. Among newspapers, the indispensable source for local events and opinion, the *Fresno Republican* gives access to opinion and events in the San Joaquin Valley. Also important are the San Francisco papers (the *Call*, *Chronicle*, and *Examiner*) and the various Kern County papers, including *Kern County Californian*, *Kern County Gazette*, and the *Southern California and Kern County Weekly Courier*. These papers are available on microfilm; many of them are indexed in the California State Library in Sacramento, although the index is not complete.

TABLE OF CASES

Page numbers are cited for those cases mentioned by name in the text.